D1429214

AFTER THE AVANT-GARDE

Robert Boyers is the editor of the quarterly *Salmagundi* and Professor of English at Skidmore College. He is the author of books on Lionel Trilling, F. R. Leavis, and R. P. Blackmur, and his essays appear regularly in such publications as *TLS, The New Republic, The American Scholar, Dissent, Kenyon Review,* and *Partisan Review.* His most recent book is *Atrocity and Amnesia: The Political Novel Since 1945* (Oxford, 1985).

AFTER THE AVANT-GARDE

ESSAYS ON ART AND CULTURE

Robert Boyers

THE PENNSYLVANIA STATE UNIVERSITY PRESS
University Park and London

Library of Congress Cataloging-in-Publication Data

Boyers, Robert.
  After the avant-garde.

  Includes index.
  1. Arts, Modern—20th century—Themes, motives.
2. Arts, Modern—20th century—Philosophy. I. Title.
NX456.B68   1987   700'.9'04   87–43001
ISBN 0-271-00609-9

For Stanley and Laura Kauffmann
and for Peg Boyers

"Art succeeds, but the situation of art is hopeless."
　　　　　　　　　　　　　　　—Harold Rosenberg

Contents

PART FIVE
CINEMATIC READINGS AND MISREADINGS

Introduction

The essays in this volume were written over the period of the last ten years. Such commonality of purpose as they suggest is owed to my obsession with particular issues and my resistance to certain ideas which have so infatuated many of my contemporaries that I cannot but think them important. Collectively the essays argue that it is both necessary and possible to distinguish between good art and bad art. They also argue that, as Clement Greenberg once put it, there is a difference between "those values only to be found in art and the values which can be found elsewhere."

But to claim that the essays collected here therefore constitute a continuous argument would be to claim that this is a unified book, and this is not the case. Whatever my reader may feel about qualities of voice and concern which persist from one item to another, the fact is that these pieces can only do what individual essays do. They are as various as the occasions and impulses which moved me to write them.

The title of the book suggests that what was once regarded as a dangerous and novel enterprise may now properly be regarded principally as a historical phenomenon, in the wake of which certain creative possibilities have been marginalized or extinguished. Though writers and artists obviously continue to make things that will strike some of us as fresh and original, the idea of a permanent avant-garde, like the idea of a permanent adversary relationship between artists and spectators, is one of the myths I have thought it useful to challenge in this collection.

So too have I probed the options available to serious artists now that the very idea of aesthetic value has been called into question. If the late Harold Rosenberg was right in contending that in our era "the whole measuring apparatus [for evaluating works of art] has been sent to the devil," is it useful to pretend that we know what we are doing when we talk about and ultimately evaluate a film or a painting or a novel? Is there any reason to suppose that one translation of a poem can be legitimately preferred to another when readers are authorized to read the original any way they wish and to reject the idea that they are guided by an authorial intention? In arguing that avant-garde creations are susceptible to readings their authors cannot have anticipated, but that a mind properly responsive to works of art may only imagine what it has been charged to imagine by the work at hand, these essays steer an unpredictable course between competing orthodoxies.

While several of the essays focus on particular films or novels, the volume may be described as a series of reflections on the artistic consciousness of our time. These reflections are chiefly posed as responses to theories that have gained—especially among literary intellectuals—an indisputable currency. Among those associated with these theories are writers so diverse as Michel Foucault and William Gass, Jacques Derrida and Susan Sontag, George Steiner and Bruno Bettelheim. What emerges from my encounter with these writers is a negative aesthetics, an inquiry into the threatened possibilities open to contemporary artists and the impositions or abuses to which works of art are routinely subjected. I ask questions not so much about the political convictions of artists—though on occasion that is an unavoidable subject—as about the politics of various influential readers and their attempt to control works of art for purposes often obscure even to the critics themselves. In accounting for various kinds of misreading or ideological abuse I try to indicate what I take to be legitimate ways of looking at works of art, remembering that our personal background and experience will have much to do with our responses. Though my essays are frequently sharp and contentious, they come at the issues with an air of resolute provisionality.

No single essay collected here may be said to encompass all of the major themes and approaches examined in the book. Neither does any one essay presume to deliver an exhaustive account of its subject. More often than I expected, widely divergent pieces strongly reinforce one another. Only the paper on "Moral Fiction" develops in a general way the case against those who believe that narrative functions best when it tells us by example how to live our lives. But the argument presented in that paper—really an extended response to the novelist John Gardner—is substantially deepened by my dispute elsewhere in the book with Bruno Bettelheim on the subject of Lina Wertmuller's notorious film *Seven Beauties*.

Just so, though I take on in a general way the case for works of art as exclusively self-referential objects only in the essay on "Real Readers and Theoretical Critics," the argument presented there receives its truest support in the paper on Jean-Luc Godard. There, I respond to Susan Sontag's view of Godard as an artist who properly refuses to explain anything, arguing on the contrary that a successful film by Godard necessarily explains itself in its own terms quite as fully as more conventional narratives do. That willingness to explain and to engage our lives, I go on to show, is bound up with a film's inability to exist for us as a perfectly autonomous object.

Of such matters there is always more to say, and I can only hope that the essays themselves do modest justice to their subjects. Obviously some readers will welcome my views on certain subjects more than my views on others. The editors of periodicals who originally commissioned the essays were well aware that some would stimulate protest. Not all of the essays go against the grain of received opinion on a given subject—the essay on Ingmar Bergman's women characters, for example, defends him against feminist attacks by elaborating perspectives which are anything but eccentric.

The paper on John Ashbery, on the other hand, in its original periodical incarnation seemed sufficiently provocative to become more or less at once the target of a criticism which has moved to establish that gifted, clever, but decidedly minor poet as the presiding genius of his age. What matters, in these various performances, is not that one critic has or has not bought into a currently dominant orthodoxy or consensus. The point of it all is that, in discussing this or that work or idea, I may—deliberately or inadvertently—make contact with those cultural issues which most exercise the contemporary imagination. If, like the artists I discuss, I am more interested in raising questions than in resolving them, I would like to think that I have at least made it harder for my readers to be tempted by the fashionable theories and conceits which have made useful talk about the arts increasingly rare in our culture.

To the magazine editors who originally published the essays in this book I here express my gratitude. Most especially I wish to thank John Gross, who, as editor of the *London Times Literary Supplement* (*TLS*) in the late 1970s and early 1980s, commissioned six of the essays in this book and offered me additional opportunities to write at length on a wide range of subjects. Though I devoted most of my time in those years to book-length studies, I recall the months I gave to the *TLS* assignments as some of the most rewarding time I have spent as a writer.

Robert Boyers
Saratoga Springs, N.Y.
December 1986

PART ONE

Modern and Post-Modern Theories of Value

Visionary Avant-Garde

Octavio Paz, *Marcel Duchamp: Appearance Stripped Bare*, translated by Rachel Phillips and Donald Gardner (New York: Viking Press).

The avant-garde is by now a historical phenomenon. To intone the names of Picasso, Stravinsky, Apollinaire, or of more recent figures like John Cage and Jackson Pollock, is to remember that the phenomenon has been with us for almost a century, that we have talked it to death, and that no object is any longer likely to offend even the most ardent philistine. Though participants in the avant-garde may be variously described, we have been able to put the movement as a whole "in perspective," as historians like to say, and no one may doubt that something permanent has been effected in the way we look at works of art. We may not be entirely pleased with the advanced works produced in our time, but they are with us to stay. It is foolish to suppose that we might have done better to indulge pious sentiments on behalf of old-fashioned realism in literature or harmonic limitation in music. One needn't be a determinist to argue that what happened had to happen, and that the avant-garde was a movement as open to talent and intelligence as earlier movements had been.

More and more, in recent years, artists and critics have come to identify Marcel Duchamp as the true exemplar of the avant-garde. Though the movement may be said to have produced greater artists, none of these would seem to have promoted so peculiar and elusive a sense of his calling as Duchamp. Nor has Duchamp, like

From *London Times Literary Supplement* (*TLS*), January 18, 1980.

most others, cluttered the scene with a great variety of works requiring some discrimination of better from best. With but a few "major" works to his credit, Duchamp invites us to engage his project as an idea whose validity may be considered apart from its capacity to generate masterpieces. In the extent that we can take Duchamp seriously without believing that he is himself a great creative genius, we testify to the power of his example.

Though nothing he invented may move us, his works remain interesting and, at some level, stimulating. They inspire contemplation—not of this object or that, but of what we have come to expect in our transactions with works of art. A Duchamp invention is immediately "historical" in the sense that it is patently a theoretical gesture without significant power to pass beyond its status as idea. In drawing attention to what it is not, and to the reasons for its failure to be satisfying in itself, it quickly assumes the status of a phenomenon rather than an object. Though camp followers of various sorts may like to think of Duchamp as a free spirit and a marvelous inventor, he is more properly regarded as an intellectual presence, a critical force.

It is no secret that Duchamp's fundamental contribution has been critical rather than imaginative. His central work, *The Bride Stripped Bare by Her Bachelors, Even* (also called *The Large Glass*), is meant to be "read" with the assistance of an accompanying text-manual entitled *The Green Box*. Nor is the manual to be regarded as essentially distinct from or inferior to the work it explains. In the commentaries of Octavio Paz and of other writers committed to Duchamp's work, the text seems at least as important as *The Large Glass* itself, and little attempt is made to think about the object independent of the affirmations Duchamp wishes it to make. To compare Duchamp's work with a modernist work like *The Waste Land* is to see at once how little Duchamp's productions conform to expected patterns. Eliot's poem may rely in part on the apparatus of notes and references he attached to it, but the poem has a life and presence of its own. It is not itself merely a reference to a range of ideas beyond its compass but an object with depths and a variety of competing energy centers. One may justly speak of it as creating tensions which it sustains and into which it draws readers. By contrast, the viewer of a Duchamp glass or assemblage becomes at once an alienated witness, encouraged to move around and outside of the surfaces of the work, to think about it rather than to engage it in or for itself. To speak of Duchamp as a critical presence is simply to say that he is interested in ideas more than in experiences, that thinking is for him an activity valuable apart from any more total experience it may enable. His *Large Glass* is, as Paz has it, "a machine for producing meanings"; as such, it goes against the grain of the sensuous apprehension we take to be crucial to our experience of works of art.

In fact, Duchamp's work constitutes a deliberate rebellion not only against academicism or realism or romanticism but against the modernist spirit itself. Though the creations of early modernist masters like Stravinsky and Braque and Eliot were deeply intellectual, all were finished works with purposes very different from the production of meanings or the avowal of ideas. One says of the works of such men that they are invariably more than their ideas, that they evoke or make use of meanings without being at all reducible to them. Of *The Large Glass* one says that it means something or it is nothing, that it enforces a particular attitude or position or it is a whim, a gimmick, a tactic without a program. Duchamp seems to many people so important because he suggests by implication what has happened to the modernist experiment, how it has gone wrong. In his refusal to do what the modernists did, he recommends a strategy of avoidance and a means of spiritual rejuvenation. One may not wish to follow him, but he does certainly enable sharp registration of the recent state of affairs in the arts.

No one is better equipped to discuss this state of affairs than Octavio Paz. His new book on Duchamp, though it collects and extends earlier pieces, is as fresh and provoking as it seemed in previous monographic versions. Picasso discovered how to say yes to the age in an astonishing variety of ways; but, Paz argues, it was Duchamp who resisted the age, who taught us how to go against the grain of movement itself and of that continuous impulse to change which is the modernist spirit. In this way, by adopting Duchamp as focus and culture-hero, Paz can recommend a view of art which is decidedly antique without having to reject the particular productions of this artist or that. "The art of the last two centuries has borne a common stamp," says Paz; "it has deified aesthetic values, which have been cut off from other values . . . It is against this conception of art that Duchamp rebelled." The rebellion is mounted in a series of works—actually only a relative handful—which raise indifference to a primary principle. Not the work in itself but the idea it wishes to transmit is important. By creating objects that seem not to have any of the attributes we value in other aesthetic objects, Duchamp rejects the thing in itself in favor of what is merely hypothetical. "Duchamp devalues art as craft in favor of art as idea," Paz insists again and again. The modern hunger to consume works of art, to possess them or, in turn, to be ravished by them, is challenged by an art that refuses to be taken in by the hungry eye or to overpower us with signs of patent creative vitality. Attaching us to what is not, to a virtuality without substantial presence, Duchamp counters the progressive movement which began in the Renaissance and reached its culmination in the modernist period, namely, "a transition from *vision* to the perceptible thing." Paz understands the consequences of this transition better than any other critic I know, but even he has trouble getting at it in a way that will be at once clarifying and hopeful.

The goal is not, of course, to debunk the art of two or more centuries. The goal must have more to do with indicating what is meant by the term *vision* and how it is possible to reconcile the general charge against modernism with the appreciation of works by the great modernist artists. Duchamp is surely an interesting figure, and Paz has much to say that we cannot ignore; but Duchamp is decidedly less important than the tradition he throws into such bold relief. We describe him as an exemplar of the avant-garde to indicate that he sees himself as perpetually working against the grain. He makes things we are to consider not because they are good but because they are unique—at least in the way they are presented—and provide an occasion to exercise and therefore to strengthen the mind. By contrast, a modernist painting by, say, Paul Klee puts us in mind of a specifically human content, just as the so-called impersonality of a modernist poet like Eliot is inconceivable as anything but an expression of personal tensions carefully evoked and only tentatively mastered. Such tensions are entirely beside the point for avant-gardists like Duchamp, who have no genuine interest in personal problems or in psychological exploration. Their attachment to art as idea is part of a refusal to be taken in by works that confuse the working out of psychological and expressive tensions with spiritual achievement. Though modernist art may be said to be rigorous and austere in several of its manifestations, it seems to Duchamp and his colleagues too committed to aesthetic sensation to satisfy ultimate demands. The avant-gardist may do all he can to make us laugh at works with serious designs upon us, but his purposes are likely to be "pure" and lofty in a degree not often conceded by casual observers of his whimsically self-deflating inventions.

Paz has his hands full doing justice to Duchamp, whose "purity" and dryness must be made to show by contrast what we ought to miss in the more characteristic art of this century. For Paz, Duchamp is the master of an ironic mode so cunningly deployed that it subverts at once the aesthetic predilections of hopeful observers and the merely negative or satiric appetites of disaffiliated skeptics. If the modernist work appeals to us as an incarnation of some drive to achieve an end that yet remains in doubt, the avant-gardist work may be said to deny genuine ends and the prospect of satisfactory incarnations. In Paz's terms, such works "distill criticism of themselves." They invoke possible meanings only to destroy them. They are visionary in the sense that they detach us from relation with works that celebrate themselves and the acts of creative imagination that bring them into being. A masterwork by Duchamp is, according to Paz, "an open space that provokes new interpretations and evokes, in its incomplete state, the void on which the work depends. This void is *the absence of the Idea*." In provoking us to entertain a variety of "lower case" ideas, the work bears witness to the absence of an organizing principle or myth that might properly validate our exertions. What emerges from encounter with the perpetually ironizing artifact is the conviction that we have but a single idea we can bear to hold or share: the idea of Criticism, an idea that seems particularly thin and unstable as it functions in the avant-gardist invention. Duchamp so appeals to Paz because he refuses to believe in anything he can see and insists ever so playfully that there must be something even he can't manage to mock. It may require charity to "read" the avant-gardist enterprise in this way—as a visionary project without a discernible spiritual object or center—but the reading does effectively suggest how desperate we've become for alternatives to the modernist theory of art.

Perhaps we can say more clearly what is at stake in Paz's defense of the avant-garde by remembering that Duchamp really made his mark as the "creator" of ready-mades. His paintings of the *Nude Descending a Staircase*, shown in New York in 1913, did not go unremarked, but the ready-mades may be said to have made a statement about the condition of art that was peculiarly telling. By presenting anonymous objects as works of art, Duchamp initiated the critique of value and of aesthetic taste which continues to inform much of the "higher" criticism of the visual arts today. Though more than one admirer has spoken of the graceful lines of Duchamp's urinals and of the chaste symmetries of his bottle racks, Paz is surely closer to Duchamp's intentions when he argues that "good taste is no less harmful than bad" and that "there is no essential difference between them." Duchamp did not want his ready-mades to be studied and "appreciated" in a way that would make possible observations about their charm or grace or symmetry. He wanted to show that anything at all could be made to seem acceptable if it became familiar enough, and that modern art could be useful only if it refused to appeal to values or to constitute a value in itself. The readymades were to be seen as critical gestures, expressions of an ironic disdain. For Paz they signify the artist's freedom from conventions of value, craftsmanship, and inspiration.

The notion that the artist is at his best a free man and that the works to which he puts his name are expressions of his freedom is bound to seem confusing to anyone who takes seriously the visionary dimension of the avant-garde. American critics, like the late Harold Rosenberg, could speak persuasively of the artist's freedom because they thought him to be genuinely creative and to be rightly involved in expressing his own eccentric view of things. Though the painter might, as in the case of Jackson Pollock, struggle to achieve "a state of grace" rather than a polished or pleasing surface, he was free in the sense that he could intensify in his own way the relation developing between his expressive impulses and the requirements of his canvas. Rosenberg's free artist operates in relation to something he can see, which he knows himself to have had a hand in bringing to life. Paz also wants the artist to be free, though what he makes has no value in itself, is in fact nothing but "a medium, a cable for the transmission of ideas and emotions." Duchamp is not, for Paz, the man who has a rich inner world which he works to shape or externalize. He is not, in that sense, free to share with us something that belongs peculiarly to him and is a function of his temperament. He invents "works in search of a meaning" that he cannot locate or embody through any operation of his own craft. If he is free, he is free only to wait and to witness the palpable insufficiency of his own project. Paz's formulations might be more acceptable if he described Duchamp as free only in the negative sense: free from anxiety about the status of his works, free from the temptation to express himself or to direct attention to his "genius."

Duchamp's ready-mades are indifferent objects, to be sure, and they appeal neither to good taste nor to bad. Why they should seem on this account rigorous and chastening it is not easy to see. For what exactly do they criticize? They function in a universe of discourse that necessarily excludes those who care only for old-fashioned novels or academic painting. Insofar as they can have anything rigorous to say they must address other artists, must stand in ironic relation with other emerging and more energetic works. Can it be said that these other artists have need of an embodied critical irony, or that their creations are somehow chastened by being forced into tacit relation with resolutely indifferent objects? Artists like Braque and Mallarmé were already involved in the critique of aesthetic value when Duchamp emerged. But their works, in moving *through* gestural negation to a new affirmation of created value, were rigorous and provoking in a degree far exceeding Duchamp's. Criticism may be the only "upper case" idea we trust, but it can hardly claim to be rigorous when it is programmed to say nothing but *no* and to pretend there is no possibility it may wish to change its mind.

The avant-gardist work as medium is important to us only so far as it can be made to channel creative energies which are otherwise misdirected. According to Paz, the ready-mades succeed because they say *no* to the headlong rush into ever more inventive "solutions" and ever more exciting evocations—no, that is, to high modernist art. Because they are more or less unitary objects without discernible intrinsic tensions they may be described as inert, and though Paz may object, he does consider Duchamp's later complex inventions more promising. This is hopeful, for *The Large Glass* does at least open up a plausible discourse about the relations among its parts and about the nature of its own potential meaning. The ready-made has no intrinsic energy center and invites no aesthetic reflection. Its meaning is entirely extrinsic, in the sense that it invites no collaborative reading of its dynamics; its immobility and muteness may provoke a response, but the response remains always external to the work. Even the amused observer is an alienated witness who prefers feeling superior to feeling involved. This is not an aesthetic preference but a cultural attitude entirely subject to the vicissitudes of fashion. *The Large Glass* is a more promising enterprise in enforcing a more challenging relation to its objectives and in mobilizing interpretive energies which have, quite clearly, a difficult work to accomplish.

Paz's book on Duchamp is an interpretive commentary, an analysis of *The Large Glass* and of *Etant donnés,* an assemblage housed along with most of the artist's works in the Philadelphia Museum of Art. The first is described as "a double glass, 109¼ inches high and 69¼ long, painted in oil and divided horizontally into two identical parts by a double lead wire." Its forms are further described—by the critic William Rubin—as a series of cold mechanical figures drafted with puzzling exactitude:

A spectator unfamiliar with Duchamp's iconography would not immediately divine that he was in the presence of "a mechanistic and cynical interpretation of the phenomena of love" (Breton) but would respond to it only as a perspective study for some strange and humorous machine of indeterminate purpose. He would note that although the parts are connected mechanically, they are antisequential and unexpected in their various individual identities. A waterwheel, chocolate grinder, cloud, and what appear to be dry cleaners' blocking and pressing forms seem to function together like a very serious and carefully engineered counterpart of a Rube Goldberg apparatus . . .

As we look at *The Large Glass*, we see reflected in it our own image, which blends with the other images and painted figures. This experience, of seeing through, is the bridge between *The Large Glass* and the later assemblage, in many ways so visibly different as to seem unrelated. This culminating work, with the English title *Given: 1. The Waterfall, 2. The Illuminating Gas*, is beautifully evoked by Paz as follows:

> In the far wall, embedded in a brick portal topped by an arch, there is an old wooden door, worm-eaten, patched, and closed by a rough crossbar made of wood and nailed on with heavy spikes . . . The door sets its material doorness in the visitor's way with a sort of aplomb: dead end . . . But if the visitor ventures nearer, he finds two small holes at eye level. If he goes even closer and dares to peep, he will see a scene he is not likely to forget. First of all, a brick wall with a slit in it, and through the slit, a wide open space, luminous and seemingly bewitched. Very near the beholder—but also very far away, on the "other side"—a naked girl, stretched on a kind of bed or pyre of branches and leaves, her face almost completely covered by the blond mass of her hair, her legs open and slightly bent, the pubes strangely smooth in contrast to the abundance of her hair, . . . the hand grasping a small gas lamp made of metal and glass . . . our glance wanders over the landscape: in the background, wooded hills, green and reddish; lower down, a small lake and a light mist on the lake . . . On the far right, among some rocks, a waterfall catches the light. Stillness: a portion of time held motionless. The immobility of the naked woman

and of the landscape contrasts with the movement of the waterfall and the flickering of the lamp. The silence is absolute. All is real and verges on banality; all is unreal and verges—on what?

Paz is an agile interpreter, and he has extraordinary patience. When he finishes with Duchamp one feels that every aspect of the artist's intention has been sympathetically examined. He makes much of Duchamp's eroticism, which is taken to be fully compatible with spiritual aspiration and intellectual sobriety. But he makes nothing of the dismay even a sophisticated viewer is likely to feel as he looks in at the naked girl—might she be a teasing castrato?—on her bed of leaves, or of the fact that few observers will care to read the dimly inscribed erotic rites of *The Large Glass* in the prescribed way. Which is only to say that, after doing his best to evoke the works, Paz retreats from them as rapidly as he can. Content to treat them as ideas—the bride is once called "the copy of a copy of the Idea"—he works feverishly to unearth meanings which are thought to constitute their only reason for being. The meanings are said to be *virtually* present, each work the "projection" of an unknown to which ordinary creative gestures are unequal. The viewer will feel more eagerly involved than he did in the ready-mades, but he is likely still to feel that his central relation is to be with something he can neither see nor imagine. The works engage him only if he agrees to think persistently about their intentions, and since he cannot really tell from the works themselves what they intend—they seem if anything only curious and mildly self-satisfied playthings—he will have to dwell on the "philosophy" of a gifted ironist named Duchamp. This may not be what he had in mind, but his works do have a value that is indistinguishable from their role in his conceptual project. The project one can appreciate without at all taking a serious interest in the works themselves.

The problems are nicely focused in several of Paz's resonant formulations: (1) "The Bride is a desiring motor that desires herself . . . This desire, which cannot be reduced to feelings although it originates in them, is but a desire for being." (2) The goal of art is "to penetrate the nature of reality . . . the nature of that reality is hypothetical . . . a point of view." (3) "It is a symbol machine. But these symbols are distended and deformed by irony." (4) ". . . I prefer to call the Waterfall and the Illuminating Gas signs and not symbols. Symbols have lost their meaning by virtue of having so many contradictory meanings. On the other hand, signs are less ambitious and more agile; they are not emblems of a 'conception of the world' but moveable pieces of a syntax . . . No symbol has an immutable meaning; the meaning depends on the relation."

Point 1: To describe Duchamp's Bride as desiring anything at all is to suppose that a conceptual apparatus can register its own incompleteness. A desiring "motor" will of course experience desire in a very peculiar way, and Paz is no doubt aware that the words for saying these things are less than precise. There is a sense, though, in which Paz's metaphors cannot work. It is not possible to suppose that an apparatus which has no being can desire anything. And it does not matter that the attributed desire "cannot be reduced to feelings." The desire will have much to do with feelings or it will not be desire. Paz insists on the "desire" because he is uneasy with what he is elsewhere compelled to say of the piece—that it is "a static illustration," for example. But sheer insistence will not make a static illustration desire what it is not. When we look at *The Large Glass* we do not experience the apparatus as a "desiring motor." It is so obviously "put together" that we cannot but feel that Duchamp has included in it whatever he thought it could accommodate. If, after studying the object, we conclude that for all its shapes and forms it has no capacity to fill us with wonder, that it is merely curious, we do not then go on to think of it as desiring what it does not have. Why should we? We may imagine *for* the apparatus what it does not have and cannot make us feel, but that is obviously a very different thing.

The issue, then, is the status or sufficiency of the work itself. Works that have a life of their own may be said to generate within themselves a desire for greater fullness of being. Duchamp's apparatus can have no desire because nothing the artist says about it can bring it to life. Just as we know the difference between an illustration and a painting, so we can distinguish between a diagram of possibility and an enactment. Nor are these distinctions expressions of an arbitrary aesthetic preference determined at the level of taste. Even analytic works, cubist paintings, are enactments of a vision or a mode of vision. So are the machine-abstractions of Léger. Such works have purposes to which they are in part adequate, and their adequacy is largely caught or evidenced in what they appear to be. We experience their adequacy in a way that is inconceivable with any of Duchamp's creations. They witness not a desire for being but the artist's dread of stable purpose and palpable achievement. His aversions may entitle him to some status as a cultural hero, but they do not authenticate his pieces as works of art.

Point 2: A work that refuses to engage the world's familiar objects or to become an object of contemplation—an object with a complex being of its own—cannot be said "to penetrate the nature of reality." The reality aimed at by works of art is always, at last, hypothetical, in the sense that they represent possibilities they can never fully encompass. A painting may penetrate in the degree that it allows itself to take on a variety of expressive burdens to which it wishes to be equal. If it renounces its possibilities at once, if it is inadequate by definition, it will have nothing to penetrate. Since the reality aimed at by works of art must always be an imagined and, in that sense, a created reality, nothing may be penetrated by a work that refuses to imagine a being of its own. This is not a semantic quibble, but a way of recalling essential facts of life no practicing artist may fail to acknowledge.

Point 3: Duchamp's irony cannot be its own reason for being. It has to be good for something in order to be good at all. Otherwise it is no better than the cheap sensation produced by any number of modern works which titillate viewers without chastening any of their normal appetites. For Paz, irony is a critical passion. In the great works of modernism it is part of an "aesthetics of surprise." But in Duchamp the irony lacks a crucial dimension: It fails to be "infatuated with the very thing it denies." This critical dimension, elaborated by Paz in his book *Children of the Mire,* ensures that works be present to us as Duchamp's refuse to be. Paz, strangely, does not miss this dimension in Duchamp. So taken is he with the wit of Duchamp's negations and their visionary promise that the tension characteristically sought in works of art seems not to matter. Paz speaks of the distension and deformation of Duchamp's symbols, but the symbols are self-denying artifacts to begin with. Paz does not see that irony is a hollow gesture when it has no passionate embodiment to work against.

Point 4: Paz is least to be trusted in his discussions of the symbol. Though here and there he is comfortable with the idea of the symbol as a meaning to be denied, elsewhere he grows anxious and wishes to renounce the symbol altogether. To speak of the elements in *Etant donnés* as "moveable pieces of a syntax" is to describe them accurately. They are not symbols, any more than the various elements in *The Large Glass.* They wish to mean, and to deny that they mean. But they are not in themselves meanings to which it is possible to make a substantial, that is, an aesthetic, response. The fact that particular elements may suggest "contradictory meanings" has really no importance at all. Genuinely symbolic works may also suggest a variety of meanings, and they are not thereby incapacitated from working towards " 'a conception of the world.' " Paz never comes to terms with the real significance of his own insight, namely, that Duchamp produces signs rather than symbols because he doesn't believe in anything at all. He is fundamentally without *serious* visionary ambition, and his works seem merely "agile" when they are not inert because he has not the force of conviction to make them stand for anything he would willingly stand by. It may be that no symbol any longer has "an immutable meaning," but that is not to say that it must fail to represent the will towards sufficient meaning which is the mark of spiritual enterprise. For all that many great works of modernist art are involved in ambiguity and paradox, in irony and demystification, they are willing also to evidence the defection of certain meaning from the materials of their discourse. By attempting to create symbols that will serve, knowing that complex strategies must be devised to prevent those very symbols from disavowing their own visionary purposes, modernist artists do combat with their own worst fears. Duchamp would seem to have capitulated prematurely, and to have forfeited the prospect either of creating alternative worlds or of telling us what it feels like to be truly bereft.

Clement Greenberg and the Modernist Theory of Value

Donald B. Kuspit, *Clement Greenberg, Art Critic* (Madison: The Univ. of Wisconsin Press).

No one who has tried to write about the art of this century has had an easy time of it. Art news journalists, who produce one or more pieces each week, may do a satisfactory job of describing the "look" or, occasionally, the apparent intention of a painting, but they must usually be content to offer in place of criticism or analysis an opinion or estimate. Critics employed by monthly or quarterly art journals may have more leisure, more space, but find that there is little they can add to the summary accounts offered by frontline journalists. Occasionally contexts are invoked, comparisons risked, a scheme of development charted. But these are most often handled tentatively, with no accompanying suggestion that any insight be taken for a general truth. Unstable and unpredictable as the art scene has been, critics opt for a genial pluralism in place of the polemic advocacy and the building of value-hierarchies that still characterize critical activity in the area of the literary arts. No wonder painters often complain that there are no more than one or two reliable voices in the current scene, that even the better critics are more interested in displaying their openness to new sensations than in trying to discriminate between one achievement and another. It may once have been supposed that avant-garde painters and sculptors resented or had no use for criticism. In fact, they have exhibited a remarkable readiness to embrace or at least to take seriously the judgments of even minimally sympathetic critics, and

From *London Times Literary Supplement* (*TLS*), October 24, 1980.

their complaints about the quality of the writing may be taken to express a genuine regret that they have no one to rely upon.

In the United States, only Clement Greenberg may be said to have gotten through to painters in a way most of them can admire.* Those he chose to ignore in the course of forty active years may feel hurt or bitter, but there is little doubt they would like to have been treated with the care he alone was able to bring to their contemporaries. Some may prefer the writings of Greenberg's brilliant and more versatile colleague, the late Harold Rosenberg, but no one who has thought about the two will think that Rosenberg was as good an art critic as he was a social and literary critic. There may be more to talk about in a Rosenberg essay on "Time in the Museum" than in a Greenberg piece on, say, "The Crisis of the Easel Picture," but Greenberg always manages to say more about sheer painting in a page than Rosenberg would in an essay. The contrast points up not the relative merit but the fact, again, that the most talented critics tend not to want to write about art as art. They are interested, quite as Greenberg argued time after time, in art as phenomenon, in art as social meaning, in art as anything but what it was for most of those who made it.

The difference between Rosenberg and Greenberg—though not as total in the end as both men claimed—may be summarized by isolating a few brief formulations. In these it will be seen that their respective approaches to twentieth-century art derived from theories of value which they did their best to apply consistently. Strangely, the two men most often agreed on what was important, and both may be said to have found in Jackson Pollock an exemplary painter whose disfavor with other artists and critics only proved how barren of decent standards was the contemporary scene. Greenberg always claimed, more than Rosenberg, to know what was what, and it wasn't often that he allowed himself to be surprised by a new body of work or by the reception it had been given. All the same, he admitted now and again to changing his mind, and conceded that the artistic climate might well affect the way even Clement Greenberg would look at a painting. Rosenberg's was the more mercurial temperament, and his best essays on art seem always to have a more speculative dimension, as if—in the absence of a firm belief in the value of individual paintings—he needed to discover

---

*Until 1986 and the publication by the University of Chicago Press of the *The Collected Essays and Criticism*, the only pieces Greenberg chose to collect were gathered in the volume *Art & Culture* (Boston: Beacon Press, 1961).

both the source of their obvious energy and of his own peculiar interest in them. Greenberg, who resisted any note of boyish enthusiasm, was content to sound like a connoisseur, so that even his changes of mind seem to emerge from a stable basis of comparison and evaluation. Rosenberg, on the contrary, seemed not to be writing predominantly for people who had given their lives to painting, but for those who, like him, had found in modern art a powerful expression of—and a way out of—the modern condition. Not surprisingly, Rosenberg is most impressive when he is talking about "the condition" of this thing or that; Greenberg is best on "internal" developments in the work of Picasso or Lipchitz or Chaim Soutine.

Rosenberg (on Pollock): "His consciousness is directed not toward an effect determined by notions of good painting but toward the protraction and intensification of the doing itself."

Greenberg: "To be categorically against or for a current artistic tendency . . . means inquiring into the motives of artists instead of into results."

Rosenberg (on American action painting): "The gesture on the canvas was a gesture of liberation from Value . . . The new painting has broken down every distinction between art and life . . . If the picture is an act, it cannot be justified *as an act of genius* in a field whose whole measuring apparatus has been sent to the devil. Its value must be found apart from art."

Greenberg: "All values are human values, relative values, in art as well as elsewhere. Yet there does seem to have been more or less of a general agreement among the cultivated of mankind over the ages as to what is good art and what bad . . . this agreement rests, I believe, on a fairly constant distinction made between those values only to be found in art and the values which can be found elsewhere."

Because Greenberg insisted so often upon invoking "values only to be found in art," he could seem narrow to readers who were less interested than he in formal properties or who had trouble seeing them even when Greenberg pointed them out. And of course, to try to distinguish between achievement and failure at a time when, according to other intelligent witnesses, the "whole measuring apparatus has been sent to the devil" is to seem pretentious and, perhaps, dishonest. Greenberg's attempt to establish a theory of value and to rigorously evaluate works of art that had in some degree broken with earlier representational norms was, clearly, an admirable enterprise. But it tended, in

practice, to breed suspicion, and as Greenberg grew more confident in his writings, he came more and more to invite fierce
resistance. This is a pity, really, since it should be possible to
disagree with Greenberg's view of a particular work without having to resist him altogether. Even where—as in his less than respectful accounts of Rouault and Alexander Calder—he fails to
persuade, he has instructive things to say, and it is intellectually
satisfying to see the man explaining to himself in general terms
what must once have seemed to him a merely visceral or personal
aversion.

To decide between Greenberg and Rosenberg, which is to say,
between one theory of value and another, may seem necessary to
someone who wishes to know where he stands on the art of the
moment. But the battles fought by the great critics in the period
between 1940 and 1970 have by now been settled, and one's position on the big issues may not finally have much to do with one's
actual response to paintings. I can say that Pollock was a painter of
major importance without accepting Greenberg's view of specific
canvases as "achieved and perfected works of art." I can reject
Rosenberg's account of the "peculiar gracefulness" and "skill" in
Pollock's late paintings without denying the radical challenge they
posed to everything else that appeared in 1955. Greenberg may
help me more than anyone else to cast a cold, intolerant eye on
what currently passes for avant-garde invention in New York or
London, but it is also the case that only a critic as intimately involved in the scene as Greenberg was thirty years ago may expect
to shape our enthusiasms as he did. The approach to paintings as
paintings remains a necessary model, an exemplary critical fiction,
if you will. But new works continue to require fresh adjustments,
and the older modernist or post-modernist works often seem only
slightly less impenetrable than they seemed a generation ago.
Whether or not you agree with Rosenberg that the value of individual paintings "must be found apart from art," you have to agree
that it's not easy to decide which one of ten Pollock or Rothko
paintings you ought to prefer.

Which brings us to the heart of the matter. If it is true—as I
believe it is—that Greenberg taught a whole generation to see the
connection between collage as practiced by the great Cubist masters in 1913 and the emergence of abstraction in America after the
Second World War; that he made the definitive case not only for
the American painters of his generation but for Monet and other
already "classic" painters we didn't quite know how to use; and

that he founded a rigorous aesthetic based upon a ready tolerance for "errors of taste, false starts and over-run objectives," why is it that he yet left us with so little confidence that each of us so educated would be able to do the job of evaluation for himself? Why is it that, when Greenberg says of *Guernica* that it proves Picasso "could not make a success of a large canvas with Cubistically flattened forms," we register only slight surprise, and go on to murmur something about the irrelevance of disagreements over particular works? For shouldn't it be that people who share certain values, a common vocabulary, and a sense of historical progress or tradition should also be able to agree that *Guernica* is or is not a successful painting? And if we cannot, as many cannot agree with Greenberg that Chagall's black-and-white etchings are far more successful than his paintings, or that Soutine succeeded as an artist only *in spite of* his expressive gifts, what is our critical education all about?

Professor Kuspit's book on Greenberg doesn't go so far as to ask that question. It does complain about the critic's refusal to countenance a phenomenological approach to painting, and argues that without such an approach the critic is forced to ignore "psychological effect, or more generally, the expressive aura of art." This aura, Kuspit goes on to say, "is the residue of intention," and no matter what Greenberg may claim, is an important part of our experience of the painting. Greenberg's attempt to validate his taste and to establish for it a consensual basis seems to Kuspit a heroic enterprise, but he denies that it is possible to isolate works of art from their cultural moment and to look at them without attending also to their referential dimension. If we cannot find a generally acceptable way of looking at individual paintings, the reason may be that we insist too strenuously on a pure or narrow view of art as the object in itself. Kuspit offers no alternative, apart from his vague sense that we ought to make room for a "psychological" reading of the work. In practice, the alternatives have usually been embodied in an impressionistic criticism that is frankly personal and oriented to surfaces; in a historical criticism that defines and evaluates the work against the tradition in which it must be set; or in a literary criticism that humanizes the work by discovering or inventing a content that will be relevant to the ordinary concerns of ordinary men and women. Kuspit seems not to believe that these are the only alternatives but provides no working model of his own. Though he tries, with considerable skill and intelligence, to set himself apart from Greenberg, he is on the whole reduced to paraphrasing the master's views and seconding his conclusions. The problems remain very much what they seemed to those of us who have for years lived with Greenberg's essays as a bracing bedside companion.

The temptation, in addressing these problems, is to start at the beginning, but one soon concludes that this is useless. It may be interesting to know what Picasso was thinking when he tried his hand at landscape painting in the early fifties, but his intentions are after all aesthetically significant only in the degree that they are manifestly inscribed in the works themselves. What we then choose to make of the paintings is another matter, and I have not the slightest doubt that many of the artists Greenberg covers would have difficulty recognizing themselves in his account of their intentions. What did the sculptors Calder and Noguchi think of his statement that, in them, " 'the *modern* is treated as a convention with a closed canon of forms,' one of which, 'the emphasized contour,' they use decoratively"? This is not, clearly, a descriptive statement pure and simple, but an implicit reading of intention. Suppose Noguchi denied that for him the modern was reducible to a particular *look* or decorative gimmick. Suppose he was supported in his denial by other reputable artists and critics. What would this prove? Greenberg is careful to say that the modern is *treated* in a given way by Noguchi, not that Noguchi thought to succeed as an artist by figuring things out in the way Greenberg describes. In any case, actual intention is not crucially at issue. What counts is the impression made, the way in which the thing invites us to respond to it by working at a style. To start at the beginning is to start with a first impression of the work.

That first impression, of course, will not *tell* unless it is the impression of a person who can truly judge. When Greenberg wrote that "the best taste develops under the pressure of the best art and is the taste most subject to that pressure," he meant to exclude from the serious consideration of art the "urban masses" and the country "folk"—those, in other words, who will always "set up a pressure on society to provide them with a kind of culture fit for their own consumption." In no discernible way sensitive to the obvious charge of elitism often leveled at him, Greenberg has consistently maintained that the attempt to make high art popular can only lead to the creation of kitsch, an art that "pretends to demand nothing of its customers." The genuine article, he contends, is usually hard to take, at least at first, and its effects will be felt only by those who have trained themselves to look for and to sustain the impression of irreconcilable tensions within the work. Kuspit, like Greenberg, sees these tensions as in part provided by the artist's ambivalent commitment to verisimilitude, which can take the form either of a straight representational impulse or of a desire to "imitate" or to "express" his own emotional state. Either way, the artist is almost bound to find his commitment an "obstacle to pictorial unity," which he will achieve if at all only as a "dialectical illusion." Greenberg's term, following Kant, suggests that the tension experienced by the viewer will be phenomenally *real* in a way that cannot be matched by his experience of pictorial unity. The viewer who is likely to have a fruitful first impression will need to keep these different kinds of experience apart and to resist the idea that, as he becomes more familiar with the work, there will cease to be division in his experience.

Nor is it the case, in Greenberg's view, that the tension and the different levels of experience he describes will be limited to one's encounters with twentieth-century painting. The history of Western art shows that the "dialectical fluctuation between abstraction and representation," as Kuspit has it, between design and expression, has been constant. Even a radically abstract or intellectual painter like Barnett Newman Greenberg describes as keeping "within the tacit and evolving limits of the Western tradition of painting." This sense of the tradition Greenberg most often supports by showing how good painters always work with a sure sense—sure even if inarticulate—of the "tacit and evolving limits." Even the viewer operates, as it were, in these terms, so that our perceptual capacities are constantly conditioned by what we see and what we learn to admire. If, at a certain point, we find it hard to like Renoir, find that the necessary tensions to which we are alert have been unduly softened, the cause will lie in our evolving relation to, say, Matisse or the later Monet. For if we learn, in coming properly to appreciate them, that what matters in painting are "simplification, broadness, directness"—Greenberg's terms—then it may be that Renoir will suddenly seem too picturesque, too bent on the "sure-fire effect." This impression too will probably come to be modified under the pressure of other aesthetic experiences, including perhaps renewed encounters with paintings of an earlier age whose qualities had similarly to be retrieved from the impression produced by their more obvious effects.

Wherever we look, adjustments in our perceptual habits are required to keep pace with our experience of new works and with our changing conceptual grasp of the tensions to which all interesting works bear witness. The development of collage in 1912 may have produced "a more vivid *idea* of depth" than any previous painting had achieved, but the dynamics of the actual work, like the tensions produced in cubist art generally, had still to be understood in "traditional" terms. Greenberg quotes, in his great essay on collage (1959), a famous passage from E. H. Gombrich's *Art and Illusion*, in which the "dialectical fluctuation" is described as the relation between illusion and contradiction. I don't see how it is possible to improve upon the formulation:

> If illusion is due to the interaction of clues and the absence of contradictory evidence, the only way to fight its transforming influence is to make the clues contradict each other and to prevent a coherent image of reality from destroying the pattern in the plane. Unlike the Fantin-Latour, a still life by Braque . . . will marshal all the forces of perspective, texture, and shading, not to work in harmony, but to clash in virtual deadlock . . . Cubism succeeds by the introduction of contrary clues. Try as we may to see the guitar or the jug suggested to us as a three-dimensional object . . . we will always come across a contradiction somewhere which compels us to start afresh.

Though the goal of the modernist work is to shift the balance of force from illusion to contradiction, the element of tension remains to distinguish the experience as an aesthetic experience. Gombrich's account of the revolution wrought by the cubist masters in no way disputes Greenberg's sense of historical continuities. The best answer to the charge that Greenberg is a historical determinist, that he is willing to see development only when he can account for it in terms of the already evolved tradition, is that he has read the tensions inhering in paintings always *as if* he were confronting those particular tensions for the first time.

More difficult to answer is the charge that Greenberg has too decisively limited his discussions of modern art. When Kuspit challenges his "insistence on the logical priority of the medium to what it conveys," our impulse is to side with Greenberg, until we consider all that is entailed in the proposition. Does Greenberg's insistence on the material character of the work of art commit him to Valéry's view of art, in terms of which "the real connoisseur . . . is necessarily he to whom the work suggests nothing"? And if this is so, does it follow that people with the best taste will *naturally*—directed not by imposed cultural imperatives but by "common sense"—incline to consider the medium apart from anything it might suggest?

Consider a typical instance. The connoisseur is confronted with a painting by Rouault entitled *The Old King*. What does he see? He recognizes a figure in profile. He registers the fact that the figure is rather blocklike in its solidity and that, despite its several luminous colors, the painting achieves remarkable pictorial unity. This he attributes to Rouault's method of compartmenting his colors, encasing his shapes in heavy black borders which are clearly intended to call to mind Gothic stained-glass windows. The viewer may not care to read in the old king's face the "mood of resignation and inner suffering" that means so much to textbook writers like H. W. Janson, but he will no doubt feel there is a heaviness in the figure that has at least to be considered as an aura. The painting has a mood. He may not like that mood, may feel that it excludes him in some way. But he will need to come to terms with it, to give it a name and assign it a purpose before deciding what to think of the painting.

Greenberg would say of the mood that it is inevitably a function of the "artistic personality" embodied in the work, and that a personality like Rouault's should inspire "distaste." The judgment, he would insist, is aesthetic, not personal, and is arrived at by attending to Rouault's handling of his medium. Yes, there are the obvious "interventions" of black or brown borders in Rouault's paintings, and yes, they call to mind stained-glass windows. But what is the use to which Rouault puts these things? The connoisseur will know, surely, that the "interventions . . . offer a safe way of guaranteeing the harmony of other colors." Rouault offers himself as an artistic original with a traditionalist religious orientation, but in fact he simply sought and found an easy way of unifying his surface. The bordering technique helped to articulate and "emphasize" the surface in a hopeful way, but Rouault only "seemed to be settling the conflict between pattern and illusion in favor of the immediate, sensuous effect of the former." Live with the paintings a while and you will see that "the unifying conception . . . remains oriented toward a standard illusion in depth, and the result, for all its ornamental accents, remains essentially conventional." Rouault's artistic personality is rejected because it "masks a conventional sensibility behind modernist effects." It is, in this sense, dishonest. The aesthetic distaste has what might be called a moral component, whatever Greenberg wishes to call it.

But let us return briefly to the question of the tension embodied in the work. Though he does not choose to dwell upon it, Greenberg's account of Rouault does clearly demonstrate that there is the requisite tension in his characteristic paintings. And it is, roughly, the tension between illusion and contradiction or design and expression elaborated earlier. Greenberg rejects the work not because the tension is resolved too entirely or too prematurely but because it is resolved in the wrong direction. The painting "remains oriented toward a standard illusion in depth." But what does it mean to say this? Not, surely, that any illusion in depth is by definition "standard," or that Rouault's image is drawn to appeal to an easy notion of mechanical skill or lifelikeness. If Greenberg wishes to speak for tension in the work of art, he must show that he is committed to the "dialectical fluctuation" rather than to an up-to-the-minute postmodernist resolution. This is precisely where the aesthetic falters. For what justification has Greenberg to say that any version of the illusion in depth—no matter how original that version—will indicate "a conventional sensibility"? To my knowledge, no one ever claimed that Rouault drastically challenged our perceptual habits in the manner of a Picasso. But that is no reason to dismiss his efforts as dishonest or to pretend that the tensions implicit in his work have no valid expressive content. If his paintings show a genuine involvement in issues of design and pattern, he should at least be said to have been aware of problems to which others may have contributed more various and inventive solutions.

Greenberg's insistence on the priority of the medium doesn't prevent him from arguing, with Rouault as with others, that the artist's handling does finally have something to do with content. "Rouault's manner," he complains, "seems to have a life independent of the subjects to which it is applied. We come away remembering paint instead of single pictures." Here it is necessary to object not to the fact that the critic rejects in Rouault what he praises in others—sheer painterly touch—but to the way in which he tries to "get" Rouault, as it were, coming and going. First he is accused of settling for standard illusions in depth, then of working for a pure manner complete with painterly refinements. The fact is, were Greenberg as ready as he claims to approach the work without a repertoire of limiting principles, he would find in Rouault a manner obviously geared to his subjects. If we do come away from *The Old King* "remembering *paint*" instead of the subject—an arguable proposition in any case—that is only because mood and medium are so deftly integrated that to think of the paint is to think of subject and necessary effect. The protagonist in Lionel Trilling's story "The Other Margaret" who looks at the Rouault painting and notes that its "rude blacks . . . might seem barbarically untidy" doesn't feel that the manner is independent of the subject. His observation of the king's "fierce quality" doesn't prevent him from feeling that he is "human and tragic" or that the painting as a whole breathes an air of impersonality that lifts it beyond our capacity to identify too entirely with any aspect of it. Greenberg cares more than the Trilling character about Rouault's laying on of paint, and he obviously knows more about the options available in a "conflict between pattern and illusion." But he is more ambivalent than he admits about content in painting, and his aesthetic principles often force him to be unfeeling towards paintings he has every reason to like better.

The weakness in his position is again pointed up in what Greenberg takes to be a conclusive contrast between Rouault and the modernist painters he prefers: Rouault, he argues, is "a narrow virtuoso who favors a certain kind of content mainly for the sake of style—unlike Matisse and Picasso and Mondrian, who work at a style in order to achieve content." A tricky business. What exactly is the content favored by Rouault? Clearly, for Greenberg, it has something to do with the tragic solemnity we have noted in his figures. This aura or suffusing emotion the critic rejects as in some sense insincere or vaguely wishful. It stems from a religious conviction, a "modern" Catholicism which when deliberately expressed in a modernist painting inevitably comes off as religiosity. When he writes that "Rouault's manner seems to have a life independent of the subjects to which it is applied," Greenberg means precisely that even the figure of the king who has no specific religious affiliation will seem to express the content of the painter's vague religious faith. And the style? " 'Profundity,' " says the critic, "is the term that gets associated with religiosity in these days." Rouault's is an unsatisfactory style because it lends itself to the impression of an *obvious* profundity. His content is shallow because it is manipulated in the end for the sake of a certain look. And a look, Greenberg has elsewhere written, is "an affair of standardized categories . . . within reach of uninspired calculation."

If we reject the critic's case against Rouault, we are yet compelled to agree that he has his reasons and that a certain skepticism about artists who inspire confident assertions on the quality of life in general is usually warranted. We may be less willing to agree that the great modernist painters work "to achieve content." A painting like *Guernica* Greenberg dismisses without making any mention of content. Hans Hofman he praises for fertility of "vision" though he never once offers his version of the content of that vision. Matisse, Picasso, Mondrian? He says of the latter that he gives us "islands radiating clarity, harmony, and grandeur—passion mastered and cooled." Is this content, we wonder, intrinsically more acceptable than Rouault's? Kuspit argues that the high modernist aesthetic— which so clearly prefers Mondrian to Rouault, for example—is a partisan position: "it sets limits prematurely; it avoids confusion, but its clarity blinds us." Mondrian, I should say, whatever his originality and his radical capacity to work out the terms of his enterprise, is a prime example and mover of this modernist bias. He is, no doubt, a more important artist than Rouault. But are his paint-ings better paintings? Is their content more sincere? Have they a greater power to move and affect us? Do we remember single pic-tures by Mondrian more clearly than we remember *The Old King?* For Greenberg, as Kuspit shows, Western art has now triumphantly entered its "positivist phase," which is to say, it "is now explicit— abstraction is the form this openness takes—about what has always been implicit in it." A mature art, by this token, always knows what it is about. Its content is not stated in the work but is inferred by a viewer who is in touch with its underlying objectives. It does not contain its reflected effect but gives oblique access to that effect. Thus it is that an art like Rouault's must be rejected. In its attempt to suggest a content by predigesting for the viewer its central objec-tives, it operates too comfortably like an earlier Western art that concealed its material character in its overt commitment to represen-tation and illusion. The content of a Mondrian or a Matisse doesn't have to be underlined, because the quality of the invention is self-evident. How do you know it is self-evident? You know. And the content? "You know that a work of art has content because of its effect." You cannot compare the effect of a Rouault to that of a Mondrian unless you misconceive entirely what is meant by effect. The one does not so much achieve as deliver over an effect that it has received; the other moves us because its content is so entirely a function of the attention it pays to its own material composition.

Obviously, those who have learned—at whatever cost—to prefer Mondrian to Rouault and who experience that preference as a vis-ceral attraction and revulsion will hope to find in Greenberg an adequate support. But no matter how thorough Greenberg may be in substantiating this claim or that, he remains ultimately elusive just where one expects him to be definitive. His feeling for painters like Pollock or for the sculptor David Smith is consistently mounted as an appreciation of those who know how to "accept the surprises of their temperament," who perfect an art "beyond accomplished-ness, facility or taste." Always an opponent of "the safe way," he celebrates in Renoir the "fading of the desire to please," in Monet the point at which "he stopped correcting himself and became slap-dash." To many of these favored artists it is possible to grant the highest compliment: that they "impose the greatest possible organic unity upon the greatest diversity." But if "economy" is a necessary element of organic unity, as Greenberg also supposes, then it is hard to see how Pollock rates. And if "the greatest diversity" has to do with anything beyond originary, inexpressive intention, it should be hard to make the case for Mondrian or Barnett Newman. Even the case for the great cubist masters may seem confusing when Green-berg speaks of their "encasement in a style that, so to speak, feels for the painter and relieves him of the anguish and awkwardness of invention, leaving his gift free to function almost automatically." I cannot help feeling that the same insight, derived from an encounter with another kind of painter encased in a different style, would take on a negative valuation and lead Greenberg to dismiss the painter. For to say that a style feels for a painter is after all to say that he does not feel for himself. And a gift that may be said to function "almost automatically" may not be said to actively risk the "false starts" and "errors of taste" that come with a more temperamental approach to painting. I conclude, with Kuspit, that Greenberg's aesthetic is defi-cient, his attempt "to articulate . . . the premises of his own sensibil-ity" only a partial success. If he is the greatest critic of twentieth-century art we have had, he has shown that neither the best taste nor the best intelligence can fully compensate for the absence of a tradi-tional, consensually validated hierarchy of aesthetic values.

Heresies
of Modern Art

Xavier Rubert de Ventos, *Heresies of Modern Art* (New York: Columbia University Press).

The injunction to make it new in the arts has lately been extended. For more than a decade, artists and academic fellow-travelers have insistently recommended that random experimentation and irregularity be introduced into the precincts of ordinary behavior. This recommendation has been associated—particularly in the United States—with the radicalism of the 1960s, and many of us have wanted to believe it would disappear with the peculiar frenzy of that period. Some may even have thought that the tendency to aestheticize ordinary experience, to impose aesthetic categories upon family and work patterns, would refresh the body politic and help to clear away outworn assumptions. From the first it was clear that the leaders of the so-called counterculture entertained immoderate ambitions for the renovation of society. But those of us who had been taught to admire artists for the things they made, and to believe that intellectuals had an obligation to propose drastic adjustments without supposing that anyone would take them seriously, could not get it into our heads that some changes really had taken place. The recent book by Señor de Ventos helps us to gauge the magnitude of those changes and to consider the fate of radicalism in our culture.

Heresies of Modern Art appeared originally in a Spanish edition in 1973. A scholarly work, it at once proposes to deliver a "history" of

From *Bennington Review*, Spring 1981.

Western art and to repudiate our central traditions by securing for the new arts a primacy that is everywhere related to recent developments in social life. These developments it reports with a combination of dismissive *brio* and revolutionary optimism that will seem oddly unsettling to any but the most convinced true-believers in cultural revolution. For de Ventos, instead of arguing his case, is content to cite the testimony of others whose views support what he thinks he has to say. Nor does the book unsettle us by making us confront what we've never considered before. Though it is one of the more ambitious scholarly works to come out of the experience of the 1960s, it is an important example of the ravages wrought by the continuing divorce between criticism and learning. The fact that this book passes for criticism even among gifted critics like Richard Sennett—who has written the preface to the volume— only indicates how ready some of us are to credit anything that proclaims disenchantment with the organization of control in our society. And what do we mean by the divorce between criticism and learning? We mean the inclination to believe that a series of descriptions of a given state of affairs—provided they have been accumulated from respectable sources—will suffice to demonstrate the cogency of conclusions drawn from those descriptions. No thought is given to the possibility that, quite in the way that official views are built up out of a managed consensus, alternative views may also be built up by drawing upon a very narrow range of sources and by contriving to suppress anything that cannot support those views. Did Mr. Sennett never wonder, as he read this book, why de Ventos pays so little attention to worrying details which, by the logic of his case, he should be forced to entertain?

An example. At one point, working himself up into a perfect ecstasy over the possibilities of Artaudian theatre of cruelty, de Ventos is forced momentarily to remember what Walter Benjamin wrote on the aestheticization of politics: that war is the only necessary and sufficient culmination of that process. Since Benjamin is now important, since his views on these matters are well known among radical intellectuals, de Ventos cannot pretend not to know that he exists. That is how de Ventos operates: He is a "knower." And so, Benjamin is introduced. But one would not imagine, from the way in which de Ventos ignores Benjamin's insight, that it is utterly central to much in his chapter, indeed, to his entire book. For de Ventos, there is simply an opportunity to indicate that he has made contact with an essential source, and an occasion to reiterate what is always on his mind: the notion that any theory or practice which relies upon convention—as even the gestures associated with Artaudian theatre must—is repressive and "puritanical." Benjamin's more than cautionary perspective cannot be permitted to stand in the way of one who knows where he is going.

But let us consider rather more closely the specific thrust of this book. De Ventos argues that the arts of Western culture are typically puritanical, whatever artists may tell themselves. By puritanical, he means that they typically serve some purpose beyond the production of pleasing surfaces and the satisfaction of the artist's expressive needs. If, for example, a novel wishes to say something about politics in the Napoleonic period, it is impurely motivated and, therefore, puritanical. Were such a novel willing to present events with no intention of addressing *particular* problems or a particular historical period, it might be more satisfactory by present lights. Works of art in general are most successful when they exalt pure vision or pure sensation, when they do nothing but *show*. Works that legitimize their operations by putting us in mind of transcendent categories, or utility, or moral questions, fail to exercise our freedom as they should. What we want from works of art is a display of gratuitous invention that will stimulate us to undertake our own flights of gratuitous exploration. We want to move beyond all of the familiar conventions. Action painters who worked to do away with representational norms thought they were free, while in fact they were sadly struggling to fulfill other requirements: for good taste, more intricate design, greater originality, and so on. Even Nietzsche, according to de Ventos, was a hopeless puritan, for was he not infected like the others by "the *esprit du serieux* of his period and his class"? Did he not, while insisting upon art as game and artifice, affirm "the order of fiction, of artistry and deceit—in a word, of culture"? For de Ventos, anything to do with function is by definition puritanical and, in that sense, repressive. He will accept nothing but surface and appearance.

Now de Ventos is ready to concede that the definition of art varies with the expectation imposed by particular cultural systems. Definitions seem to remain relatively stable within stable cultural systems, and to break down or contradict their own predictive norms when the society is in crisis. De Ventos does not so much wish to legislate attitudes towards the arts of the past as to indicate why those arts are no longer suitable. Now and again he confesses to a passing weakness, a nostalgia for settled and familiar forms, but he asks us to take control of ourselves and to see the situation as it is. The modernist artists, right up through the abstract expressionist painters of the

1950s, were obviously sincere in their desire to opt out of the expressive systems they had inherited from another age. But they were fatally limited by their "labelling as *aesthetic* [only] the activities and objects to which it was thought legitimate in their period to apply imagination." They did not see that the cultural system could no longer be trusted to furnish satisfactory ideals with which to legitimize anything. What matters in art, what has always mattered, is "pregnancy," and this, says de Ventos, is an "inherent possibility of any experience, activity, or work." The definition of art in terms of what is not art seems to de Ventos a sterile and reactionary reflex that owes more to outworn social systems than to our current situation.

The theory comes to us complete with a psychology. Art, for de Ventos, is "the symbolic rejection of a system of control." What system? *The* system. If you're looking at the thing from, say, the United States, it will do to say, for system, capitalism. If you're standing somewhere else, you may speak of systemic repression in other terms. De Ventos isn't as interested in social or political analysis as he seems here and there to be. He is interested in formulating his theory at a high level of abstraction, and his task is made easier if he can simply say, when the spirit moves him, system of control, and expect that his reader will instantly *know*, and nod approval. With this attitude safely assured, the reader will also know about the psychology of those whose lives must be shaken and possibilities re-created by the example of art. For is it not a fact that we are all of us weak creatures, afraid "of being the masters of our own fates"? Is it not true that we have been conditioned to accept "the great axiom of the consumer society: whatever desire, dream, or aspiration one has, there is always an institution that channels it and an object that satisfies it"? And if this is true, why then it must follow that the only experience that can possibly wean us away from our expectations will be "nonpragmatic, unpredictable." As participant-observers in chaotic mixed-media events designed to exert minimal control, we must unlearn the controlled behaviors we live by. In the degree that we are normally carried along by a sea of encompassing stimulations, we shall more and more crave experiences that are "irrational, anomalous, and individual." Art alone, conceived as de Ventos would have it, can train us to tolerate and to create such experiences.

The stress on experience is of course a familiar feature of 1960s-style cultural radicalism. In the writings of R. D. Laing and others it came to signify a sacred precinct that might be approached or protected but could not be penetrated by others. Systems of control in the West would destroy individuals by getting them to believe that their personal experience was invalid, *merely* personal, a projection of simple fantasy or need. Those who spoke, as they so often reminded their audiences, *for man* encouraged people to trust their intuitions and to resist the injunctions of authority wherever they might be met. Experience could be preserved only by those who allowed themselves to register what they were feeling, who refused to submit what they thought they felt to an executive board for unscrambling, placement, and evaluation. In the extreme, this translated to encouragement for schizophrenics and other persons formally labeled as mentally ill, persons who might now be thought to have acknowledged what they were feeling in a way the rest of us were too well conditioned to permit ourselves. In the arts, this meant the relaxation of standards of value in the quest for experiences that were free, unprogrammed, even arbitrary, provided only that they did not call up responses that were learned or in any way correct.

De Ventos's book is not a brief for any one kind of art, but the author's working definition of conceptualism does aptly describe a characteristic bias. "Conceptualism," he says, "does not aim to absorb the spectator into the work, but to refer him to the concept or process which lies behind it." The intellectual dimension inscribed in the enterprise, so defined, is not invariably present in the aesthetic experience as de Ventos celebrates it. But he does invariably insist upon that which is unpredictable, a mode—whether in literature or painting or theatre—which is exercised neither by plausibility nor typicality. In fact, as we examine the several key formulations closely, we find that de Ventos doesn't really object to a certain kind of absorption into the work. He objects only to what he at one point calls "discursive processing." It is quite alright for the work to absorb the spectator, provided only that the stimulation be pure. "In the movies or the new theatre," de Ventos exclaims, "the protagonist can again be the Event, the Violence itself, without the mediation of an Ego or a Discourse that represents them." Which is to say, only *mediation* is truly forbidden those who wish to know on their pulses (with art, the only valid place to know) what they feel. It may be necessary to have recourse to an originating idea or conceptual process, but this will necessarily delay the more vital and immediate gratification it is our business to win.

Why the consistent opposition to mediation? De Ventos is heavily influenced by the constellation of European philosopher-intellectuals—most especially Michel Foucault—for whom discourse has almost become synonymous with the history of oppression and control. To mediate an event is, for such people, to submit it to the official interpretive codes by which events of a particular kind are neatly assimilated to the type or pattern of such events and stripped of their ability to astonish or to inspire fresh response. De Ventos assumes that we are familiar with these views of discourse, and that we will share with him a desire to avoid it at all costs. A conceptualist artifact at least asks that we perform a two-part operation before we agree to submit the work to discursive processing. At least, in the space of time before we arrive at a conceptual pigeonholing of the work, we can try to separate it from its apparent stimulus-function. Confronted by the thought of an intention apart from the work itself, we may be able to think further to a nexus of pure intention or feeling that is not susceptible to exact representation. The goal, here as elsewhere, is to avoid that which is predictable and can be responded to conventionally, with the interpretive apparatus typically mandated for such operations. De Ventos tolerates the processing intrinsic to a conceptual art because the goals of the mediation it entails cannot be rigidly determined or securely realized. It is one thing to think intention, quite another to move to see that it is fulfilled. To be touched by a classic work—a Tolstoy novel or a Vermeer painting—in a more or less decorous and expectable way (a way de Ventos would have us avoid) is to submit to a process of mediation with a determinate end in view. And ends, once again, call to mind the consideration of origins and, ultimately, of control.

The problem with all of this is that de Ventos really has nothing better to offer as alternative than his fixed conviction that irregularity and experiment are good for people, and that art succeeds best when it denies itself obtainable goals. For all his obvious facility in charting the evolution of artistic forms, he does not understand the variety of purposes—expressive and social—at work even in the most austere and controlled classical forms. His view of art is too mechanistic to account for what goes on even in the objects he cites. No doubt, if all that is involved is "the satisfaction of needs and the exercise of abilities," as he claims, then there is not much more to say than he says. A particular work either does or does not satisfy, does or does not provide the exercise. By these criteria, a masterpiece formerly avowed as such by generations of educated people may cease at once to seem worthy as soon as members of the present generation determine that it does not answer their needs or exercise what they take to be their real abilities. No other consideration is relevant. The recommended procedures for appropriating and dismissing aesthetic experience make of persons—as of the objects they confront—something less than we should like them to be. If persons are more than needs and appetites, so the objects that satisfy them may be more than inspired devices geared to service those needs. De Ventos does not see how surely his theory works against the image of human being he wishes to assert.

In what is perhaps the most interesting passage of his book, de Ventos adopts—temporarily—a McLuhanite perspective, and argues that the ethics of mass consumption are inherently unethical. For they amount in effect to a re-creation of "a *slave* morality (enjoyment, irresponsibility) opposed to a master's morality (responsibility, prestige, power)." In this scheme the consumers are the slaves, the artists the masters. The one group agrees to be gratified, the other to manage or control. So put, the arrangement is self-evidently unsavory and reactionary. But nothing de Ventos can say against it can alter the fact that his vision makes just such an arrangement inevitable. What does he recommend to counter the emergence of a slave morality? Participatory forms, and an endless series of experiments—aesthetic, familial, sexual—in which artists and fellow-traveling avant-gardists accumulate failures. "With uneven success," de Ventos claims, artistic imagination of the appropriate sort is spreading into "all the areas of theoretical or practical activity." Failure is no longer a thing to fear but to confront head-on. People who take risks will throw off their chains and cease to be slaves. Former masters, less secure in the prospect of manipulation and control, will cease to be exalted over their constituents in an unseemly way.

What is absurd here is the talk of failure when there is no determinate enterprise to fail in. Without a goal or a coherent scheme of values by which to measure progress, how is failure to be gauged? De Ventos wants to have it both ways. He wants, on the one hand, to encourage people to get involved, to refuse to be passive consumers, to be more than the needs and appetites ascribed to them by market analysts and movie companies. He also wants to encourage random experimentation, the emergence of gratuitous activity in which the experience of failure ceases to produce anxiety. He does not see that these are incompatible goals, that his idea of gratuitous activity runs counter to any possible notion of individual responsibility and purpose. Another definition or version is required. Gratuitous activity, after all, need not be mindless or infantile or without an element of skill or control. What is essential is that the control be exerted *by* the actor for purposes that he assigns and that are not outside the range of the activity itself. Painting ceases to be gratuitous when the painter calculates what will sell before setting down his strokes. The reader of a novel ceases to be engaged in a gratuitous activity when he considers, as he turns each page of the book, how he will represent the dominant theme to his class. But de Ventos debases the very idea of play when he suggests that those who play have no thought of failure as a consequence to be avoided. To welcome failure is not to care about one's activity. Does de Ventos believe that, on the tennis court of a weekend afternoon, one would as soon miss the ball as place it deftly just out of the reach of one's opponent? And does he think that, to take satisfaction in that placement, in that achievement, is not to have a gratuitous relation to the game? If so, he has never played at anything, never grasped what it means to be passionately engaged in an activity for its own sake with no thought of reward apart from the doing. To be so engaged is of course to be in touch with the prospect of failure and with the goal of avoiding failure. To speak of blithely accumulating failures is precisely to frame activity as an irresponsible and mindless pursuit worthy of slaves. De Ventos would make of skill or excellence but two more repressive goals imposed by a society committed to technological control.

The most terrible aspect of de Ventos's theory is its vicious attempt to fetishize the idea of play under the banner of freedom and to propose that art and life are one. It is bad enough that he should try to reduce art to a sterile ideology of gratuitous frivolity. But that he should go on to proclaim the aestheticization of reality as an objective worth aiming at is unforgivable, particularly when the evidence marshaled to support the effort is so paltry. Ours is a period "with a chronic scarcity of the gratuitous," he says, as if masses of people were not routinely engaged in just the kind of mindless play he exalts. What we need is an art committed to "tearing down our defenses against the unexpected, freeing up our feelings, . . . liberating our narcissism," and so on, as if there were not portents to indicate how sick of unbridled self-expression and liberationist enthusiasms many have become. But the main thrust of the argument is centered in de Ventos's appropriation of short-lived cultural fads to assert that things have started to go his way. Look to television and comics, he says; that is "where people search for inspiration these days." Consider how far along we've

been brought by the art of popular film, "the images and sequences" of which are, thank god, anything but " 'reticent.' " In
all, opposed though we are to the consumer society, we cannot but
be pleased by some of its creations, and pleased as well by the
emergence of "alternate" styles that go against the grain of our
usual concern for "originality," "beauty," and "exclusivity" in the
objects we admire. Here at last, in the recent popular acceptance of
kitsch and camp and pop, we have a positive sign that older valua-
tions are giving way. For is it not true that, though none of the
newer styles "works with new ideas, . . . neither do they put you
down or overwhelm you like those artistic or cultural forms that
people feel obliged to experience or to understand"? The key terms
here are "put you down" and "obliged." If we are hereafter to think
of our lives as a species of aesthetic play, we shall want to accustom
ourselves to an art that makes no extravagant demands, that is as
superficial and painless as the new "arts" generated by mass culture have in fact become.

But consider more closely the very idea of an art that does not
"put you down." De Ventos holds up to derision the "artistic or
cultural forms that people feel obliged to experience or to understand," presumably on the grounds that people do not come to
those forms freely but are programmed to "appreciate" what at
bottom they detest. But if it is the case that many people do pretend to appreciate what they really do not like or understand, is it
not also the case that others genuinely learn to discriminate better
from best for *themselves* and to enjoy what once seemed forbidding
or impossibly difficult? Is it not the case that de Ventos's objection
to demanding artistic or cultural forms is itself not so much an
objection to forms as to the educational values and practices that
encourage people to make arduous discriminations? De Ventos
cites with approval the radical "deschooling" proposals of Ivan
Illych, and there is no doubt that he wishes to do away with anything that has about it the aura of structure or system, hence, of
control. Obligation, whether freely chosen or not, seems to him a
repressive emotion, bespeaking an implicit valuation of experience
and a corresponding refusal to take things more simply, as they
come. Objects that oblige us to exert ourselves in a particular way
extend the system of control by which we have been made to lose
ourselves. Such at least would appear throughout to be de Ventos's
position. By contrast, objects that do not "put you down" may be
related to more casually, with a kind of easy indifference. If nothing much is at stake, nothing much invested either by the artist/

entrepreneur or consumer, the control exerted will be minimal. With each person encouraged to get involved, though at a very low level of intensity, and generally on a temporary basis only, no one is likely to be hurt, and no invidious distinctions promoted.

Need I say that de Ventos drastically underestimates the resilience of most educated persons, and that he shamelessly overstates the conditions obtaining in contemporary culture? For one thing, it is simply not true that most people who have a capacity to be moved by works of art are inspired by television, comics, or any of the other dreck served up by the mass culture industry. Serious intellectuals who have flirted with camp and pop and kitsch and have even admitted to an appetite for such things have not in the main confused them with the objects they most admire in the arts. Fewer still have imagined that a culture growing more and more "desublimated" can afford to dispense with cultural forms that remind us of an earlier and possibly still attractive dispensation. The idea that a tolerance for fiction as a more or less plausible structuring of experience leads *eo ipso* to a devaluation of "reality" and a susceptibility to "discursive processing" is not widely held in the Anglo-American intellectual community. One who wishes, like de Ventos, to describe the cultural situation has got to indicate what are the main currents and what, like it or not, are at best marginal or eccentric operations. It is important to note that the appetite for fiction of a kind that would have been recognizable to Mann or Tolstoy remains substantial *among people who read;* that representation has become respectable once again even among painters; and that the modernism we have learned, according to de Ventos, to go beyond seems to most educated persons as central to the understanding of art as it did twenty-five years ago. De Ventos's view of the scene as having shifted *entirely* in the 1960s is pitifully shortsighted.

Of course more than shortness of vision is involved. De Ventos's view of art is a muddle, but it comes out of and is in the service of a view of social process. When he tells us that the "classical" avant-garde of the 1940s and 1950s dropped the old representational requirements only to fulfill requirements for good taste and so on, we remember that the formulation, to work, would have to accommodate, say, Allen Ginsberg, Jackson Pollock, and Günter Grass, and we move on, satisfied that we'll have to discover useful analysis elsewhere in the argument. Then we discover that, though we're grateful to de Ventos for bringing to our attention so many curious "views," and for putting the case for a new art so boldly, he does no better in his approach to social process. The best moments are provided, in quotation marks, by other critics, like Simmel, and by Sennett, whose valuable insights de Ventos does not know how to use to strengthen his argument. Yes, Sennett proposes in his books "*the suppression of external and bureaucratic control*" in the life of cities. But there is not much that bureaucratic control has in common with the control exercised by an artist in his workshop, a teacher in his classroom, or a journalist on his beat. Such distinctions are routinely ignored by de Ventos in his quest for a theory that will encompass everything. His view of social process in fact shifts with the shifts in focus mandated by the overambitious reach of the book. When he is speaking of Sennett, or of the American social critic Philip Slater, he briefly adopts their perspective and grows enthusiastic about adaptation, struggle, negotiation, and—*qué horror!*—the "quality" of life. Elsewhere he is ready to dabble in chic frivolities, to embrace theatrical violence and cruelty, and to espouse a view of the beastly bourgeois as too hopelessly one-dimensional to calmly or usefully negotiate anything.

In all, de Ventos has not much to say about social process. Though there is some ideological chatter about "specific repression" of this and "segregation" of that, he doesn't really seem to be interested in the fate of particular groups or persons. What he cares about, as he insists, is "the symbolic rejection of a system of control," a rejection best managed by an art conceived as routinely available to and within the capacity of anyone. What he will not see is that "the irregularity which may be introduced into everyday activities" by this aestheticization of common experience is nothing more than the mass market entrepreneurs and the television industry executives are already eager to provide. Art and life? Who knows better than an ad man how to suggest that value and easy pleasure are one, that novelty is more important than a "substance" that is bound to wear out or to soon seem no longer desirable? To assign radical virtue to "irregularity" is to forget that even irregularity can become a control device in an economy built on rapid obsolescence. What do American movie producers do but program "irregularities" into their products in the hope of appealing to the bottomless appetites of American audiences for novelty and thrills? De Ventos wants a "symbolic rejection" of control systems, but the rejections he imagines are empty tokens, gestures of denial, firm only in their refusal to acknowledge their inability to change anything at all. By denying to art any of the values it has always depended upon and nurtured in its audience—values like disinterestedness and, yes, seriousness—de Ventos denies to it the radical power to affect us. What better than an attitude of scrupulous disinterestedness, after all, can enable resistance to the appeals of the market and the "art" it typically promotes? The liberated art de Ventos proposes as an answer to our disaffections was already, at the time he wrote his book, a commodity with a market value that diminished as quickly as its novelty eroded. His notion of experimental life-styles, like his view of art as gratuitous play, was bound to seem empty and delusional once it became clear that the absence of value could never be the basis of renovation in a society that had all along taught us to abandon value if we hoped to accomplish the good life.

"The Dehumanization of Art" Revisited

Near the end of his famous essay on "The Dehumanization of Art," Ortega informs us that "the new art has so far produced nothing worthwhile," or at least that he is "inclined" to think so. We recall that, when he wrote the essay in 1925, Braque and Picasso had already produced a major sequence of cubist paintings; Stravinsky's *Firebird* and *The Rite of Spring* had been performed; Eliot had published *The Waste Land*, Rilke *The Duino Elegies*, Joyce *Ulysses*, and so on. It is reasonable to wonder what Ortega had in mind and what made his essay an influential statement of a position shared by many more people than were willing to stand up and be counted.

In fact, Ortega is careful to qualify much that he says, and is well aware of the way in which philistine readers might be encouraged by his essay; but the essay does promote a view of modernist art that is deeply confused and likely to appeal to persons at once too wary to dismiss the new art out of hand and too sensible to be caught paying it much attention. These were not persons typically resistant to new ideas. On the contrary, they welcomed new ideas and new works of art as opportunities to demonstrate what a refined intelligence could do to accommodate what was difficult and unfamiliar. The critic Harold Rosenberg says of the class of such people that it believes "in cutting all ideas down to size, its size, which it declares to be the size of man." It is peculiar that the writer who expressed such palpable distaste for the masses should have found common cause with them in resorting to the idea of dehu-

From *Bennington Review*, Spring 1983.

manization. And it is distressing that Ortega was unwilling to consider rather more scrupulously what he took to be not only the size of man but the character of an exemplary art that might have done justice to his idea of man.

But what, more precisely, is the confusion to which Ortega succumbs? He defines the new art, by which he means the art of modernism, as resolutely antipopular, an art that is designed not to be understood by ordinary people. It is an art, moreover, dominated by irony, in which the recognizable human content has become so thin as to be negligible. The creators of such works, says Ortega, consider what they produce of no consequence, and deride the older artists for taking things seriously, as if the business of art were to deal with the materials of real life more or less earnestly and directly. The central impulse of the new art is to be seen most clearly in cubism, where the representational imperative has been denied and subverted. "From painting things," Ortega writes, "the painter has turned to painting ideas. He shuts his eyes to the outer world and concentrates upon the subjective images in his own mind."

Already, in his elementary definition of modernist art, Ortega's confusion is discernible. It is not accurate to say of Eliot and Joyce and Proust and Mann that they held their own creations in contempt, or thought them of little consequence. This might with some qualification be said of avant-garde artists like Duchamp or the notorious Dadaist painters who sought to discredit the idea of value itself. But without making these and other distinctions, Ortega cannot hope to persuade us that he knows what he is talking about here. Neither is it legitimate to speak of irony as if it were a unitary phenomenon more or less regularly associated with the play habit of mind. It is a long way from the irony of Eliot's "Portrait of a Lady" to the irony of Mann's "Death in Venice." And if irony is a dominant factor in Proust, it is hardly to be associated with sheer aesthetic play.

So Ortega identifies irony in a particular modernist work and makes it a central characteristic of modernism. He thinks of the play spirit as manifested perhaps in Duchamp's urinal and thinks it must be said to inhere as well in Braque's cubist still lifes. And he thinks of the Baudelairean imperative to *epater les bourgeois,* so present in the gaudy excesses of Joyce's *Ulysses* and the reticent stringencies of Mallarmé, only to overlook Thomas Mann's reminder in *Tonio Kroger* that he succeeds as a writer by virtue of his continuing though ambivalent affection for what is ordinary, even banal. The will to theorize leads Ortega astray, much as it does contemporary theorists who ignore elementary discriminations in their quest for an explanatory principle that will justify their enthusiasms and establish a ground for their aversions.

Ortega has no feeling for modernism. He sees in it a movement beyond the acceptable limits of stylization established in the past. His allegiance is not to the past as such, not to a particular style or tradition, but to what he calls the living subject. Works of art that do not hold before us the living subject, that do not make us perpetually aware of that which is sacrificed or overcome in the act of stylization, are in Ortega's terms dehumanized. We are not to demand of a poem or a painting what it can never provide, but we are not either to ignore the price we pay when we acquiesce in an aesthetic vision. All art, in this sense, inclines toward dehumanization. To be concerned primarily with form and with the invention of objects that are not imitations of already existing realities is to devalue the familiar human content of our ordinary activities. But the modernist artist has gone further. He has taught us to believe that the ordinary world does not exist in the way the artist's world exists. He has—or so says Ortega—put a ban on pathos and labored to create objects in which there is little vestige of living forms. The result? Nothing worthwhile has been created, and persons who submit routinely to modernist works are likely not to turn back to the world quite so enthusiastically as they may once have done.

Ortega writes very well, of course, and no one has said more powerfully what every artist often feels, namely, that "an object of art is artistic only in so far as it is not real"; or, "preoccupation with the human content of the work is incompatible with aesthetic enjoyment proper." But these statements may mean very different things to those who hear them or utter them as their own. Some will wonder, and quite rightly, whether it is possible even to conceive an "aesthetic enjoyment proper," as though in one's relation to a work of art one could banish sentiments and thoughts typically associated with other activities. Obviously, reading a poem is not the same thing as eating a piece of cake, and one wants not to confuse one kind of pleasure with another. But the idea that there is such a thing as pure aesthetic apprehension and that it is devoutly to be cultivated is hardly apparent even to artists given to making rigorous demands on their constituents. And the idea of the poem or painting as resolutely unreal is also provocative, though it is apt to seem tempting as well. Ortega assures us that, when he walks up to a painting, he is not disposed to regard what he sees as an answer to life's mundane questions. A painting at most proposes solutions to formal problems which it raises. And it proposes its solutions with a clarity that can only be achieved when the artist's private sentiments are not permitted overtly to control what is shown. Aesthetic pleasure, Ortega insists, must be "a seeing pleasure."

It is reasonable to suppose that when Ortega speaks of "a seeing pleasure" he is referring to the pleasure we take when we master something, when we feel that we have penetrated to its principle of organization and possess it. In his *Meditations on Quixote*, Ortega tells us that "culture is . . . that aspect of life in which, by an act of self-reflection, life acquires polish and order." Aesthetic pleasure, as a constituent of life in culture, confers upon us the sense that we can order our lives because we can perceive order in something that has been made by persons more or less like ourselves. The emphasis, as always in Ortega, is upon thought, upon the activity of the mastering intelligence. But Sir Herbert Read and other critics have questioned Ortega's ideal of clarity, and recommended in its place what Read calls "an affirmation of the positive nature of doubt and indeterminacy." Where Ortega prefers unambiguous values, in art as in politics, his critics support "subtle shades and indefinite outlines," the setting out of questions in a way that will resist not only the elaboration of definite values but the idea that such values would be useful if we could bring ourselves to agree on them.

Ortega is so uncomfortable with modernist art, then, because it refuses to do what he believes art at its best has always done. He misses the elaboration of an orderly perspective within which definite values may be permitted to emerge. He says he appreciates the demonstration of certain faculties, but he wants the work of art to reach out to us, to address us as human beings with a disposition to take hold of sense objects and convert them to ideas in the interests of clarity and order. He concedes, as we have shown, that typically works of art present unreal objects and are more intent on adding to reality than on illuminating what we have all learned to take for granted. But he also complains that "with the objects of modern pictures no intercourse is possible." The intercourse he craves, presumably, is not a transaction in which the work of art ceases to be itself, an object subject to its own laws. Ortega demands an exchange in which the dignity of our quest for reality is affirmed. This can happen only when the work of art honors the reality to which it adds. We can have fruitful intercourse only with a work that does not despise the object world into which it is cast, and that refuses to feel contempt for those who are necessarily engaged in the labors of that world. A painting that wishes to seem entirely self-sufficient, perfectly autonomous and—so far as is possible—without antecedent, is in Ortega's terms dehumanized and of little interest.

Ortega is a good deal more ambivalent about all of this than he admits, and it is his refusal to admit to ambivalence that makes so much of his aesthetic seem arbitrary and confused. If he said, simply, that modernist art tends to be cold and aloof and to negate its own importance by cutting itself off from the idea of worldly consequence, we might feel less inclined to conclude that he was blind to the objects he discusses. If he argued that modernism had produced a number of richly conceived and brilliantly executed works for which he could feel no affection, that too would make a kind of sense we might follow. To say that modernism has produced nothing worthwhile is to confuse us entirely; and to contend—since artists always accept the imperatives imposed by the time in which they live—that nothing can be done to counter the adverse influences of modernism is to turn one's own theory into a fact of life and to acquiesce prematurely in one version of what is an ever shifting state of affairs.

Ortega's ambivalence is a function of his entertaining two radically incompatible sentiments. He is proud of his capacity to adopt a properly aesthetic attitude towards works of art. He dismisses the beholder who seeks in the novel or painting "nothing but the moving fate of John and Mary or Tristan and Isolde." He also dismisses as insufficiently human all of those ambitious modernist works that in effect make it their business to ensure that no one approaching them will have in mind exclusively "the moving fate of John and Mary." It is not Ortega's responsibility to make up his mind. It is his obligation as a critic to address the incompatibilities in his approach and to call them by their rightful names. This he does not do in an adequately candid or consistent way. What is most impressive in his writings on art, namely, the lucidity with which he states his premises and marshals conclusions, is also responsible for our seeing that the premises are sometimes insupportable, the conclusions more often than not irrelevant.

Consider one premise on the basis of which Ortega concludes that the modernist artist has definitively lost touch with the human. This premise has it that "the metaphor [typically] disposes of an object by having it masquerade as something else." The modernist artist, in Ortega's view, has no use for things as they are, and thus installs at the heart of his enterprise a metaphor that is conceived exclusively as a weapon. By means of this weapon, the poet "turns against natural things and wounds or murders them." This he does because he hates reality, is afraid of the world and its laws and relations. Primitives may have had much the same thing in mind when they resorted to metaphor, but they at least did not think to permanently turn the affections of men from the world they inhabited to obviously special objects. With the objects they created, intercourse was possible. The modernist artifact, by contrast, seeks to seduce us more or less entirely from our habitual concerns and assumptions. It is inherently subversive.

The problem in all of this is, first, that metaphor does not typically dispose of an object "by having it masquerade as something else." Masquerade, a singularly misleading term here, suggests that the poet resorts to metaphor in the spirit of the magician's sleight of hand, anxious chiefly to put something over on his credulous partisans. Good poets, of course, do nothing of the kind. Their metaphors are not created to dispose of objects. They resort to metaphors to embody a truth, not to flee from it. When Eliot, in a metaphor grown slightly stale with familiarity, describes Prufrock with the words "I should have been a pair of ragged claws / Scuttling across the floors of silent seas," Prufrock himself does not disappear. The figure—both what he is and what he might well be—is powerfully apprehended *through* the metaphor. This it would seem almost too obvious to say. What Ortega must have intended when he spoke of metaphor in so misleading a way I cannot guess.

But there is another problem. It is equally hard to say why Ortega thought that the modernist work had gone so far beyond any previous kind of art. Had he seen in the operating metaphor what is obvious to all who read Eliot's lines, he might plausibly have felt that a change had occurred. Surely, in Mallarmé or in a number of the more austere symbolist poets, metaphor at least *seems* not to work as it does in Shakespeare or Keats or Tennyson. But one who views metaphor as characteristically a means to evade or dispose of real objects should not have been able to discern a drastic change.

The issue, needless to say, has been discussed at considerable length by many observers, though no one has illuminated the change in the status of metaphor as well as the critic Erich Heller in a now famous essay on "The Hazard of Modern Poetry." There he demonstrates how, in the literature of the last 150 years or so, a split has developed in the previously indissoluble relation between the represented object and the metaphorical language used to body it forth. Like Ortega, Heller dwells upon "the ambition of the human mind to dominate the real world to the point of usurping its place," but unlike Ortega, Heller's sympathies are fully engaged by the effort of the great modern artists to realize their terrible ambitions. And those sympathies he allows himself to express are a consequence of his tracing the modernist impulse not to a characteristic aggression against reality in metaphor itself but to the artist's inability to believe in the commensurability of language and object. Where Ortega misconceives the nature of metaphor and complains of dehumanization, Heller identifies a flaw in the modern soul and writes with properly rapturous distress of the modern poet's effort to express the inexpressible and to heal the very fabric of belief.

In part, Ortega's inability to deal satisfactorily with the phenomenon of modernism is the result of his drawing his distinctions too schematically. Consider the sentence: "Being an artist means ceasing to take seriously that very serious person we are when we are not an artist." No wonder Ortega regards aesthetic sentiments as "secondary passions." He identifies the artist generally with the Flaubertian pathology, in terms of which the words on the page refer only to themselves, and the paint on the canvas is nothing but paint. The artist in this view is reduced to what Sartre calls an "idiot," one whose "signifying activity" never satisfactorily "reaches beyond its instrument toward the world." The artist, when he is an artist, is not a serious person. He is not interested in issues; his primary goal is not to communicate something that matters deeply to him; he aspires only to compel admiration for the wonderful things he has made and for his overcoming of material reality. Sartre at least considers Flaubert a special case, and treats him as such. Ortega writes as though, in describing Flaubert, Sartre identified the nature of art itself. And if the artist is as artist not a serious person, then the modernist artist, by moving further and further from committed writing, by engaging reality ever more obliquely, must cease actually to be a whole person capable of creating a human work.

By conceiving the central issue in this way, Ortega in effect refuses to acknowledge the many different things that artists do; and in discussing modernism as though its sole object was to subvert reality rather than to unsettle our perceptual habits, he conveniently ignores, for example, the very serious person Yeats was when he wrote "The Second Coming" and "Easter 1916." Not all modernist artists were given to drawing mustaches on reproductions of the Mona Lisa. Ortega, after making it quite clear that he has no use for modernist art, suggests that it may yet bring forth something valuable. One may ask questions about the new artists, "and yet they provide no sufficient reason for condemning them." But of course one is not particularly interested in whether or not Ortega condemns the modernists. One wants him to understand them and to establish an acceptable procedure for evaluating what they produce. This he cannot manage.

Near the end of "The Dehumanization of Art," Ortega does say one further thing we ought briefly to examine. For the "present-day artist," he writes, "the kingdom of art commences where the air feels lighter and things, free from formal fetters, begin to cut whimsical capers." Is it true that, in modernist works, things are "free from formal fetters"? Consider the severe formality of Stravinsky's mature style, or the rigorous formal language of the cubist painters. In these and other modernist efforts one sees how problematic the idea of formal constraint has become. But one cannot possibly consign the idea to irrelevance.

More interesting is Ortega's contention that in modernist works "the air feels lighter." Ortega seems to feel that, as a work dwells more and more on its own substance, it inevitably develops a whimsical attitude towards everything. Only the world outside the artist's created universe can inspire us with an idea of consequence. When Ortega says that "the air feels lighter" in modernist works he confesses that he misses in them the accent of Necessity which ennobles or authenticates an enterprise. But of course it is precisely Necessity that is so unmistakably inscribed in the great modernist works. Ortega would seem to feel that a seemingly casual or spontaneous surface destroys all impression of Necessity. But what does Proust give us if not his own version of that "inexorable necessity" he identifies in the exchanges between piano and violin in the sonata that dominates a part of *Swann's Way?* And what can be more fraught with palpable consequence than the terms of the necessity inscribed in a poem by Paul Valéry?

Ortega refuses to see that modernism at its best is a critical response to the devaluation of man and his works by our culture. A culture that is determined to make every man a customer will try to make every object into a saleable commodity. These are commonplaces of contemporary critical discourse, but they do help us to see what is absent in Ortega. He does not see how complicit a so-called traditional art can become in affirming the procedures by which even beautiful things are degraded to the level of commodities. The philosopher T. W. Adorno was as skeptical as Ortega about many aspects of modern art, but he appreciated what it was designed to accomplish, and honored those works that succeeded in establishing some independence of market values. "Only in so far as it withdraws from a *praxis* which has degenerated into its opposite," Adorno wrote, "from the ever-changing production of what is always the same, from the service of the customer who himself serves the manipulator—only in so far as it withdraws from Man, can culture be faithful to man." By creating a structure within which everything is consequential and elements are bound to one another by an inexorable necessity whose laws are clear for any scrupulous observer to see, the modernist artist forces us to confront reality as it might be. The degraded reality in which everything is up for sale to the highest bidder and in which every object comes to seem commonplace is subverted and resisted. Culture, as Adorno argues, in the modern world can be faithful to man only by withdrawing from the fetishized conception of Man to which Ortega would recall us. The dehumanization of art ought not to be the issue. The issue, more properly, is the dehumanization of man by the forces of production. About this Ortega sadly has little to say in his writings on art.

PART TWO

In the Realm
of Babel

Language Theory and the Promise of Translation

George Steiner, *After Babel* (New York: Oxford University Press).

George Steiner's new book is not only the best thing he has done; it is one of the centrally important works of our time, a work that instructs us in so many ways that readers will not know how amply to express their pleasure and gratitude. Its subject is bewilderingly large and complex: What, Steiner wants to know, is the nature of language, and how helpful have previous writers on the subject been? What is the relation between actual discourse and everything in human experience that is fundamentally inexpressible? What, finally, do we know about the dependence of culture, and the transmission of its various codes, on the constraints built into formal language structures and the impulses to conventional subterfuge and privacy which underlie those structures? It is a pleasure to observe that, though Steiner does not have definitive answers to such questions, he has considered the options, taken due measure of the liabilities implicit in his own and other approaches, and organized the available information with scrupulous attention to essential detail and speculative context. The reader of *After Babel* will feel that, probably for the first time, he has been armed with the sophisticated equipment required to make his own assault on some of the more daunting theoretical and practical issues of our time.

Steiner proposes to study our language and thought by examining the practice and theoretical discipline of translation. Instructively,

From *American Poetry Review* (APR), November-December 1976.

he dwells at length on linguistic transfers from one language to another, on the procedures by which gifted men have sought to wake into resonance in their own native tongues what was given initial shape and expressiveness in other tongues. But the design of Steiner's book requires that he establish for the idea of translation a "totalizing designation . . . because it argues the fact that all procedures of expressive articulation and interpretative reception are translational." What the American poet does when he prepares an English-language version of Pablo Neruda is in many ways precisely what we do when we receive ordinary speech messages or read newspapers, or make our way in nonverbal communications matrices. Translation, Steiner contends, is an act we perform more or less routinely, acknowledging at least implicitly as we do so that we never mean exactly what we say, and that we may never hope to penetrate confidently to the substance of another person's discourse. We "translate" what we are told into meaningful and acceptable messages whether or not we have been able to make good use of every suggestive detail in the original message-unit. Our own utterances intentionally or unconsciously mask half of what we feel, so that we "translate" our sentiments into a shorthand of plausible and mostly inoffensive commonplaces. It is a *gross* commonplace, of course, that verbal language must always stop short of the inexpressible, that there are areas of feeling for which mute gesturings or grunts may be more appropriate than articulate speech. Steiner's radical contribution to the theory of communication, and to a theory of mind, is to argue that the process of translation that underlies and organizes our reception and creation of discourses, verbal or otherwise, is the key to understanding not only the routine dynamics of exchange but the very fabric of our thought, and the nature of language itself. It is at once an audacious and attractive idea.

What makes Steiner's argument so appealing, apart from the learning and panache he brings to the task, is the disappointment so many of us have felt with alternative approaches to these very large questions. To read, in *After Babel*, that "the study of language is not now a science," and that, "very likely, it never will be a science," is to have some useful confirmation of impressions many of us have dimly, uncomfortably entertained. Anyone who has tried, as I tried some years ago in graduate school, to discover what possible uses Chomskyan transformational grammar might have in an analysis of a complex linguistic structure—say, a modernist poem or novel—will share the feeling of relief one experiences in following Steiner: His procedures are various, the analysis close-grained and rigorous. At every point the primary intention is to resist reductive explanations of linguistic capacity and invention, to insist upon the shifting terms and unstable dynamism of all human conception.

Steiner had dealt at some length with Chomsky in an earlier book entitled *Extra-Territorial*, and the two have conducted a more or less continuous debate over very intricate and technical matters. *After Babel* is, in a sense, Steiner's *Summa*, a full account of his recent scholarly labors, and there is no mistaking the fact that in part at least the book is conceived as a further answer to Chomsky, though Steiner addresses his antagonist directly only here and there in the book. What is fundamentally at issue is the whole notion of "deep structures" in language and thought, the presence of substantive universals, whether in the human brain or in the fabric of discourse or in particular words, which will genuinely account for the things we say and think. For Chomsky, linguistic theory must aim at a description of linguistic universals that will establish a sequence of grammatical rules of such precision and general validity that they will account for the generation of *any* language. Part of Chomsky's procedure involves a search for reliable semantic universals, of the kind he posits in *Aspects of the Theory of Syntax:* ". . . the condition that color words of any language must subdivide the color spectrum into continuous segments; or the condition that artifacts are defined in terms of certain human goals, areas, and functions instead of solely in terms of physical qualities." Steiner's contention is that, though such semantic descriptions are ingenious and have some plausible validity, Chomsky's underlying procedures are in no sense consistently productive, so that Chomsky has himself lately felt it necessary to scale down his claims. *After Babel* argues that if there is no consistent point-by-point correspondence between grammatical elements of all languages one cannot contend that there are universal structures susceptible to meta-mathematical formulation. This is neither a glib dismissal nor an impossible demand for superficial coherence: Steiner concedes Chomsky's point that universals may not fruitfully be sought at a phonological or syntactic level. But he is skeptical as well of the notion that it is fruitful to work from a theory of "innate components of the human mind" which generate formal linguistic operations. For Steiner, social content is a crucial component in the examination of thought and language. "To know more of language and translation," he contends, "we must pass from the 'deep structures' of transformational grammar to the deeper structures of the poet."

Among the many services it performs, *After Babel* surveys the history of the theories of language to discover a whole range of theoretical "deep structures," each of which has encouraged particular programs for the transmission and preservation of actual languages. Thus, "the occult tradition holds that a single primal language or *ur-sprache* lies behind our present discord . . . This Adamic vernacular not only enabled all men to understand one another, to communicate with perfect ease. It bodied forth, to a greater or lesser degree, the original logos, the act of immediate calling into being whereby God had literally 'spoken the world.' " Following this tradition, and its impact on Renaissance thinkers like Jakob Böhme and on such recent writers as Walter Benjamin or Stéphane Mallarmé, Steiner invokes a puzzling and determinedly unverifiable theory of translation: "A genuine translation evokes the shadowy yet unmistakeable contours of the coherent design from which, after Babel, the jagged fragments of human speech broke off. Certain of Luther's versions of the Psalms, Hölderlin's recasting of Pindar's Third Pythian Ode, point by their strangeness of evocatory inference to the reality of an *ur-sprache* in which German and Hebrew and ancient Greek are somehow fused." This is, of course, not the sort of thing that one can easily prove, and Steiner, for one, is not at all certain that a proof need be undertaken. Possibly the best one can do is to work closely with a variety of texts and translations, reflecting insistently upon the dynamics of language transfer and the relative effects produced by plausibly similar locutions and single words taken from different languages and employed in highly charged fields of discourse.

Steiner is highly selective in the texts he examines, and usually abandons his analysis after working on what he takes to be a representative fragment of the chosen text. He is especially illuminating in his discussion of the German Romantic Hölderlin, who produced a number of remarkable though defiantly eccentric translations, and who had much to say about what he was doing. What stands out in Hölderlin's work is the element of simultaneous submission to the conceptual/linguistic authority of the original text and insistence upon correction and improvement. Confronted with *Antigone*, the German translator must perform a sequence of complex and in part contradictory procedures before committing himself to an alternate version. Preparation for the task at hand will include frequent reminders that, in the language of T. W. Adorno, "the only true thoughts are those which do not grasp their own meaning." All impulse to merely literal approximation must be resisted, so that the translator may acknowledge that we generally communicate not facts but, in Steiner's words, "motivated images, local frameworks of feeling." Such observations have as much to do with ordinary conversation among native speakers of a language as with transfers of meaning from ancient Greek to nineteenth-century German. When, following Hölderlin, Steiner writes that "the correction made by the translator is latent in the original; but only he can realize it," and that "there is in this visionary pre-emption a touch of madness," one is encouraged to think of the related though more customary and unimpassioned corrections all of us will make as we try to make sense of our experience.

But what can it mean to correct or improve a classic text like the *Antigone*, especially when no disrespect or dissatisfaction with the original is involved? And what, moreover, may be said to be "latent" in any linguistic "original" which the author of that discourse, no matter how gifted, could neither discern nor intend? Steiner circles persistently around such questions, not because he wishes to avoid them, but because each penetrative thrust in his inquiry, each tightly drawn hermeneutic circle, as it were, itself constitutes a center or focus with considerable power to hold. Steiner's discourse is not constructed with a single core around which various contingent elements revolve; there are in fact several cores in the discourse, each capable of attracting to it the other key symbolic elements, which submit only long enough for the author to suggest how the complications in the argument require a constantly dissolving and moving focus. Running through it all, though, as the idea of translation itself remains a more or less dynamic constant, is the related notion of language as creative fiction, of mind as deceiver. To deal with the issues of latency in a text or oral discourse, or with translation as correction or improvement, Steiner posits his own hypothetical "deep structure," an account of the origins of language which locates the central impulse in every formulation. Working with concepts drawn from Nietzsche, from the linguistic speculations of Benjamin Lee Whorf, and from a variety of other sources, Steiner concludes that "the evolution of the full genius of language is inseparable from the impulse to concealment and fiction." In this view, words

> . . . encode, preserve, and transmit the knowledge, the shared memories, the metaphorical and pragmatic conjectures on life of a small group—a family, a clan, a tribe. Mature speech begins in shared secrecy, in centripetal storage or in-

ventory, in the mutual cognizance of a very few. In the beginning the word was largely a pass-word, granting admission to a nucleus of speakers. "Linguistic exogamy" comes later, under compulsion of hostile or collaborative contact with other small groups. We speak first to ourselves, then to those nearest us in kinship and locale. We turn only gradually to the outsider, and we do so with every safeguard of obliqueness, of reservation, of conventional flatness or outright misguidance. At its intimate center, in the zone of familial or totemic immediacy, our language is most economic of explanation, most dense with intentionality and compacted implication. Streaming outward it thins, losing energy and pressure as it reaches an alien speaker . . . In brief: I am suggesting that the outwardly communicative, extrovert thrust of language is secondary and that it may in substantial measure have been a late socio-historical acquirement. The primary drive is inward and domestic.

Each tongue hoards the resources of consciousness, the world-pictures of the clan. Using a simile still deeply entrenched in the language-awareness of Chinese, a language builds a wall around the "middle kingdom" of the group's identity. It is secret towards the outsider and inventive of its own world. Each language selects, combines and "contradicts" certain elements from the total potential of perceptual data. This selection, in turn, perpetuates the differences in world images explored by Whorf. Language is "a perpetual Orphic song" precisely because the hermetic and the creative aspects in it are dominant. There have been so many thousands of human tongues, there still are, because there have been, particularly in the archaic stage of social history, so many distinct groups intent on keeping from one another the inherited singular springs of their identity, and engaged in creating their own semantic worlds, their "alterities" . . . Or to put it simply: There is a direct, crucial correlation between the "un-truthful" and fictive genius of human speech on the one hand and the great multiplicity of languages on the other.

The "deep structure" in a language, then, is more or less peculiar to that particular tongue: The operant conceptual notion is Whorf's *cryptotype*, a mysterious principle of meaning underlying a given language which, though it is nowhere specifically apparent, may be said to create the grammar and define the potential range of idiom. How do we know such a principle exists? Surely a large degree of intuition is involved, but we know as well by comparative analysis of different languages, of the formal structures required to say the same thing in French and in English, for example. In one case Steiner briefly conducts such an analysis to show, persuasively, that "in French, phenomenal appearance, epiphany are categorized and conceptually prepared-for as they are not necessarily in English. This is not a question of poorer means, but of metaphysical insistence." Such observations, interesting in themselves, are primarily important in building a foundation for the broader theory. What is latent in a given discourse is implicitly present in its grammar, frequently in its most familiar combinations of ordinary words. This latent content is, however, literally inexpressible because in its very nature it insists that speakers of the language know what it is without calling attention to it or to their knowledge. Once it is given a name, established as a palpable fact which speakers may argue over or seek to change, it is altered. No wonder, Steiner reminds us, the German Romantic Herder fought to protect language from translation, for no tongue would preserve its "vital innocence" against the harsh scrutiny and penetrative ambition of the translator.

The idea of latent content has remained important in the study of language despite the fact that linguists rarely agree on what the idea is worth. Steiner insists upon its importance in explaining what takes place in virtually every human contact, and in so insisting makes the idea considerably less mysterious and inaccessible than it had been. What takes place, in fact, has much to do with the establishing of contexts within which communication can successfully occur. Even in casual conversation we instruct one another in the relevant assumptions required both to take in what is essential in the present utterance and to maintain contact for as long as the participants wish. In part, of course, this has to do with the linguistic, intellectual, and temperamental dispositions of particular individuals, but Steiner would contend, I think, that larger and more impersonal conventions are at work in such ordinary contacts. In an epigraph to *After Babel* he quotes Heidegger: "Man acts as if he were the shaper and master of language, while it is language which remains mistress of man . . . For in fact it is language that speaks." More than four hundred pages later he writes that "freedom derives meaning from constraints." When we speak with one another, then, we inevitably affirm community within the expressive resources and constraints of a given language. The community ethos is binding upon us insofar as we are sensitive to the underlying conventions which govern discourse. This kind of sensitivity is not the same as good manners, which refer to social behavior and strategies of a more or less deliberate nature. Sensitivity to latent content involves a mostly intuitive grasp of expressive conventions that constitute the ground of good sense and reasonable particularity in a language: How much are we to say when a friend asks how we feel? How will we best express feelings of sincere bereavement when others are inclined to mistrust elaborate declaration? What is reasonable detail in setting a scene or evoking a milieu? These are questions to which no reliable answers may be formally given, but which each of us will know implicitly how to answer when we are called upon to execute customary linguistic routines. If we know all *too well* what is required, the conventions of utterance presumably will have stiffened, and the language we speak will have begun to grow inflexible and unresponsive to the legitimate expressive aspirations of native speakers.

When Hölderlin spoke of the "correction" made by the translator he effectively described the elaboration of context which to some degree occurs in every communication. The latent content of the original is, as we have seen, inexpressible in any other language. Approximation to the latent content thus requires fleshing out the literal equivalents of the original words, by providing what Steiner calls an "illustrative context" in a procedure that is basically "circumlocutionary." A healthy language points implicitly to a wealth of unarticulated suggestion coursing just beneath the surfaces of discourse. It maintains an unbroken tension between public utterance and private intention, a tension vividly realized in a poem whose ideological superstructure is regularly violated or compromised by textural details which seem to accumulate by a momentum of their own, not owing to any conscious design of the poet. The translator acknowledges the inherent tension and labors to express it in his own verbal idiom. When the translator aspires to "correct" the original text he means to discover its latent content and articulate it in another way. He "corrects" the original by explaining it, by providing that "illustrative context" unnecessary for those sensitive to every nuance of the original but indispensable to outsiders.

For Hölderlin the translator's ideal is yet more strenuous than anything we've indicated, though one doubts that it can serve as a practical model for most of us who interpret and explain. His is an extreme sensitivity to the kind of false meaning we associate with

deceptive simplicity in a discourse. The position, as sympathetically recapitulated by Steiner, is very close to Roland Barthes's
thesis in such works as *Writing Degree Zero* and *S/Z*, and we can
only wonder why Barthes is not so much as mentioned in a book as
encompassing as *After Babel*. This view holds that words in themselves are potentially explosive, that they are rich in a historical
content which they yield to those who can "hear" their previous
uses even as they attend to the current definitions attached to the
words. "Provide them with an enforced smoothness and linearity,"
argues Steiner, "and you will have betrayed the literally daemonic
potency of definition, of action, encased in the human word." Conventional sentence structures progressively distract the mind from
any focus on individual words, so that we come more and more to
acquiesce in a facade of logic and agree to ignore the resonance of
particular terms. Obviously, linguistic "compromise" of this sort is
required to carry on the business of mundane experience, though it
is undeniable as well that we shall miss out on much that is important to us if we do not occasionally fall silent and try to replay in the
mind's ear essential passages of the exchanges to which we have
contributed. The task of the poet demands that he resist deceptive
surfaces altogether, so that his discourse carries its justification and
definition in every word and trope. Just so, the truly gifted translator, in Steiner's terms, "invades and seeks to break open the core of
alien meaning" by resisting the "enforced smoothness and linearity" of a merely general or approximate reading of the original.

The example of Hölderlin is surely instructive here, as is Roland
Barthes, but no one has so powerfully demonstrated what it means
to break open the core of single words as Martin Heidegger, to
whom Steiner intermittently returns in the text. Who better than
Heidegger has understood that all insight is penetrative, that we can
come to terms with things-in-themselves only when in some basic
sense we have made them our own, translated them? Steiner does
not refer to Heidegger's fragmentary reflections on tragedy, and did
not, apparently, find them of sufficient interest to incorporate them
into his earlier book, *The Death of Tragedy*. But they are entirely
germane to the purposes of *After Babel*, for it is Heidegger's contention there that man is what he is—"the strangest of the strange," he
calls us after Sophocles—by virtue of his tenacious will to unnatural
incursion into the domain of the familiar which he has helped to
make and to strengthen *against* unnatural incursions. Conceived
linguistically, we may suppose, the familiar is the syntax and vocabulary we establish to protect ourselves both from too much light and

too much darkness—from overexposure to blunt considerations which threaten our confident habitation in traditionally sanctioned modes of discourse; or from unchecked solipsism, a compulsive reflexiveness that would make mind its own worst enemy. The familiar as language is the medium within which we transact ordinary business. Neither the language nor the idea of the ordinary, however, is genuinely available to experience according to Heidegger, except insofar as we invade and seek to deflect the natural course of things. Hölderlin in his translation works towards a strenuous verbal monadism, a wrenching of single words out of their enforced linearities, frequently exaggerating the resonance of a given particular and risking absurdity. Heidegger similarly stresses the impulse to create anew by sinking down into the very bowels of the familiar to experience at once its consoling and terribly provoking, unyielding constraint. For it is only as we experience this resistant otherness, "the thing that is because it is there," that we feel called upon to take account of our own powers and to affirm both identity and distinction in the combat that ensues. What Heidegger calls *techne* is the creative gathering power that draws upon every available resource to assault the fortress of the familiar—in language and in the various institutional norms of culture—knowing itself throughout as acting within a medium whose origin is not the self but the intersecting conventions which together articulate the parameters of selfhood in a particular era. The dialectic of aggression and constraint is beautifully realized in Heidegger's formulation.

What we do when the words are broken, the encased meanings approached, has nothing to do with a comfortable or wholly achieved relation to the world in which we live. There are always impulses to concealment and reinvention to contend with and to savor. As we successfully appropriate to our own perspective formerly alien meanings and move to share our achievements with others, we call into play those customary safeguards "of obliqueness, of reservation, of conventional flatness or outright misguidance" to which Steiner regularly refers. For nothing entirely worth having is easily shared, and so eager are we to experience ever freshly the gratification of fruitfully aggressive intercourse with the alien particular that we routinely banish achieved meanings and press for others. In a somewhat Heideggerean formulation, Steiner settles upon the term "interanimation" to describe what happens when we translate and, in more encompassing terms, submit to the verbal imperatives by which a culture enlivens and makes meaning possible for its constituents: "there is annihilation of self in the other consciousness and recognition of self in a mirroring motion." Somewhat later, when he speaks of the "almost bewildering bias of the human spirit towards freedom," Steiner completes the perspective in a way yet more recognizably congruent with Heidegger's view.

The penetrative thrust by which encased meanings are appropriated is not, ideally, an ungenerous exercise: This we have seen. In every serious encounter with an alien figure there are several component disciplines no interpreter/translator can afford to overlook. Of primary importance, in Steiner's view, is what he calls trust, "an instrument of belief . . . in the meaningfulness, in the 'seriousness' of the facing or strictly speaking, adverse text." And this, as Steiner goes on to show, is no easy matter, for careful examination of the verbal details of a discourse may impress us only with their resistant particularity, their dependence upon all details of the autonomous message-unit, without whose supportive and precise elaboration the original meanings grow elusive. Or we may find that so many meanings accumulate around given words that they threaten to swamp further inquiry—for if particular details may finally refer to almost everything, they may seem more and more to mean nothing.

The most helpful of suggestions obliquely addressed to this dilemma comes from Wittgenstein, whose more elaborate linguistic theories Steiner is otherwise avid to reject. "For one may well frame the problem," Wittgenstein writes, " 'How is this joke (e.g.) to be translated (i.e. replaced) by a joke in the other language?' And this problem can be solved; but there was no systematic method of solving it." In these terms, to trust the adverse text, the encountered discourse, is to believe in the equivalent status of another text whose possibility is foreshadowed in the original. One does not, then, seek to refute or overthrow the autonomy of the original but to give shape to an alternate version of comparable integrity. One does not dismiss the very *idea* of systematic inquiry into the given translational problem, but one comfortably concedes that solutions here are likely to be provisional and largely self-consuming: The dynamics of interaction with an original discourse may come to seem more important, finally, than the product of that interaction, and no interpretation is likely to be accepted as definitive by all interested parties. What we do when we read a book has much in common with the translator's discipline: In Steiner's terms, "we re-enact in the bounds of our own secondary but momentarily heightened, educated consciousness, the creation by the artist."

Nor need the text in question be a poem or a novel, the author an artist. The procedures Steiner outlines, with the help of the distinguished predecessors he compulsively cites, suggest how close are the relations among reading, translating, explicating, conversing, remembering, and thinking itself.* For we cannot approach a discourse, actual or potential, without in some sense acknowledging our plural identity, an identity produced by the many formal and extemporaneous texts we have engaged, which have taken possession of us. Similarly, the texts themselves, no matter how assiduous they are to announce their singularity, will call to mind other texts, other possibilities, and thereby stir readers to conceive their own inventions by submitting to the sympathetic vibrations sounded on the air. In negotiating a contract with the discourse, say, with Wittgenstein's joke, we agree that it has a potentially fruitful relation to us, and aim to liberate to some semblance of consciousness the originals of that discourse *already present* within us. Whether or not we intend to formulate in words what has been borne in upon us, we shall know by the stimulation of the urge to respond *specifically* to a coded provocation that we are in relation, that we must reenact in our own terms what we have been given. And we shall know that not consumption but the play of imagination may restore to us both the original intermittently suspended in space and awaiting translation, and the self anticipating a sequence of fragmentary communications it feels *elected* to complete—clarify—strengthen.

In his concluding chapter, Steiner asks, "To what extent is culture the translation and rewording of previous meaning?" This construction informs Steiner's reflections throughout *After Babel*, and it has the merit of suggesting the expandable quality of his primary focus on translation from one language to another. At the same time, it raises troubling questions we are not likely to answer satisfactorily. What, for example, do we make of *truth* in terms of this construction? If every discourse is but a fragment, what may be said to contribute the whole from which it is derived, in the direction of which it inevitably gestures? What manner of *authority* resides in the "previous meaning" we aim to translate? No theory of culture can fail to address such questions, for it is clear that, as cultures organize truth, they make it available to us only in frag-

---

*On this crucial point, *we must note*, Steiner differs entirely from recent French theorists, from Barthes to Derrida, who consider the printed *text* as distinct from any other kind of discourse.

ments, and that an implicit authority must direct our attention to some discourses at the expense of others, to the renovation of *these* meanings rather than *those*. Culture implies discrimination, and it implies the ordering of perspectives. *After Babel* is truly cognizant of such matters, but determines not to dwell at length on issues of cultural truth and authority for fear of obscuring its linguistic focus. Probably this is just as well: Ranging as widely as it does, Steiner's book might otherwise get out of hand, tempt us to look in it for fundamental instruction on every particular of knowledge. The question of culture itself is not properly the subject of *After Babel*, but it is difficult to imagine future theories of culture which will not wish to make good use of Steiner's book. It is, at once, an indispensable contribution.

Translation and the Status of the Poem

Ben Belitt, *Adam's Dream: A Preface to Translation* (New York: Grove Press).

More than one recent poet or critic has thought to remind us that poems are made with words, not with ideas. Others tell us that, if they do nothing else, poems inevitably call attention to the verbal medium and may be judged exclusively by the way in which ascertainable meanings are produced by words clearly selected to evoke precisely those meanings. Readers unhappy about contemporary verse are asked to concern themselves with the adequacy of the words to purposes clearly designated, to worry less about the informing vision that may or may not have anything to do with the experience of the given poem.

There are others, of course, who come at the issues in a very different way. These will say that the best poems derive their organization from nature, that what seems a lack of control is a vital sign that the poet's energies are in touch with the only things that matter. The poet's carelessness with language, his insistence upon saying—and seeming to say—the first things that come into his head, are part of a principled resistance to poetry as craft or repressive discipline. Yes, poems may be made with words, but, finally, almost any words will do so long as one has something to say and no reluctance to get it said. The poet's vision may not improve the world or have much in common with any other vision, but it will move us to wonder and approval so long as the articulating accents are robust and sincere.

From *London Times Literary Supplement* (*TLS*), December 7, 1979.

The debates on these and related issues are no longer likely to edify, and poets of whatever persuasion seem properly determined to do the things they do without bothering to consult disinterested "experts" for advice. Apparently there are no reliable rules about how to make good or interesting poems. But there are, it seems, preferred ways of reading poems. And if this is so, there may well be acceptable rules to help in translating them. In fact, nowhere are the questions "What is a poem?" and "What may it be said to know?" so loudly debated as they are within the fraternity of translators. For translation has lately become a big business and a respectable academic subdiscipline. So much is this the case that the works of foreign-language authors with very limited appeal are sometimes available in several competing English translations. And the relative merits of these translations are now and again argued in the pages of magazines whose readers have never learned to read a word of the originals from which the competing translations were made. Poets working in their own language are mostly content to do their individual "thing"; translators are avid to justify their works and to persuade readers to a view of the poem that will explain their own procedures. Neruda's Chilean readers do not have to ask epistemological questions when they read the master's *Canto General;* they may take it for what it is without asking what it is or considering overmuch whether they are to be persistently attentive to the verbal medium for its own sake. The American or English reader, confronted with one of several translations, will want to be assured that it is Neruda he is reading. And he is not likely to conclude that, because the translated poem has intrinsically a certain cogency and authority, it is true to the spirit of the original. He will want something more, and is sure to become frustrated and indignant when told that there are many plausible "readings" of Neruda, and that the poet was himself unwilling to single out one preferred version to the exclusion of others. The debate over vision and word, discipline and personal idiom, while "academic" and indifferent for many of us, will never seem anything but immediate to those who have a text to translate.

It is as a translator of texts that Ben Belitt came to write the papers collected in *Adam's Dream.* Most are, in fact, prefaces to the volumes he has translated in the course of a long career. A poet of the first rank—though without the following ordinarily accorded major poets—Belitt turned to translation for the first time in the forties. He was for a long while largely responsible for introducing to English-language readers the poems of Neruda and some of the more exotic works of Antonio Machado, Rafael Alberti, and Garcia Lorca. In recent years, as the Neruda industry especially has picked up considerable steam, Belitt's translations have come in for some heavy criticism, and though Neruda continued to celebrate the translator and his work, Belitt could not altogether ignore his critics. *Adam's Dream* is at once an extenuation and declaration of the translator's calling; it is, as well, a series of reflections on Neruda, Belitt's chief inspiration and, as it were, his beneficent alter ego. The chapters on Neruda are full and sympathetic, as one might expect them to be; the pieces on the theory and practice of translation are alternately speculative, comparative, and combative. With the dissemination of Neruda's verse proceeding satisfactorily, we shall be forgiven for addressing ourselves exclusively to the more general issues Belitt opens out so nicely without feeling called upon to decide them for us. More than once in his book he describes the translator as an amateur, and in a sense it is fair to describe his speculations on his craft as the brilliant fragments of a virtuoso in love with the wayward and incomplete. No one is going to complete Belitt—the subject is too elusive, the poet-translator himself too eccentric to encourage anything reductively practical. But it should be possible to say something more about the status of the poem and its properties than Belitt himself wishes to say; once, that is, we have come to terms with the propositions he wishes us to entertain.

Foremost among these is the view that the poem is more than it can say in so many words; that the poem "speaks in its own right . . . as a pure tissue of possibility"; and that—following Coleridge—"in the beginning of every poem was a *passion* rather than a word." No doubt some poet will argue that his poem began with a word, not a passion, or that it manages to say quite as much as it intends, thank you. But Belitt proposes a sense of the poem that is likely to appeal to most poets and readers. No one need discount the conscious element in the crafting of the poem to believe in an originating passion. Nor does the "possibility" to which Belitt refers commit the reader to an easy acceptance of vague approximations and trivial novelties of diction. The poem may be said to suggest possibilities only some of which may be programmed or predicted, but Belitt is assiduous to remind us of constraints imposed by the poem and by pressures brought to bear by particular elements within it. The reader, like the translator, must see to it "that all the elements have been subjected to atomic scrutiny." Only so will he be in a position to know what is the legitimate business of the poem, what it intends beyond its capacity actually to tell us.

Now most of us feel we know what a poem is, even what it means or intends, when we say we have mastered it, that we have lived with it and come gradually to take hold of it as though it belonged to us. But it is another matter entirely to reproduce that knowledge, either by stating it in the form of a prose summary or, more difficult yet, by creating another poem that will affect its "natural" audience quite as the original item may be supposed to have affected its readers. This is, of course, the dilemma that confronts the translator, who will need to perform both operations—the first only in an informal or provisional way—in his pursuit of an acceptable text. Even the translator who, like Belitt, refuses to believe in literal equivalences will believe there is some unmistakable essence within or about the poem which may not be traduced. Those who accuse Belitt of taking unforgivable liberties in his translations may be surprised to read that "the poems must be rendered *as they are*," that "they must be given safe and passionate passage." The protection and preservation of something that is said to exist, though in its new incarnation it must assume a different sound and texture—it may even assume a somewhat different shape and structure—are apt to seem an implausible enterprise for the translator. But if he believes, with Belitt, that poetry is not *information*, he may find that there is something fundamental to which others may be helped to gain access. To master the poem, in this sense, is not to memorize its words or diagram its structure. That is to think of it as information. Truly to master the poem is to take possession of an "imaginable truth" which is everywhere approximate and imperfect. Our object, as readers or as translators, must be to "imagine or re-imagine the process of a poem's embodiment." This alone is the truth the poem may authentically propose. A literal translation of a great poem, focused at the level of the word, aiming to achieve an unexceptionable correctness, denies by definition the imaginable truth to which the original bears witness. The literalist, scrupulous to a fault, dedicated and cunning, will be seen in the end to "lay a dead mouse at the feet of the master."

What, then, does the poem know, and what part of it may the translator undertake to convey? An achieved poem will, of course, know a number of things that no other poem may be said to know in the same way. Just so, a good translation of a poem—any poem—will inevitably be shown to know some things the original cannot know. But the achieved poem will nonetheless betray a kind of knowledge that will be reassuring to readers of other successful poems. It will have the quality of a thought for which certain objects are more significant or compelling than others. It will know what it is meant to accomplish, and it will elaborate a point of view on the basis of which one object may be made to stand clear of every other. This compelling object may be an object in space: I think of Randall Jarrell's meditation on "The Bronze David of Donatello." Or it may be a perfectly fantastic object, like the tower in "Childe Roland to the Dark Tower Came." Or, at last, it may be nothing more than the intersection, the implicit though unnameable focus of a series of reflections, as in Robert Lowell's "Waking Early Sunday Morning." Whatever the status of the object privileged by the poem, the poem will itself be a procedure, a mode of inquiry conducted from a more or less identifiable point of view. And that point of view will know what thoughts it may and may not accommodate; will know, too, what kinds of thoughts a reader may be permitted to entertain if he is not to compromise the quality of the attention he is asked to pay to the poem itself.

Such observations are mostly commonplaces, to be sure, but so strident are the spokesmen for another view entirely of the business of poetry that even commonplaces may be thought useful. If Ben Belitt has had to fight long and hard to win a proper hearing for his conception of translation, the reason has had much to do with the diffusion of various influential though misleading propositions about the objects of poetry. For example, those who believe that poems teach us how to live—a view lately more popular in the United States than in England—will have also to believe that poems, and poets, know more than we have given them credit for; also, that this knowledge can be efficiently extracted from poems without utterly dismantling the tenuous structures in which they are housed. Belitt's view is that the poem is what it knows. It offers its knowledge only to one who is prepared to abide patiently with a thought that is everywhere deeply interfused. The translator of a poem works to reimagine relations because the poem has no significant meaning apart from the embodiment of those relations. To say that a poem teaches us how to live is to say that it has meanings which are not subject to the laws generated within the poem, that it knows something which may be isolated in these words but not in those, or isolated in a formulation fully separate from the poem. Belitt's insistence upon the poem's "full orchestration" is an insistence upon the poem's knowledge as a mode of saying. The translator's point of view, like the poet's, ensures that there can be no fact, no meaning, that is not everywhere and immediately a function of that special angle of vision.

To say that the poem exists only in its "full orchestration" is to deny, of course, that any translation can give the original "safe and passionate passage." This Belitt understands. All the same, he argues, the translator proceeds *as if* it were possible to do the job. What he wants, obviously, is to minimize the loss, the damage. Many believe that this can be accomplished only by the translator's taking the vow of "poverty, chastity, and obedience." In place of this, Belitt recommends the play spirit, an acknowledgment that the work to be accomplished cannot be accomplished to the entire satisfaction of anyone involved. Because the elements of the new work—the translation—will include sounds, textures, implications that cannot have been elements of the original, there will have to be, in place of equivalence, uneasy approximation.

Strangely, or so it may seem at first, poets themselves are more tolerant of translations of their own work than anyone else. Committed to what Belitt calls "a workable dissemination of the world's avowedly irrecoverable originals . . . in the search for a shared humanity," the poets welcome various approaches, many voices. And who better than they should appreciate the impossibility of the translator's task? What more can they demand, Belitt asks, than that their translators allow them "a little character, for heaven's sake!" The poem may be made of words, and the verbal texture may mean a great deal to those who care for the poem at all, but there must be something more. The poet who demands that the quality of "character" be preserved or intimated will know that the poem moves always in the direction of an object it cannot name. If Jarrell's "Bronze David," in the original, "thrusts its belly out a little in exact / Shamelessness," a translator's object will be to get at the combination of passive, narcissistic satisfaction and deliberate self-imposition that is so central to Jarrell's poem. But he will want as well to avoid the impression that Jarrell's intent was merely to turn the Old Testament legend on its head and to celebrate not David but Goliath. To isolate the object of the poem in this way is to limit oneself to what the words, one by one or in small clusters, can say. And to think of the poem in this way is to think of it as an exercise in idol smashing, an adolescent's display of the "knowing" insight that levels and confuses. Jarrell would have to wish for a "reading" sensitive to the poem's muffled undercurrent, which sings praise of David—of the sculptural object and the biblical character—even as the figure is deftly subverted and chastised for being what it is: proud, victorious, and wonderful. Character, in this sense, would be the capacity to hold several "objects" in the mind at the same time and to do implicit justice to all of them—without, of course, losing sight of one's central purpose. What poet would not be pleased to see this sort of character preserved in translation, even at the expense of several passing effects or particularly impressive locutions?

Gains and losses, losses and gains: These are the tallies feverishly kept and pored over by every serious translator who ever lived. But so elusive is the quality of character we would wish to preserve in so many poems that the tallies must frequently be kept provisionally, as if a present loss might soon assume the status of a gain. The poem, as Belitt has it, is responsible to itself, to the originating passion it has determined to express and to make at once intelligible and significant. If the passion is utterly single-minded and its expression, as a consequence, all too accessible, the poem is likely not to please. Possibly it will move some readers, but only for so long as the originating circumstance—say, a major public crisis—seems relevant or threatening. Character, in such a poem, will seem to be little more than the capacity to take an acceptable public position or to give voice to an approved sentiment or opinion. As the poem will go about its business in a clear and fundamentally unambivalent way, whatever the obligatory admixture of irony or doubt, the translator will have a sure sense of what it is that needs "safe and passionate passage." The gains and losses will be easy to measure. Nothing unduly provisional here, though there are always factors that escape precise computation.

But what of a poem whose character, though clear enough, is not a matter of particular sentiments or opinions? What of a poem whose character has to do with the assumption of a voice, an identity coursing through reflections of bewildering variety and intensity? How will gains and losses be figured there? Belitt reports, in the course of a vigorous interview with Edwin Honig, that Borges himself pressed upon his translators a notion of poetry and of translation fully astonishing to many of them. His intention, in working with a cadre of translators assembled by Norman Thomas Di Giovanni, was to get them to subject his originals to a thoroughgoing "Anglo-Saxon decantation." "If Borges had had his way," Belitt goes on, "—and he generally did—all polysyllables would have been replaced by monosyllables." The poet betrayed a persistent "mania for dehispanization." Why? Because, presumably, the texture of the originals could no longer be supposed to embody the quality of character Borges had wished to invest. The Spanish of the originals Borges had come to regard as "jejune." Translation into an English resonant with an Anglo-Saxon bluntness might be just what was needed to revive the poems and let them speak what they were intended to speak. In place of the "youthful" and "latinate," Belitt and his colleagues would decant something "wiry, minimal." The original poem, as an assemblage of particular words and sounds, had its right to exist, but its character could be preserved only by paying attention predominantly to something else. In the beginning was a passion: atomic scrutiny of all the parts, to be sure, but accompanied by a renovative urgency in touch with "the afflatus that imagined the parts."

The Borges translations are astonishing and splendid things, but no one would think to take them as models. They have something to say about the nature of poems—some poems—and about the tolerance of poets for the inventive stratagems of translators. They don't help us at all to explain how a translation can know essentially what the original knows when the poems are in fact different poems. Borges did not after all take the time to help a dozen or more translators to create new poems of their own. He assumed that the new poems would be in some important way versions of his own, that the knowledge of his originals—like their character—would be freshly communicated. This knowledge, in Borges, in Neruda, in any good poem, is the process in which the poem as thought takes shape. It is not a process in terms of which one Latinate word leads inevitably to another by means of a (largely unconscious) sympathetic vibration. Such a process may account for the draft of a poem, but not often for a finished poem. The Latinate element in Borges is but an element, and is not the knowledge to which the poem bears witness.

What matters, ever so much more, is a tension of the mind, the way the mind manages materials it can never fully control. The poem knows something in the sense that it knows a good deal about its own powers and about the material it wishes to treat. It proposes, implicitly, a question of adequacy: ends to means, ideas to sensations, and so on. The translator aiming to reproduce a process of embodiment will concern himself especially with the relation between ends and means broadly conceived. Not this word or that so much as this effect as produced by this *kind* of cause will concern him. If Belitt or Borges and others are provisionally optimistic about the enterprise of translation, they are so in the spirit of Valery, for whom the translator "reconstitutes as nearly as possible the *effect* of a certain *cause* . . . by means of another *cause*."

Often, of course, translators are accused of substituting for a cause that is an entire orientation toward experience a mere linguistic cause. Belitt, for one, is often accused of hoping to convey "Neruda's boldness by novelties of diction in English." If Neruda uses the word "duro" (hard) over and over again in a single poem, the translator must respect that decision and refuse to select alternate versions of the word. "Obdurate," "durable," "refractory" are forbidden to anyone who would give passage to the original. The translator's vow of poverty and obedience must prevent him from taking measures that visibly go beyond the language of the original.

The fact is that Belitt has never taken that particular vow and has never believed that his readings were to be focused on words in isolation from one another. George Steiner, in *After Babel*, describes precisely the kind of circumlocutionary tactics to which Belitt, like other translators, must resort if they are to communicate the spirit of the words of the original. "Duro" may say what Neruda wants it to say to Chilean readers; that is, it may say here "durable," there "refractory," and so on. But "hard" is not going to do as well in the English-language version of Neruda's poem. The translator must flesh out the implications of the original, implications inscribed in the unique history of the Spanish word and selectively invoked by the line in which the original word is set. If Belitt selects various terms to take the place of "duro," he does so not "to avoid saying 'hard' "—the suggestion is absurd and unimaginative—but to get at Neruda's intention. No doubt, something is lost when a word like "duro" cannot be repeated over and over again with the confidence that each time it will say something other than it said before. But in a Belitt translation that is a calculated loss. Abandoned in the instance is a certain kind of boldness. Is it in fact the boldness we most associate with Neruda? Certainly it is not, and Belitt has always insisted upon a variety of ways to "embolden" his verses to reconstitute—"as nearly as possible"—the required effects.

The issue is not, then, Neruda, or the absolute integrity of the word, but the general effect to which an entire poem may tend. This effect is, in turn, something the poem knows but may not be able to isolate in every single word. And if the original itself will be hard put to invoke its knowledge at every turn, how may the translation be expected to carry over that knowledge in every corresponding turn? Belitt's so-called "novelties of diction" have at least the character of restless invention that is so fundamental to Neruda's voice. By contrast, those who uphold the sanctity of the original word produce deliberately "simplified" versions that reduce the voice to the stern and elemental as conceived by the laureates of the American middle-western prairies. For flash and color and presaging enigma they produce a safe version that is comparatively flat and chaste. Reading the Neruda translations of the poet Robert Bly, for example, one is put in mind of Eliot's still wonderful musings: "Because one has only learnt to get the better of words / For the thing one no longer has to say, or the way in which / One is no longer disposed to say it." In Bly's hands, Neruda knows all too well what he wants to say, knows so well that he cannot possibly have been interested in saying such things over and over again for fifty years. Bly's versions "immobilize" Neruda's diversity, quite as Belitt argues, as though Neruda had had only a few things he really wanted to say, and was content to say them with a certain tough bluntness and clear-sighted conviction from which he never wavered. Again, by contrast, in Belitt's versions, the poem knows many things. Its adequacy is measured by the degree in which the articulating voice bodies forth a mind hungering for a knowledge just beyond its grasp. That knowledge even when explicitly invoked is never perfect, rarely self-limiting in the ways of a poetry anxious to disclaim its affinities for the tenuous and murky. Belitt's translations remind us that the poem "is never the sum of its parts," that the process of its embodiment—a process fraught with uncertainty and only marginally fueled by ideas—is the knowledge it most wishes to convey.

But again, it is not this translation or that version that is here primarily at issue. The issue is the status of the poem and, in some unmistakable way, the future of the poem. A recent anthology of poetic translations from several languages (*Another Republic*, Ecco Press, New York, 1976), edited by the American poets Charles Simic and Mark Strand, will serve to focus the issue very nicely indeed. The editors describe, in their preface to the volume, "the growth of an international style which is dominant in poetry today." This "style," they claim, has taken hold so firmly that the work of young American poets especially "seems more influenced by the poems of Popa and Amichai than by those of Stevens, Eliot, or any other of their American forebears." A striking idea, to be sure, and if true, an idea bound to upset a great many assumptions. One of these is the view that the words in an original poem rely upon depths of implication or suggestion that need not be explicitly invoked to affect our sense of what it knows or intends.

But the supporting context must be rich, full of possibility. The international style that has come into being through the enormous recent popularity of translated verse is the consequence of a view of language that threatens to impoverish the poetry of the near future. Already this impoverishment is palpable in the works of several of the poets and translators assembled in the Strand-Simic volume. These works are content to know very little, and to strive as little as possible for the linguistic abundance and implication that make a poem's unfolding worth attending to. If translation is the misguided leveling of the poem to what Belitt calls a "denotative pudding," then an original poetry inspired by such work is bound to be a paltry thing.

The critic Hélène J. F. de Aguilar, in an article in the journal *Parnassus*, contends that "a poet, as artist, cannot be *influenced* by this language. He can only derive from it a certain dispirited sensibility, a reluctance—or an inability—to expend more energy on poetry than that which will get the lines to the printer." Though not all works in translation will have this effect, obviously, the tendencies are nonetheless ominous. "This curious deadness of language," she goes on, "stripped deliberately of as much subjective resonance as possible, is probably what is now passing undefiled from tongue to tongue, 'internationalizing' art." What is at stake, she concludes, is "the proper balance between disinterested investigation and art." Just so. If Belitt has refused to countenance a view of the translator as "nobody in particular," he has done so in the belief that the poem knows its business in a way that is fully personal and *interested*. And that is the spirit in which the translator as well confronts the alien object he must reimagine. It is perfectly acceptable to think of poems asking to be rendered *as they are*, but one must not consent on that account to strip them at once to their bare essentials, as if they were aggregations of minimalist signs and practiced reticences. The poets have it in their hands to make of poetry in our time something decidedly less than it can be. How strange that it should fall to the new legion of translators—ostensibly committed to the preservation of an art that counts fewer and fewer adherents—to bring the crisis to its present head.

PART THREE

Real Readers and Theoretical Fictions

Real Readers and Theoretical Critics

William H. Gass, *The World Within the Word* (New York: Alfred A. Knopf), and *Fiction and the Figures of Life* (New York: Vintage Books).

We're apt to hear a good deal these days about realism, anti-realism, and all of the many related sins that critics and reviewers are equipped to dabble in. The French structuralists and their epigoni in the United States especially have taught us to dwell solemnly on issues that should have resolved themselves long ago. Consider a passage from a recent paper by the critic Robert Alter, who presumes to take on the structuralists in a sensible way:

> We seem now, however, to run some danger of being directed by the theoreticians to read in a way that real readers, on land or sea, have never read. If one insists on seeing all novels as congeries of semiotic systems intricately functioning in a pure state of self-referentiality, one loses the fine edge of responsiveness to the urgent human predicaments that novels seek to articulate. The greatness of the genre, both in its realist and in its self-conscious modes, has been to present to us—through the most inventive variety of artifice, whether disguised or manifest—lives that might seem like our lives, minds like our minds, desires like our own desires.*

*Alter, "Mimesis & the Motive for Fiction," *Tri-Quarterly* (Spring 1978), pp. 228–49; see also the special Fall 1978 issue of *Salmagundi:* on "The Politics of Anti-Realism."

From *London Times Literary Supplement* (*TLS*), November 3, 1978.

Now Alter is no doubt right about these things, though it is tiresome to insist that there are things in the world—and in books—more important than signs and artifices and the tradition of the novel. Only when we feel that a book has nothing really to say do we suppose that a novel may operate "in a pure state of self-referentiality." And when we are driven to suppose that, we suppose too that the novel we read addresses us not as a mind addressing other minds but as a system making up to a series of skilled receptors. To put the matter so may load the argument, but we needn't be embarrassed to put things where we think they belong. There is really no cause to pretend that novels are so special as to defy ordinary powers of comprehension, or that only practitioners of *nouvelle critique* are equipped to make the elementary distinctions by means of which naive readings may be blissfully avoided.

But let us consider more closely what is at stake here. A number of influential critics argue that literary works do not represent the real world, that they are self-referential sign-systems with encoded meanings. Readers are said to work at these meanings with no sense that anything conclusive is at stake. Whatever may be thought to correspond to experience outside the given text will give itself away as an illusion to which trained readers will be fully resistant. How, after all, can a novel that organizes its material manage to represent what is at best random and intransigently elusive? This is the kind of question that lies at the bottom of the new criticism that has demanded our attention. Not that "advanced" thinkers are likely to put the issues so boldly, so innocently, alert as they are to the prospect that someone may think them foolish. But is not the question just what a freshman student is likely to bring forward in an introductory fiction class: "But what do you mean when you say that Tolstoy wants to represent a general human experience? don't we know when we read the words on the page that we are reading words on the page? and isn't it clear that a Tolstoy alternates one kind of chapter with another because he has a design? and doesn't he make Anna's husband susceptible to this sort of emotion to bring us slowly around to her view of him? and would it really be possible for someone who knew Karenin to know him as we do, without seeing him, as it were, so consistently in the round? Really, you know, these are just formal conventions, and you cannot expect us to be taken in by them as though we were witnessing actual human beings going through their lives—now can you?"

Of course it is tolerance and geniality we want when we confront our students. We do not want to shut off their questions and tell them that Madame Bovary is like no other creature who ever lived or that Levin is a configuration of verbal elements with a particular narrative destiny. We resist the temptation to settle things definitively, largely because we do not wish to falsify what is a very complex sense of what Levin is and how peculiarly Madame Bovary may be like no one else and also much like anyone who's ever wanted something he couldn't have. But the practitioners of *nouvelle critique* aren't students, and they don't ask plaintively. They come to excoriate naive readings and to abolish all proprietary relations to texts but their own. One cannot address them genially unless one pretends that it doesn't matter who is right or what our experience amounts to. And so I am compelled to ask who actually believes that literary representation is so unitary and simple a matter as the structuralists say we do? Who but a French critic or an impressionable American could believe that the failure to achieve exact correspondences is a measure of the absence of any correspondence? Robert Alter quite rightly speaks of "the either-or rigidity" of recent structuralist formulations, and it is clear that something better is required if the general position is to be taken seriously.

And that is why I have decided to turn my sights not on the structuralists but on William Gass, who is so much more gifted and sensible, and who disposes us to like what he says by the sheer beauty and wit of his saying. Now Mr. Gass is hardly a structuralist philosopher, but he has written works of fiction—*Omensetter's Luck* and *In the Heart of the Heart of the Country* are his best-known works—that give heart to the structuralist enterprise, and his essays may be said to promote the attack on realist aesthetics. Those essays, originally collected in *Fiction and the Figures of Life* and recently reissued by David Godine, constitute the most vigorous anti-realist literary "programme" we have had in our time. His new collection of essays, not as dedicated to system-building as the first, but no less teasing and brilliant, sustains but does not substantially develop his theory. When the earlier book first appeared, a reviewer for the *New York Times* called it "a defense of 'poesy' in a time of need." The time is always needy, of course, and it is more than "poesy" that Gass defends, but the reviewer was not mistaken to state that Gass "calls our attention to art." To do so, need we say, is to remind us as well of all the things that art is not, and ought never to be asked to be. Gass calls our attention to art not by instructing us in the decipherment of signs or in the chastening of sentiment but by underlining all of the things art will not do, and celebrating the very special things it has to do.

Gass's theory is elaborated more or less obliquely in the new book. In essays on Faulkner, Valéry, Malcolm Lowry, Proust, and others, he treats us to a ripe display of mind sifting the claims of language, distinguishing rhetoric from enlightenment, "indelible evaporations" from fatuous whimsy. If he tends, in a very long study, to make more of Ms. Gertrude Stein than some of us approve, he does successfully indicate what it is in the standard "authorial voice" that she stood against and why she should seem to him so exemplary a figure. The essays on metaphor and on what he calls the ontology of the sentence do not so much deepen as exacerbate the issues pursued in earlier pieces, but they are rewarding as only the antics of a genius given to persistent verbal acrobatics can be.

But Gass's theory may best be understood by examining the famous set pieces in *Fiction and the Figures of Life,* including the title essay, "Philosophy and the Form of Fiction," and "The Concept of Character in Fiction."* Here we find that the theory rests upon an analogy Gass draws persistently between the literary and visual arts. It is an ingenious device, this analogy, and very provoking in its way. Here are two of the key passages:

> On the other side of a novel lies the void. Think, for instance, of a striding statue; imagine the purposeful inclination of the torso, the alert and penetrating gaze of the head and its eyes, the outstretched arm and pointing finger; everything would appear to direct us toward some goal in front of it. Yet our eye travels only to the finger's end, and not beyond. Though pointing, the finger bids us stay instead, and we journey slowly back along the tension of the arm. In our hearts we know what actually surrounds the statue. The same surrounds every other work of art: empty space and silence.

A beautiful passage, no doubt, and teasing in an entirely genial way. We shall have more to say of Gass's figure after the additional, re-enforcing passage:

---

*Explicit support is offered in shorter essays on Borges, Donald Barthelme, Henry James, Robert Coover, and other "moderns."

There is a painting by Picasso which depicts a pitcher, candle, blue enamel pot. They are sitting, unadorned, upon the barest table. Would we wonder what was cooking in that pot? Is it beans, perhaps, or carrots, a marmite? The orange of the carrot is a perfect complement to the blue of the pot, and the genius of Picasso, neglecting nothing, has surely placed, behind that blue, invisible disks of dusky orange, which, in addition, subtly enrich the table's velvet brown. Doesn't that seem reasonable? Now I see that it must be beans, for above the pot—you can barely see them—are quaking lines of steam, just the lines we associate with boiling beans . . . or is it blanching pods? Scholarly research, supported by a great foundation, will discover that exactly such a pot was used to cook cassoulet in the kitchens of Charles the Fat . . . or was it Charles the Bald?

And on it goes, in terrific mockery not merely of literary scholarship but, as Gass says, of "half the history of our criticism in the novel." It is all quite devastating, and amusing. But what part of it is reasonable, as Gass would have us ask?

Let's return to the business of the statue, the novel, and the surrounding void. We follow the pointing finger, stay at finger's end, and journey, as the man says, "slowly back along the tension of the arm." Now what would be the equivalent in reading a work of fiction to that journey back, and what in the text would point like the single and purposeful finger? The finger would seem to point to something in front of it, we recall, to something not *there* in the arrangement of statuary elements. And the finger may be said to constitute the extension of the curve of the work as a whole, the outer limit of the movement to which it inclines—a movement that is built into and reflected in every muscle of the torso. In this sense we may say that the work of fiction has a purpose, a structure which is fundamentally of a piece. It inclines, it has a direction, its curve is perceptible as a movement that directs the mind. Now Gass's contention is that the mind does not incline beyond the stretch of the furthermost extension of the words of the text. As the eye is trained not to lurch beyond the extension of the pointing finger, so the mind must be disciplined not to strain beyond the reverberant tensings of the novel's culminant passage. This *is* reasonable, as Gass surely knows; but it isn't an accurate description of the way things happen in fiction. There isn't a single purposeful

finger in the novel; neither the finger that John Barth's silly character in *End of the Road* uses to pick his nose nor the finger Madame
Bovary uses to turn the pages of her romantic novel may be said to
be purposeful in the way Gass suggests. Extension in the novel is
not what it is in a statue. The novel points and extends in many
directions at once; so, to a lesser degree, do short stories like those
collected in *In the Heart of the Heart of the Country*. We know this to
be the case when we compare responses to statues and fictions.

Everyone looking at Gass's striding figure can follow the curve of
the torso through the finger and back along the arm. Responses to
Madame Bovary or to *The Magic Mountain* are likely to identify a
number of curves and pointers and to be directed back through the
work by various routes. A phrase on a character's lips is likely to be
redolent of phrases remembered from another novel, or another
sequence in the same book that rightly seemed inconsequential
and utterly forgettable to some of its readers. It is not just that
novels require an attention different in kind from anything required by a statue; it is that novels repay our attention in a very
different way. Where the statue in a sense stops the movement of
the eye from its headlong flight beyond the finger and draws it
gracefully back, the novel opens up possibility and encourages
movement back and forth among a variety of counters. Some of
these counters are located within the novel; these we know by the
names they carry or the events they may be said to initiate or
conclude. Other counters we fill in for ourselves, as it were, directed by what we are given, always inclining to go too far, restrained by that sense of reasonable possibility elaborated in the
formal constraints of the novel. If there is no single and purposeful
finger, we must say, there can be no unitary and utterly inevitable
movement back along the curve of any arm. And without that
movement, the experience of the novel is bound to be unstable and
tempted in a way our experience of the statue simply doesn't have to
be.

But let us follow William Gass and put flesh on these bones. The
very type of a unitary construction in fiction is Tolstoy's novella,
"The Death of Ivan Illych." As such it should serve the purposes of
Gass's analogy more perfectly than any other work I can name. The
torso is shapely, a more or less stately though inexorable unitary
motion that begins at the end—in death—doubles back through
the life, and works itself around again to the protagonist's long-
anticipated demise. The outcome, given in fact and implication in
the opening pages, is never in doubt. Nothing is left to chance. The

reader's eye is carefully directed, we may say, through every significant line of the story's musculature, tracing a pattern that is vivid
and everywhere clearly a function of a master-program, a design.
Nothing is permitted to distract the eye from its attention to the
essential curve of the protagonist's death-in-life and final recognition of his condition. There are secondary characters, but they are
never more than instrumental to the development of Tolstoy's thesis and demonstration. We see them only insofar as they refer to
the life and death of Ivan Illych. In its unitary structure, the story
comes as close as any story can to drawing the reader's eye back
along the tension of an arm raised to support a pointing finger. If
the finger is the actual felt death of Ivan Illych that concludes the
story, the pointing the implicit awareness he achieves, then the
movement back along the curve of the arm would correspond to
the mind's retracing its steps to the original announcement of the
protagonist's death on the first page. Does this figure adequately
describe our experience of the story? That is another question.

The argument about literary realism depends upon our sense of
what actually happens to the mind when it reaches the very end of
the pointing finger. Until that point, we may say, the mind will
largely agree to confine itself to the internal dynamics of the story,
to counters developed within the narrative structure. At the point
of recognition—which is not in Tolstoy coincident with an Aristote-
lian reversal—the mind will incline to look beyond the finger into
the surrounding void. Gass would have us turn back, in implicit
recognition that there is nothing after all to look at, nothing relevant to the arc of the experience in which we've agreed to participate. Tolstoy doesn't agree. For him there is neither vacancy nor
silence around the churning figure of his protagonist. He reminds
us throughout that Ivan Illych is a man like other men whose
names we don't need to know that they exist. Not all writers operate that way, but even those who resist the temptation to general-
ize and universalize have their ways of drawing our attention beyond the pointing finger. Is it sheer vacancy we find out there? It's
not easy to think so when you listen to the way the words themselves point. They don't say "This is true" or "Remember what
you've come through" or "Aren't you glad you're here"; or, if the
words say these things at all, they say them tentatively, complexly,
so that "This is true" sounds much like "This mightn't be true at
all" and "Aren't you glad you're here" might just as well be "Don't
you think you might have done better." Because nothing is certain
in a fiction, because even fully formulated works encourage us to

linger over what they are not or might have been, we tend to dwell more than a little on possibilities beyond the assigned words of the given text.

In Tolstoy we imagine what Ivan Illych might have done to improve his life, what may be of help to him in the moment of his death. We imagine not because we are unsophisticated readers but because we are instructed to do so by the work itself. When, in the final pages of his story, Tolstoy invokes the divine "He whose understanding mattered," we accept the invocation as just not because it has been literally prepared by any prior words in the story but because we too have been looking for a way to console Ivan Illych. The invocation comes as the answer to a wish we have felt it reasonable to share. The answer, such as it is, is hardly sufficient under the circumstances, but it is surely a legitimate reference. It's not sheer vacancy we find as we thrash about with Ivan Illych because the mind has been encouraged to imagine possibility partly in the shape of its desire. And that desire cannot be said to confine itself to the shapes explicitly given by Tolstoy.

Perhaps we can get at all this more efficiently by considering for a moment Gass's observations on the painting by Picasso. "Would we wonder what was cooking in that pot?" That is the question the philosopher puts to us. The answer: Of course we wouldn't wonder. Why should we? The experience of the painting in no way inclines us to wonder about the contents of the pot. A large part of our experience there might, though, incline us to think about color. We might consider why Picasso painted the pot blue instead of red. Now there is no red pot in the picture, and probably no other painting by Picasso with just that configuration of objects with a red pot. Yet our thought might be perfectly legitimate. I might, in thinking about the picture, begin to wonder why I remember it always with a red pot in place of the original blue. Perhaps as I reflect on the picture, no longer before me, I remember always, after a while, that the pot *is* blue. But I have imagined, if only briefly, something not given in the original. And I may say, if I am careful and explain quite precisely, that the other colors in the painting justly cause me to imagine how the pot would look if it were painted red. Now the issue here isn't realism, but the liberty of the mind to imagine what it's been charged to imagine by the work at hand. Though we oughtn't to think about what's cooking in the pot, we may respond to possibilities not actually drawn in the painting.

To say that we are always at comparable liberty when we read a novel is to say what seems to me self-evident. I may not wonder what Ivan Illych would be like had he been an entirely selfless, saintly man. The story doesn't give me leave to dwell on such thoughts, so completely out of the range of Tolstoy's speculation. But I am surely free to consider why Tolstoy made Ivan so utterly colorless and predictable that he must seem to his creator and to us just like others of his class and training. Now the story doesn't tell us in so many words what Tolstoy thought he was doing in making his character so typical, but we feel we know without having read the letters or a biography. We may not be correct in what we say of Tolstoy, but so heavy and visible is his hand as he moves his characters about that we feel perfectly at liberty to think about him and his ulterior designs upon us.

Obviously it is appropriate to describe some works as realistic and others as something else. What is true for Tolstoy cannot be indistinguishably true for every other writer of fiction. But Gass wants us to believe that we may not imagine what is in the pot, even when our sense of the work at hand may incline us to wonder about just that, or about something even less palpable, like the divine "He whose understanding mattered." And I submit that, whether or not the work at hand is a patently realistic work like Tolstoy's, we read fiction realistically. We read, that is to say, as readers who imagine what it's like to live a certain way. We are involved in a degree that inclines us to imagine possibility in the shape of our desire; and though our desire will be responsive to what is given in the text, it will insist upon what it needs, and make *various* uses of the materials at hand.

Mr. Gass doesn't think that James invites us "to discuss the moral motivations of his characters *as if* they were surrogates for the real," but of course James offers just such an invitation every time he bothers to make an action plausible. "The moral problem of *The Portrait* becomes an esthetic problem, a problem of form," Gass informs us. And of course he is right. But what does it mean to say that a moral problem becomes an aesthetic problem? Simply, that as readers we cannot consider an issue apart from the narrative strategy that has made it significant and ordered a certain kind of response. And this takes us back in turn to the moral motivations of characters. We treat characters and their problems *as if* they were real. We do not yield entirely to the fiction that they are real, but we imagine what our life in particular and life in general might be if they were real. When we ask what is in the pot, we ask without supposing the dish will be served to us for dinner. If we aren't invited to ask, we hold back only because we've other questions to ask, have our eye on other fish someone's apt to fry. That's a different thing from believing nothing is in the original pot unless it's been prepared and labeled.

Gass's books are wonderful books because they raise all of the important aesthetic issues in the starkest and most inventive way. The writing is informed by a moral passion and a love of beautiful things that are never compromised by the author's compulsive addiction to aestheticizing formulations. We all know what Gass is writing against, including the tiresome use of novels for purposes of unitary moral uplift and penetrating "world-view." What he detests is the goody sweepstakes, in which works of art are judged not by their formal complexity or nuances of verbal texture but by their ability to satisfy easy moral imperatives. Gass has had some hand in discrediting the kind of righteous moralism that so corrupts ordinary apprehension of the literary arts. That is good. But the essays in his two collections have also served to confuse some readers about the art of reading. Insofar as the essays suggest that realism is necessarily a debased aesthetic, they encourage a view of reading as a specialized activity to which we bring special passions—like the passion for form—and from which we rigorously exclude others. This is not, it seems to me, an entirely useful way to record what really goes on when we read a book. Strange to say, I think William Gass knows better than the rest of us what goes on; and one day he may even decide to tell us.

Moral
Fiction?

Why do writers periodically issue statements or position papers on the state of their art? It's a question that's hard to answer and harder to avoid. In the face of sometimes irrelevant, sometimes mischievously obtuse declarations issued under the name of this literary figure or that, one is compelled to wonder how the distinguished creator of novels or poems can have so little of value to say about the thing he does best. We have to be interested in the fact that the man who wrote *Anna Karenina* also wrote an absurd little treatise called *What Is Art?* And we have to be interested in the fact that one of our most gifted contemporary writers thinks enough of Tolstoy's reflections to take some of them over in composing his own recent treatise. "Moral Fiction" is the title of John Gardner's recent provocation,* and though the author of *Grendel* and other splendid works doesn't quite have the accent of Tolstoy at his most oracularly sententious, he is apt to give some readers a mild scare. More than one, I suspect, reading how "real art creates myths a society can live instead of die by," will be sorely tempted to reach for their pillows.

No doubt Mr. Gardner believes most of the things he has to say in "Moral Fiction," and this alone guarantees that some of us, at least, will want to pursue his thoughts. There aren't so many good writers around that we can afford to ignore their formal statements. But what are we to make of them? Critics often argue that

*"Moral Fiction" appeared in the Winter 1977 issue of *Hudson Review* and was later included in Mr. Gardner's book of the same name (Basic Books, 1978).

From *Bennington Review*, Spring 1978.

writers can be counted on to describe the art in ways that implicitly justify and honor their own work. From this point of view, Mr. Gardner's piece is interesting only because it provides some notion of how he wishes us to regard his own books. If, incidentally, he actually proposes something useful, we shall have to take it as a bit of good luck, and refrain from anticipating more of the same. Classic statements like T. S. Eliot's "Tradition and the Individual Talent" have lately fallen before just such "suspicions"; what were, a short while ago, thought to be substantive formulations are increasingly taken to reflect Eliot's problems as a writer and his desire to win the day for a certain kind of literary expression. Personal considerations aside, I should hate to accuse Mr. Gardner of writing propaganda in the guise of literary theory. For one thing, it would be hard to prove. For another, novels like *Grendel, October Light,* and *The Wreckage of Agathon* are so different from one another that they don't seem collectively defensible in the terms of a simple theory.

If "Moral Fiction" is neither an apologia nor a genuinely satisfactory piece of theorizing, what function can it be said to perform? The question persists. Clearly, it elaborates a position which literary people will have to regard as unfashionable. It argues that the moral content of a successful fiction is clearly related to the presence of "good" characters whose behavior a reader will be moved to emulate. Great fiction, by this standard, will humanize author and reader alike, instructing us in the imagining of "life-sustaining myth" by which we may "lay the foundations of our future." Mr. Gardner is well aware that this rather programmatic "definition" is far from describing the more ambitious fictions of our own day. And this, not surprisingly, is what he must take to be the central virtue of his thesis. By framing his "definition" as he does, Mr. Gardner provokes a confrontation with the standard literary practice of our day, and challenges us to refute his contention that good fiction has always been bent on performing a certain kind of moral function. If the literary culture had not been so assiduous to claim for works of art a freedom from moral imperatives, Mr. Gardner's thesis would lack the force it has. Under the circumstances, its force is largely a function of its novelty, and Mr. Gardner surely knew what he was doing when he invited curmudgeons like Tolstoy and Aristotle to "witness" his performance. The reader trained in the theory of modernism—and what serious modern reader has not been so trained?—will find Mr. Gardner's paper curiously old-fashioned, perhaps amusing. He may also think that it is wrong-headed in a way that important writers are often anxious to impose upon their loyal readers.

"Moral Fiction," then, assigns itself a distinct function. Its business is to help establish a standard by which serious fiction may be evaluated and understood. This is no easy matter, and Mr. Gardner has his hands full balancing aesthetic and moral claims, trying to make them look identical. At one point, for example, conceding that *Macbeth* is a masterwork "no writer living can come anywhere near," he suggests that it is "morally secondary." Why? Because "it is easier and more natural to be moved to right action by the model of an admirable character than it is to be moved by recognition of an evil man's mistakes." But is this to be taken as an acceptable standard, sufficient in itself to help us discriminate between one work and another? The expression "morally secondary" is particularly troublesome, and one has to wonder whether Mr. Gardner is at all aware of the position to which it implicitly commits him. For if *Macbeth* is morally secondary, so too must be "The Death of Ivan Illych," and "Notes from Underground," and all seven volumes of *Remembrance of Things Past;* so too, I would argue, a work like "Death in Venice," which Mr. Gardner clearly loves and does not think to label "secondary." Though the character Aschenbach in Mann's novella can hardly be called an evil man, he is far from "admirable" in the behavior we are invited to witness, and no one would be so foolish as to take him for a model of "right action." If major works by Shakespeare, Tolstoy, Dostoyevski, Proust, and Mann are "morally secondary," of what possible use is the designation? These writers are not willful immoralists; neither are they experimental technicians of the word committed to self-promoting prestidigitations. Each had a complex vision to impart, and the staying power to make it persuasive over a considerable period of time.

Mr. Gardner wishes to distinguish between "true fiction"—which is moral—and something else which succeeds in engaging our attention in spite of itself. To manage this he must resolve a simple contradiction to which his argument is subject at every turn. If "true" fiction, so called, is, must be, moral, then works that do not measure up in moral terms cannot be said to succeed as fictions. It is hopeless to say of John Barth that he writes superb fictions, only to conclude that "such fiction is closer to the sermon than to the true short story or novel." Mr. Gardner has identified fiction in general with a certain kind of novel, the product of a sensibility for which imitation is a suitable and potentially ennobling procedure. John Barth, in some of his work, is another kind of writer. His fiction cannot be said to be moral or immoral on the grounds that it does or does not conform to Mr. Gardner's specifications. If Barth's fiction succeeds, it will succeed at least in part on its own terms, and it will be moral in the best sense if it makes readers think and feel and imagine as well as they can. So much seems to me unarguable, despite what Mr. Gardner says. If he is serious about his claims, I would go on to contend, he must do one of two things: either, (1) stop pretending that he is describing fiction in general when he speaks prescriptively of moral dimensions; or, (2) deny validity to fictions that are not drawn to his specifications.

When we look more closely at Mr. Gardner's theory, we discover that he actually speaks very little in what we should ordinarily call moral terms. He does describe a writerly ethic, but this is only marginally related to explicit moral imperatives of the sort that disfigure and confuse the argument. Fiction is "a way of thinking," says Mr. Gardner, who proceeds to demonstrate what this means. It means, quite simply, that good writers are responsive to their own words and faithful to their characters; that they search out the implications of expressions that make their way across the page; that they don't unduly impose themselves upon their creations, who are permitted to conduct lives of their own according to the given laws of their being. This is elementary stuff, but useful all the same. Readers who don't understand the role of honesty and faithfulness in the creation of successful fictions do not know what matters most in the things they read: This is a persisting element in Mr. Gardner's paper. I can't say I appreciate his chauvinistic contention that novelists and poets are better equipped to understand these things than critics, but the substantive point remains useful.

In fact, Mr. Gardner more than once indulges the snobbish temptation to exalt bardic instinct by playing it off against critical plodding. The writer—not the critic—"tests his ideas in the process of writing." Perhaps. But what does this say? Mr. Gardner thinks to claim on this basis that writers discover the truth by being forced to submit to a system that is rigorous and compelling. But to argue on this basis is to forget what Mr. Gardner knows as well as anybody else: that writers differ drastically from one another in talent and ambition; that writers, in creating their own test cases, in submitting to their own "laws," have it in their hands to make things difficult or relatively easy for themselves. This might be said as well of critics, who have, after all, given limits to negotiate and respect, and who have always to be testing their ideas by reaching for "cases" that will prove or compromise what they believe. The novelist, like the critic, will routinely see ways of simplifying his task by pretending that alternative views or approaches are less threatening or tempting than in fact they are. Only the best novelists and critics will insist that the alternative "models" be admitted and given their respectful due. Moral fiction, as Mr. Gardner intermittently concedes, stirs us because it is willing to go against the grain of its own certainties. The good writer is not afraid to discover as he writes that a premise or an assumption needs to be revised; that an "original opinion was oversimple." The distinction here separates good writers from bad; it does not distinguish between writers and critics.

Probably the most hopeful formulation in "Moral Fiction" is the contention that "the effect of great fiction is to temper real experience, modify prejudice, humanize." This is a rather more bracing and generally significant claim than the view that writers test their ideas as they write. But the two claims are decidedly related. For if, in testing ideas, writers learn a new respect for truth-telling as an arduous enterprise, they will presumably become practiced in overcoming prejudice. They will become more human as they learn to imagine what it is like to be a person different in crucial ways from themselves. This is Mr. Gardner's view. As far as it goes, it seems plausible. Is it accurate in describing what happens to writers? Anyone who has been close to distinguished poets and novelists will wonder what Mr. Gardner was getting at. Are writers notably more free of prejudice than other human beings? Are they more generous and humble than their average reader? The answer, of course, is that they are not; that, while their superiority has a great deal to do with character, they are rarely praiseworthy in moral terms. The issue is not so important as Mr. Gardner wanted it to be, but one cannot refrain from recommending to the skeptical reader a volume like *The Selected Letters of Theodore Roethke*, or a life of Balzac, or the Lawrance Thompson biography of Robert Frost. In these accounts, as in documentary records of other great writers, one finds that the best writers are as likely to be monsters of egotism as charitable human beings. The effect of the writer's experience is likely to be a narrowing of sympathies and an intensification of focus on particular aspects of experience at the expense of others. Character, insofar as it may be said to be involved at all, is mainly evident in the writer's single-mindedness of purpose, in his refusal to be seduced from his lonely rigors by the usual blandishments most of us take to be consistent with the good life. The ferocity of the writer's pursuit is not often likely to "modify prejudice" or to "humanize."

There are writers, of course, who are, or who seem to have been, genuinely decent human beings. Some, like the poet Robinson Jeffers, will do everything they can to make readers of their verse feel that they are beyond decent human sympathies. A poet like Frost, on the other hand, who tended to put on a kindly face for purposes of the verse, may be impossible in his private transactions with family and friends. But Mr. Gardner's claims are perhaps more usefully considered in what they say of us as readers. If the effect of great literature, especially fiction, is properly to modify prejudice and to humanize, then the effect may surely be said to extend to readers. Since, in Mr. Gardner's view, the best fiction will "offer models of just behavior," readers must be expected to profit by those models. A character's "struggle against confusion, error, and evil" will inevitably "give firm intellectual and emotional support to our own struggle." Perhaps all of this is true, insofar as there are splendid persons about to profit from their literary transactions with "moral" characters. But it is not clear that experienced and educated readers are generally susceptible to the process as it is elaborated by Mr. Gardner.

The critic George Steiner, for example, has argued that great literature typically fails to humanize; that sophisticated readers may be peculiarly susceptible to a kind of inhumanity which we like to think of as touching only ignorant and "uncivilized" people. Familiar though it may have become, Steiner's argument needs to be pressed again and again, until we have come up with serious answers to the questions raised. "To Civilize Our Gentlemen" is the key item here,* and in it we find the following resonant speculation:

> Unlike Matthew Arnold and unlike Dr. Leavis, I find myself unable to assert confidently that the humanities humanize. Indeed, I would go further: it is at least conceivable that the focusing of consciousness on a written text, which is the substance of our training and pursuit, diminishes the sharpness and readiness of our actual moral response. Because we are trained to give psychological and moral credence to the imaginary, to the character in a play or a novel, to the condition of

*The essay appears in Steiner's *Language and Silence* (Atheneum, 1967), a collection that remains indispensable to everyone interested in the future of language.

spirit we gather from a poem, we may find it more difficult to identify with the real world, to take the world of actual experience to heart—"to heart" is a suggestive phrase. The capacity for imaginative reflex, for moral risk in any human being is not limitless; on the contrary, it can be rapidly absorbed by fictions, and thus the cry in the poem may come to sound louder, more urgent, more real than the cry in the street outside. The death in the novel may move us more potently than the death in the next room. Thus there may be a covert, betraying link between the cultivation of aesthetic response and the potential of personal inhumanity. What then are we doing when we study and teach literature?

I do not think that Mr. Gardner has made an adequate response to the issues raised here. And they are raised, after all, from a perspective it isn't possible to overlook. Steiner's speculations take shape under the pressure of recent events, specifically, the planned extermination of European Jews by Hitler and his comrades. "When barbarism came to twentieth century Europe," Steiner reminds us, "the arts faculties in more than one university offered very little moral resistance, and this is not a trivial or local accident." These facts—and there are others like them—Steiner insists we try to understand: "and let us not take the easy way out and say 'the man who did these things in a concentration camp just said he was reading Rilke. He was not reading him well.' That is an evasion. He may have been reading him very well indeed." To which Mr. Gardner would seem to say, in "Moral Fiction": "You cannot prove what you argue, but you can clearly see that such arguments do no one any good. Why yield to cynicism and despair when you can make everyone feel ever so much better by adopting a more positive outlook on these things? It ought to be possible to tease the mind with a hopeful view of humane literacy, just as some novelists manage to resist the 'black abyss' and create hopeful myths in their fiction."

Mr. Gardner believes that a completely successful work of fiction will be moral, and that being moral it will necessarily represent "an intensely honest and rigorous mode of thought." If it is moral, moreover, it will refuse to succumb to cynicism or despair, and it will put the reader in mind of "true" and "valid" ideas. From this basis of expectation, one supposes, Mr. Gardner would not be likely to approve George Steiner's central suggestion: that "the capacity for imaginative reflex" may be "rapidly absorbed by fictions." It is more likely, in Mr. Gardner's view, that the imagination will be exercised and primed in its encounters with fiction, so that it is in time equipped to respond nimbly in actual human affairs. Fiction is moral *because* it helps make possible a decent approach to actual experience; we support our best writers *because* they refuse to lead us where it is all too easy to go: into the "abyss" at the bottom of which we discover that what is terrible is true, what is good an idle fancy. "One tortures the reader with alternative possibilities," says Mr. Gardner. The writer performs his function properly through the "simulation of real experience," which is the enactment of an arduous freedom in a universe that gives us cause to hope.

Difficult though it is to argue abstractly with Mr. Gardner—and one would in many ways like him to be right—there is in these matters a way to decide. This is not the place for the sort of sustained textual analysis that is better done in the classroom, but we would do well to consider how a suitable inquiry would proceed. If Mr. Gardner is more or less correct in what he says of the relation between morality and fiction, we ought to be able to confirm him by examining an unmistakably moral work. Why not Tolstoy's famous short novel, "The Death of Ivan Illych"? It is a standard text, studied in elementary fiction courses and in advanced seminars in the theory of fiction; it has been almost universally admired; it is clearly the product of an imagination for which moral issues have great importance.

Does "The Death of Ivan Illych" support Mr. Gardner's theory of "moral fiction"? The reader is of course invited to conduct his own investigation. If he does, I think he will need to bear in mind the following points:

(1) Though Tolstoy's novella is the embodiment of a moral vision, it is carefully organized to make a series of points which—in one's experience of the work—are never susceptible to doubt or reversal. Mr. Gardner's general objection to thoughtful "fiction in which the writer knows before he starts what it is that he means to say" as a species of "first-class propaganda" would have to apply to "Ivan Illych" as well as to novels named in "Moral Fiction": *Gulliver's Travels*, Barth's *Chimera*, and so on.

(2) While the main character of Tolstoy's novella may be said to struggle and to suffer, he does not impress us as a notably good man whose behavior or thinking a reader would be likely to emulate. Tolstoy writes what Mr. Gardner would have to call a "morally secondary" work, since, by definition, he "leaves true morality at least partly to implication or at best in the hands of some minor

character." The minor character is Gerasim, a servant who eases his master's final days, but who cannot be said to redeem either his master or the various other characters who behave so badly.

(3) If Tolstoy believed, with Mr. Gardner, that a moral fiction must be "absolutely fair to everyone involved," why did he insist that the various characters in the first section of "Ivan Illych" react in so uniform a way to the news of Ivan's death? According to Mr. Gardner, the successful writer "plays the scene through in his imagination," and much of what he learns "he learns simply by imitation." But it is not imitation that can possibly have led Tolstoy to represent human character as the utterly predictable and rather shabby thing we find in "Ivan Illych." Consider: ". . . the mere fact of the death of a near acquaintance aroused, as usual, in all who heard of it the complacent feeling that, 'it is he who is dead and not I.' " Or, many pages later: "In reality it is just what is usually seen in the houses of people of moderate means who want to appear rich, and therefore succeed only in resembling others like themselves." Tolstoy has a plan, and an idea he is determined to communicate. He works not by imitation but by considering what will work, what combinations will produce the desired effects. If the incredible sameness of human response we find in the characters of this story will press the reader to reflect as Tolstoy desires, the story will have succeeded in the only terms that may be said to matter. We do not routinely demand of writers that they be fair to characters as we might if they were prosecuting real people in a court of law; we demand that they be interesting, and that their characters seem to operate according to the conventions established within the given fiction. The reader of "Ivan Illych" cannot believe for a moment that Tolstoy intends to be fair to anyone, for fairness is not an operant convention in his novella.

(4) Mr. Steiner suggests it may be possible to read with great care and sophistication and to behave as though one had never for a moment seriously considered the "message" associated with the text consumed. Does Mr. Gardner know what a good reader is likely to make of "The Death of Ivan Illych"? Can he be sure that a work that has designs on us will affect us as it intends? Surely it is possible that an experienced reader will resist a "moral" work precisely because he can see too well the author's purpose and does not wish to be manipulated by a work that presumes to tell him how to live. Of course, Mr. Gardner may argue that a story cannot be said to succeed if it tips its hand, if from the beginning it lets the reader in on its ultimate moral intentions. But then the work would

not be expected to provide models of human behavior for readers to emulate. It would address the reader obliquely, withholding insights and bringing him along gradually, opening up a perspective too complex for ready identification or emulation. This, I should say, is the way that Mr. Gardner's fictions work, and no one will doubt for a moment that they have very little in common with "The Death of Ivan Illych."

Fortunately for us and, incidentally, for Mr. Gardner, the first-rate novelist knows what he needs to know to give us a fiction we can love. His knowledge may not be sufficient, however, to tell him how to compose a theory of fiction or to make the rest of us feel we've been given the keys to the kingdom.

Weightless
Characters

William Styron, *Sophie's Choice* (New York: Random House).

The belief in free will is necessary to most good fiction. Without it, characters must be made to drift indifferently from one prospect to another. Human decisions will seem either not to matter or to be unconvincingly portrayed. It is not essential that the novelist himself fully believe in free will, only that he conduct the business of his novel as if he had not altogether decided against it. In practice this is something that has little to do with deliberate deception or the mastery of familiar confidence-tricks. Writers need to believe they are getting at the truth if they are to remain exercised about matters that are by nature demanding and serious. To subscribe to free will in a novel is to determine that characters will be permitted to develop in accordance with their natures, and that their susceptibilities will be plausibly various; also, that they will seem to us, as they develop, to be substantially accountable for what they do or fail to do. The novelist need not pass explicit judgments himself in order to make us feel that judgments are possible. And we, in turn, will want to feel that we have been given leave to care for this character or that without being asked to renounce the possibility of judgment. Nothing more, or less, is involved in the novelistic "illusion" of free will.

In his new novel, *Sophie's Choice*, William Styron has created a character who develops quite as variously and plausibly as one could wish. But she is made to develop in such a way that, though we care very much for her and are moved to grief and rage over what

From *Salmagundi*, Summer 1980, and from *Granta*, no. 2, 1980.

she has to suffer, we are never invited to think of her as a responsible human agent. Responsive, yes; responsible—to herself, to us, even to Styron—no. If, more than ten years ago, Styron gave us in Nat Turner a character virtuosic in assigning responsibility and in positioning himself deliberately at the bar of justice, he has here given us just the reverse. Nor is the portrait of Sophie a special instance in a novel that concerns itself almost equally with two or three other characters. Styron is here in the grip of a very simple and important idea, namely, that to counter evil one must learn to love and to express love. In intellectual terms this is to say that understanding and judgment are separable activities and ought not to be confused with one another. In literary terms Styron's idea comes across as affection for characters who do not have to earn our loyalty. Having suffered or opened themselves to the suffering of others, they assume the status of victims, and those of us who feel with them are thereby enabled to believe that we have borne witness to the central truth of our time: that *"absolute evil is never extinguished from the world."* This is a truth we can acknowledge without tracing out corresponding insights or making large and unreasonable demands upon ourselves or upon those we have come to love.

Styron's novel has taken the United States by storm, and it is no secret that, as he earlier sought to get inside the experience of slavery, he has now attempted to come to terms with Auschwitz. This he does by drawing upon the memories of a Polish survivor, who tells her story in bits and pieces to a young Southern writer immediately recognizable as the young Styron himself. In so organizing his novel, Styron can play off Sophie Zawistowska's memories against his own reflections, measuring the validity of her account against the accounts of other concentration camp survivors and writers like Hannah Arendt, Elie Wiesel, and George Steiner. From the point of view of earnest, dispassionate inquiry, Styron makes the best of his opportunity. He tries out first one idea, then another, always curious and eager to improve his grasp of the relevant facts. His respect for the historical truth and his love of ideas for their own sake make him a careful though never slavish expositor of other men's theories and opinions. And Sophie's account is subjected to the kind of tender scrutiny that makes us feel we have understood why she takes so long to get it out and to correct what had been a succession of earlier falsehoods.

The problem with all of this is that Styron nowhere feels compelled to tell what we are to make of the presented material. The refusal to fashion a perspective from which Sophie may be judged is part of a larger refusal to see people we like as anything but victims: of history, of the zeitgeist, of their own innocence or idiosyncrasy. This may be preferable to a fiction in which characters either do or do not measure up to an abstract standard of goodness or competency and are summarily dismissed or congratulated on that basis alone. But there is only so far that a novelist can go with characters for whom he feels so much affection that he cannot make us feel they are accountable for themselves in the way that others are supposed to be. No one expects the novelist to resolve every uncertainty, and the taking of positions—on persons as on ideas—has so often become a substitute for thought that the writer frequently does well to avoid it. But we do expect the novelist to follow up the issues he has set in motion, to try out the ideas that fascinate him not only on figures for whom he has no feeling but on the characters that most occupy him. To fail in this is to create confusion about what ultimately the novel intends. An ambitious writer like Styron cannot be thought to be satisfied with the evocation of terror and suffering as if these might tell us all we need to know. If Sophie, or her lover Nathan, or the narrator Stingo, are to stand, permanently, in the degree that enduring characters persist for us in memory, they must be more than the pathos or frailty with which they are invested.

Styron's Sophie is, in several respects, a powerfully realized character. What is unrealized in the novel are the ideas that are made to circulate without being allowed to settle on her fair shoulders. The title of the book tells us that Sophie had a choice, though really she is confronted by more than one. Why Styron did not call his novel "Sophie's Choices" we cannot say for sure. Apparently he felt that, having gone through Auschwitz, she had but one actual choice left her: to live or to die. But to read the character and her situation in this way is to reduce her human stature and to conclude more or less in advance that all other, less ultimate questions are of no real consequence. In this sense, it might be said that Sophie is free to live or to die, but not to live as others live, in the shadow of a succession of choices to which she is or is not equal. Nor is Styron's character a victim merely of Auschwitz, and on that account alone exempted from considerations that obtain for others who have suffered less. Even as a young woman, before the onset of war and Hitler's invasion of her native Poland, Sophie was a helpless creature, unable to do what she would intuitively have liked to do, and no less exempt from the kinds of judgment we ordinarily direct at one another. Confronted by unreasonable demands, she has a desire to run away and to save her self-respect. But she fails to move, to resist what others would make of her. Though she is revolted by a wretched anti-Semitic pamphlet prepared by her father for distribution at his university, she can do nothing but yield to his demand that she help in the distribution. "I knew that I *would* be there . . ." she recalls for Stingo, "passing out these sheets just like I done everything he told me to do since I was a little girl, running these errand, bringing him things, learning to use the typewriter and knowing shorthand just so he could use me whenever he wanted. And this terrible emptiness come over me when I realize then there was nothing I could do about it, no way of saying no, no way possible to say, 'Papa, I'm not going to help you spread this thing.' "

Was this not one of the choices Sophie failed to acknowledge and to act upon? Styron's reader may wonder why Sophie found it impossible to say no to her father, but the reader is urged again and again to move on to the "larger" issues and to concern himself with absolute evil; the failings of Sophie Zawistowska are too small and pitiful to think about in any extended way. The fact that she was revolted by the anti-Semitic pamphlet and allowed herself to feel a measure of hatred for the man who wrote it ought to be enough for us. She may not have acted well, but her heart could be counted upon most of the time to be in the right place.

It never occurs to Styron to ask why Sophie gives in so easily, why she feels she has no choice, though, for example, her friend Wanda is busy choosing frantically even when most of the better options have been taken away. He speculates bravely about less prominent characters, but is determined to love Sophie as she is, and feels this will be hard to do if he presses too hard. For all he tells us about Sophie, for all she is made to tell Stingo about herself, she remains something less than the representative human being she is meant to be. Though we feel her presence, we do not understand her: a major flaw in a novel that seeks to understand the Nazi period by examining the experience of this character especially. Is it the case that Styron would have had to face the same dilemma no matter what the name or particular background of the representative human being he decided to install at the center of his novel? Our answer necessarily depends upon our sense of Styron's options. And one of his options would have been to handle Sophie differently. Clearly he could have tried to account for her failings and in so doing made her a responsible agent. He would then have had on his hands, say, the product of a particular ethos or milieu or social class. And he would have had to indicate what chance such a person would have had to break free of inherited constraints and inadequacies. Was Sophie a typical young woman of her time and situation? This the novel does not say. Though she had a very unusual father to grow up with, she is in no way represented as a product of that relationship alone. It is surely possible that Sophie, as presented, might well have been the same kind of person had her father been a cleric or a customs official. So far as Styron is concerned, Sophie is an acceptably representative human being in the sense that she cannot bring herself to do what she likes, and suffers because there is evil in the world. To shape her nature as the product of cultural or social conditions is to become involved in something else, to distract us from what is central.

Styron also had the option, of course, of making Sophie a very different sort of person, someone more like her friend Wanda, a resistance fighter and Polish patriot whose political zeal and fervent rationality are the most attractive things in the novel. To have done this, of course, would have been not only to write a different book but to aim at a very different statement, namely, that absolute evil may be extinguished by the collective efforts of persons who do whatever they can to resist what it would make of them. That is the sort of "upbeat" affirmation that tends to embarrass modern readers—and writers—who have been taught to feel superior to affirmations of any kind. Styron is not afraid of words that, in his own account, "have the quality of a strapping homily," but he is apparently no more ready than the rest of us to embrace causes and movements.

To have made Sophie a victim who struggled bravely would have been to assign her a range of viable choices on the basis of which we might have judged her. But Styron is not interested in performance, and Sophie seems to him most definitively a victim in the sense that she cannot bring herself to choose or to act. Though, in the most terrible moment in the novel, she is asked to decide which of her two children must be taken to the ovens, she cannot be said even there to have made a choice and to have assumed responsibility. Though she "chooses" her daughter she does so without conviction or anger or sense or purpose. Nor does she seek to hold back the officer who takes the child, or follow the child's departure with her eyes. No one can say, at this point in the novel, what he would have done in Sophie's place, and the last thing one would think to do is to feel that there Sophie betrayed her humanity. What, after all, could she have done that would have been effectual? But this terrifying encounter is emblematic for us of what Sophie has all along failed to be and to do. In her suffering and dumb acquiescence she stands for some part of the human possibility. But there is something missing, and we excuse her—and her creator—too easily if we conclude that she fails only to be heroic and to transcend her ordinariness.

Our objection to Sophie as a character is not in itself a moral objection but an objection to a kind of characterization that puts unnecessary restrictions on moral reflection. In *Sophie's Choice* Styron is less interested in moral issues than in a peculiar metaphysics of suffering, and he has prompted even his more tolerant reviewers to complain that he has no gift for psychological analysis or sustained ethical reflection. As if to disprove the charge by anticipation, Styron indulges here and there a flourish of virtuosic psychologizing in a Dostoyevskian mode. Not only Rudolf Höss but a much less important Nazi officer becomes the occasion for Styron's display of psychological depth-analysis. "His strivings were essentially religious," he tells us of a Dr. Jemand von Niemand, who makes Sophie decide which of her two children is to die. Why must the man have been religious? Because it seems likely that a fellow who would do something so extravagantly monstrous—and something, moreover, quite unusual even among the atrocities committed by his kind—would have had to act in the service of an overmastering impulse. He must have seen that his boredom and revulsion were in part the consequence of an inability to commit a sin, and "that the absence of sin and the absence of God were inseparably intertwined . . . All of his depravity had been enacted in a vacuum of sinless and businesslike godlessness, while his soul thirsted for beatitude." What he determines to do is, of course, in Styron's version, "to affirm his human capacity for evil, by committing the most intolerable sin . . . Goodness could come later. But first a great sin." This analysis is accompanied by details of von Niemand's general anxiety and drunkenness, and some very close attention to the dynamics of the transaction between Sophie and her tormentor.

Though it is painful to read of Sophie's ordeal, the reader retains sufficient presence of mind to be put off by the gratuitous analysis of von Niemand. The business about his religious mania is much more inventive than anything lavished on Sophie. We're expected, no doubt, to applaud the performance, to brood on the enigma of human perversity. But von Niemand's mania is in no way related to the ambitions of other characters in the novel. It may suggest to some that radical evil is by nature extreme and unpredictable, but in that case, why should Styron make so much of efforts to understand evil, to see it as an expression of our common humanity? The analysis of von Niemand would seem useful only if it were commensurate with efforts to come to terms with what is most peculiar about Sophie. Since Styron accepts Sophie as she is, he should be less ready to work up the elements of von Niemand's unpardonable sin.

And what, after all, do the von Niemand passages contribute in the way of moral insight? Dostoyevski would no doubt have had something memorable to say of the man, and of Sophie confronted by the doctor's thirst for beatitude. Styron seems to believe that he does enough simply by invoking the syndrome. The reader will know what to make of it all by referring it to the tradition in which it belongs. But this is a dangerous assumption. Von Niemand is after all incapable of reflecting upon the origins of his sin. He may or may not actually suffer agonies of repentance once the sin has been committed. And Styron, of course, is not interested enough to make us stay around and find out. If the analysis of von Niemand were more than gratuitous, we should be made to regard him as a more important character, or we should have impressed upon us the contrast between the man and his victim. But Sophie is no more capable of extended moral reflection than von Niemand. The complex unconscious motives assigned him do not serve as a basis for understanding anyone else, and so come across as a form of novelistic exhibitionism. In an isolated passage Styron shows what he can do without bothering to consider what he has refused to do for other characters.

Some connection between Sophie and von Niemand might have been indicated. Like him, she appears to act in part out of unconscious motives that are more complex than anything Styron will allow. Even in Brooklyn, two years after her liberation from the concentration camp, she has not learned to defend herself or to do what is best for her. She seems to be playing out a drama she has no hand in directing. Styron might have made something of this, might have asked questions about her needs or had something to say about her perverse indifference to things most of us cannot be casual about. To do so, however, would necessarily have been to see her as finally responsible for herself, no matter what the burden of unconscious motivation. Is it a sin to hold responsible one who has had to bear so much? May the victim of a radical evil never be held responsible, never have her deeds or omissions subjected to overt moral scrutiny? What of the aftermath of her ordeal, when the conditions of terror have been removed and circumstances are more genial?

At a New York beach, Sophie and Stingo-Styron become sexually "involved" quite as Stingo hoped and fantasized they would. Though Sophie is still very much attached to her lover Nathan, still feels she owes her recovery to him, she advances lecherously upon the younger Stingo and concludes their session by rubbing his semen all over her face. In a moment Stingo observes that his companion is "seemingly no more touched by our prodigious intimacy than if we had done a two-step together." What to make of this? Nothing, apparently, for Styron is content to leave the narrator's observation at that. The reader is free to wonder whether Sophie's indifference has something to do with Auschwitz, with other impinging preoccupations, or with the person she has always been. Styron himself will have no part in such speculations, and will insist simply that Sophie is Sophie and nothing more need be said about it. The kind of analytic pressure applied to von Niemand is somehow inappropriate for Sophie.

Our grasp of the narrator is no better. Is he in fact the novelist himself? Are we to take everything he says as coming from Styron? Our uncertainty is bound to cause considerable—and unnecessary—discomfort, since much that he says is either puerile or insupportable. He is a decent enough fellow, and he covers himself here and there by admitting to stray prejudices and to a young man's staggering "inexperience." But it is this same Stingo who earnestly studies the holocaust literature and brings back vivid samples for our edification. It is Stingo who addresses us at novel's end in solemn accents and describes quite plausibly the vision of evil the novel is to convey. To say that he is capable of regarding himself with tolerant irony and amusement—particularly as he recalls his departed youth—is in no way to conclude that he shows an instinct for self-parody in the novel as a whole. He appears, for better or worse, to speak for Styron. We are confused by the occasional puerile observations and by much that seems arbitrary in the book because, again, Styron also fails to make Stingo a responsible agent. "All my life I have retained a strain of uncontrolled didacticism," says Stingo. But where is this didacticism in a novel that cries out for the application of free-floating ideas to the central characters? To discuss theories and formulate ideas is not to be didactic, after all, but to raise the possibility of at least provisional resolutions. These we never get, not in a sustained or serious way, and that is an element of the major flaw in this overheated work. Stingo ought to be able to reflect more satisfactorily on the material he presents, and Styron ought to indicate what we are to make of Stingo's reflections. When Stingo fails to do justice to a train of thought he has set in motion or to make adequate sense of a detail, Styron should either fill the gap or acknowledge, at least, that there is a gap; also, that there are reasons—characterological reasons—for Stingo's represented incapacity.

It is one thing to project Sophie as an absolute victim who may not be called to strenuous accounting. To some of us this may not seem legitimate, but we can entertain the idea in a serious way. But Stingo is in no comparable way a victim, and it is his experience that dominates much of the novel. In fact, only one-quarter or so of the book is devoted to Sophie's memories of Warsaw and Auschwitz. Stingo's world—his father's American South and his own adopted postwar Brooklyn—is not on the face of it terrible and intimidating. Once or twice we are reminded of violence Southern-style: racial conflict, lynchings, and so on. And there is a good deal of domestic violence perpetrated by Nathan in the Brooklyn rooming house they occupy. But for the most part this is menace on a different scale, and always it is cast into diminished perspective by the persistent dredging up of incidents from Auschwitz. Stingo is a free man. He can write his novels, fantasize all he likes about carnal transport, and pursue friendships with some hope that they will not turn sour. Styron's failure to hold him accountable for gross lapses of taste and insight is a reflection not of the novelist's self-pity but of his conviction that he is after bigger game. Why be severe with Stingo when there are graver things to deplore?

There is some truth in this view, of course. Stingo, as indicated, is not a bad fellow, and he is generously candid about his more obvious deficiencies. And there *are* larger matters for Styron to contend with. But Styron does not understand that the character ceases to matter to us as he should in the degree that his creator seems not to take him seriously. It is not enough for the novelist to show an interest in the character's ideas or to dwell to the point of tedium on his sexual adventures. To take him seriously is to invest him with the capacity to make choices and discriminations. A book that means to address the holocaust cannot afford to project weightless characters, as if the gravity of the issues might be communicated simply by insisting that people suffered and that philosophers have debated the matter passionately.

Weightless characters typically move about from one option to another without feeling pressed to distinguish for themselves between good and bad, normal and abnormal, significant and trivial. Their creator treats them as illustrations of this tendency or that and does his best to make us care about them while refusing to allow for the prospect that they might have done better. They are susceptible only to irrational guilt, never to the sense that they have actually transgressed against some presiding cultural presence or violated a commandment. To be healthy means, for them, to be flexible, to be tolerant of their own failings, and to generate signs of a capacity to respond to others. Love objects are to be relentlessly supported. Their stray gestures may seem offensive or momentarily disturbing, but nothing enacted by one of them may be thought to be wrong or genuinely symptomatic of malevolent intention. Crime, if it exists at all, is "radical" and belongs to others. Cruelty may not be ignored, but it is easy to forgive in one who shows signs of madness or contrition.

To speak of Styron's characters as weightless is to say that in some essential way they are made up, that they have no moral center. They may have a past, a parentage, a repertoire of characteristics, but they lack in any defining sense *character*. Sophie is what happens to her and what Stingo can learn from her. She is not a character who makes her fate. She suffers it as, in the novelist's conception of things, each of us must suffer the fate to which circumstance assigns us. For a man who wanted to write a book about choice and about the intersection of personal and political experience, Styron made a terrible decision. He allowed himself to fall in love with characters—including Stingo—who have not the stature required to bear witness to the treacheries of modern experience in a persuasive and instructive way. Alongside of remembrance and lamentation we should have preferred an evocation of inwardness. Styron is too committed to the advantages of confessional self-expression to write a book about good and evil.

Post-Modernism
and Politics

Mario Vargas Llosa, *The Real Life of Alejandro Mayta* (New York: Farrar, Straus, and Giroux).

In the new novel by the Peruvian writer Mario Vargas Llosa there is an arresting sequence in which the protagonist and his revolutionary comrades stop at the ancient mountain community of Quero. They rest there for two hours before continuing their flight from government troops sent to bring them back to be punished for revolutionary crimes against the state. What is striking in the handful of pages devoted to Quero is not the quality of the political ideas brought forward or the revelation of character facilitated by the protagonist's reflections. What emerges so forcefully, rather, is a powerful sentiment of disgust focused not only on the trappings of the place but on its inhabitants. That disgust, we cannot but note, is accompanied neither by qualification nor apology. "All the houses in Quero had to be like that," we read: "no light, no running water, no drainage, and no bath. Flies, lice, and a thousand other bugs must be part of the poor furniture." But if this is a sorry spectacle, we are admonished, consider the people who live in this filth: "If they had to pee at night, they probably wouldn't feel like getting up and going outside. They pee right here, next to the bed where they sleep and the stove where they cook . . . And if at midnight they had to shit? Would they have enough energy to go out into the darkness and the cold, the wind and the rain? They'd shit right here, between the stove and the bed."

This is not an isolated passage in Vargas Llosa's novel. Still in

From *Dissent*, Summer 1986.

Quero, he wants us to note that the lady of the house probably sleeps with her animals, that she has no doubt been wearing the same skirt for many years, and that it has probably been many years "since she had washed herself." Elsewhere in the book there are many references to the mountains of garbage threatening to overwhelm the city of Lima, and to middle-class citizens who grow so accustomed to it that they no longer notice what has become of their neighborhoods. Poorer citizens are described as "resigned," not only to the garbage, which they routinely throw out of their houses, but to such emblems of crime and disorder as "a decapitated body" lying untended in the street.

Some will speak of all this as part of the author's apocalyptic vision, reading the signs as a warning of the disaster that is about to befall Peru as it has already befallen other countries in the region. But more than a prediction of political or social disorder is at issue in the imagery that so pervades this novel. To be confronted so steadily with filth and wretchedness is in fact to suspect that political categories are inadequate to comprehend what is happening in places like Peru. Tempted like the rest of us to come at problems of poverty, inequality, and tyranny with the vocabulary of revolution, reaction, and reform, the novelist also seems more than a little tempted by the thought that politics inevitably misses the point. If, as his narrator has it, "Peru's going down the drain," mightn't it be the case that there's no help for it, or worse, that the people almost deserve what they've got? No such awful conclusion is drawn in this novel, but it is hard not to feel that the novelistic intelligence shaping the material has but barely managed to resist it.

Ostensibly Vargas Llosa has written a political novel. The setting alternates between the Peru of the late 1950s and the Peru of the near future. The central figure is an old-line Trotskyist disappointed in the merely theoretic communism he's pursued for twenty years. A member of a splinter party with seven members, Alejandro Mayta has had reason to feel disappointed. His one attempt to break out of the sterile round of ideological disputation and ineffectual pamphleteering was a minor revolutionary action that had no real chance of succeeding and that cost Mayta all the political friends he'd had. Vargas Llosa's narrator, who closely resembles the novelist himself, reconstructs the story of the long-forgotten Mayta and his abortive insurrection by means of interviews with those who knew Mayta in the 1950s. By the end of the novel we see Mayta as a sixty-five-year-old man whose chief desire is to keep himself and his family afloat and whose principal dream is a dream of escape to another country. He lives in an already dilapidated "new town" in the shadow of the prison in which he spent many years of his adult life. Obviously, there are grounds for despair in this narrative outline; and in the detail Vargas Llosa supplies, relentlessly, there is more than reason for disgust. Mayta himself may not inspire revulsion, but the spectacle of his failure and the humiliation of his hope is rarely edifying.

It is legitimate to wonder precisely what Vargas Llosa hoped to accomplish in this novel, indeed, to wonder whether Vargas Llosa knew quite what he was after in a work that is full of misleading details and false starts. If he wished to say, simply, that there is no hope for improvement in countries like Peru, he could certainly have examined the consequences of that observation more rigorously than he chose to. If he wished to inquire, as he did in the earlier novel *Conversation in the Cathedral,* "When did Peru get fucked over?", he could certainly have provided a more ample historical perspective, going back before the 1950s to discover what made revolutionary agitation seem attractive to so many people in his country. If, on the other hand, he wished simply to settle old scores with a Latin American left that has often seemed not to know what it was doing, he could surely have made things easier for himself by creating a less likeable protagonist than Mayta and by portraying the conditions of life in Peru as requiring something less than total renovation. As things stand in Vargas Llosa's novel, it is hard not to feel that we have been given contradictory signals: on the one hand, a situation that is ripe for revolution; on the other hand, a portrayal of revolutionary ambition that makes it seem alternately cynical or childish, and always futile. If the carefully deposited signs of filth and degradation in the novel do not finally add up as we expect them to, neither do the indications that the book is to be read as a political or historical inquiry.

Already a number of reviewers have described *The Real Life of Alejandro Mayta* as a more or less standard post-modern novel which creates narrative obstacles only for the pleasure involved in overcoming them. In such a work, some reviewers have said, we are necessarily reminded "that art is as arbitrary as truth is relative" and that "life itself is a moment by moment invention." The author of such a work insists on his own duplicity so as to assert, in Vargas Llosa's words, the author's "enormous deicidal will for the destruction and reconstruction of reality." In these terms, Vargas Llosa may be said to make common cause with those who read him as if

he were a contemporary Latin American follower of Vladimir Nabokov, measuring his success by his willingness to use "to the hilt"
the narrative instruments he elects. No doubt, as John Updike has
aptly noted, "the intelligence of Mario Vargas Llosa plays above
the sad realities and unrealities with a coolness that should be
distinguished from Nabokov's hermetically aesthetic ardor." But it
is the novelist as gamesman and master strategist who most frequently emerges from accounts of the present work.

Obviously there is much to be said for such an approach. The
novel reads like a post-modern work, moving rapidly and often
without transition from one time plane to another, mingling past
and present so dexterously as to subdue them to a single, almost
undifferentiated texture. What happened, what might have happened, and what is likely to happen are accorded equivalent status,
and the author-narrator's desire to get at the truth is explicitly
confounded with the need for a plausible basis on which to
fabulate and embellish. Though the apparent subject of the book is
Mayta and the unsuccessful uprising in which he participated, we
are so often reminded of Mayta's fictional status and of the author-
narrator's literary exertions that we might well think it chiefly important to concern ourselves with the creative impulse itself. The
advantage of such an approach—apart from the fact that it may
answer directly to Vargas Llosa's intentions—is that it forces us to
treat a novel as a novel, that it dismisses as trivial or irrelevant
questions of historical accuracy which may only confuse our responses as readers. If there is a vision at work in this novel—so we
may want to feel—it is the vision *of a novelist*. The views of Vargas
Llosa as expressed in his latest journalistic contribution to the *New
York Times Sunday Magazine* may interest us in various ways, but
they can have little to do with the vision of the novelist, whose
business is to ask questions rather than to promote a position. If
The Real Life of Alejandro Mayta is a novel of politics, we may feel, it
is also a work that refuses to endorse any programmatic reading of
its material.

The narrator in Vargas Llosa's novel is a writer who is clearly
intended to remind us of the public figure Vargas Llosa has become. Like other thoughtful persons, he is interested in the fate of
his country and knows a good deal about its history. He is also
attracted to a wide range of ideas. In sum we know relatively little
about him, but we have reason to believe that he is not a frivolous
man. Though he is something of a "possibilitarian"—Robert Musil's word describes a person who cannot forget that things can

easily have been other than they are—his words have a gravity about them that belies the seeming arbitrariness of his novelistic invention. He may play tricks on us, carefully establishing a character's identity only to reveal at last that we were misled; but we feel all the same that his games have a purpose, even if we cannot always say with certainty what it is. Kierkegaard's fear—that if everything is possible, every "fact" subject to sudden contradiction, then nothing is true—does not do justice to our sense of this work. So intent is our narrator upon his inquiry into Mayta and, more especially, into Mayta's abortive revolutionary gesture, that we cannot but feel he believes in the truth his exertions will uncover. In no way reducible to a disembodied voice speaking arbitrary words, he seems everywhere to feel that things have weight, that there is such a thing as a necessity to which even the most playful imagination is responsible. If we are occasionally irritated by the liberties he takes and puzzled by his desire to sabotage his own credibility, we are nonetheless confident that for him certain things are real, the desire to know what they are genuine and, in its way, admirable.

The notion that for such a narrator, as for Vargas Llosa himself, the traditional idea of character has been abandoned is at once plausible and misleading. Obviously the absence of linear narrative will entitle the reader to feel that he participates to some extent in the piecing together of the story. So too will the reader feel that he chooses from among conflicting possibilities so as to create characters whose identity will nonetheless remain ambiguous. But it is one thing to project possibility without motive or consequence, another to insist that there are always motives and consequences, however difficult they may be to assemble. Character in this novel is always a primary concern, the key to what may be said about the validity of an enterprise. When we think of the narrator himself, we consider not only his duplicities and stratagems but his character. We try to determine what matters to him, and we conclude at last that we know enough about him to reject certain possibilities and to emphasize others. His absorption in Mayta of course tells us more about him than anything else, quite in the way that Mayta's obsessions largely define his identity. To conclude that Mayta has no identity, no character, simply because there are unanswerable questions associated with his conduct, is to ignore how much is revealed. Vargas Llosa here affirms a traditional conception of character by forcing us to acknowledge that *we know these people*, indeed, that we can judge them by considering motive, circumstance, and consequence, quite as we would if we were working at a more conventional narrative.

Does this mean that Vargas Llosa's narrative procedures are merely a smokescreen designed to conceal the conventionality of his purpose? Those who would draw such a conclusion would then have to feel that for Vargas Llosa there is a plain truth which the novel is after, that underlying all the complex authorial derring-do there is a simple narrative of naive revolutionary aspiration and inevitable disappointment. But so obviously is there no such plain truth, no such schematic narrative program in this novel, that one cannot but concede the futility of attempting to formulate conclusions in a neatly edifying or chastening way. Our attention to character and to its elusive relation with politics will rather lead us to ask whether the novel adds up, whether its devices have something to do with its purpose.

To say that a book of a certain kind adds up is usually only to say that its various parts cohere and collectively underwrite an overarching purpose. With the Latin American novel that purpose is usually taken to include the setting out of a political conflict. Vargas Llosa's novel deals with an incident that actually occurred in Peru in 1962, though he sets the events in 1958, before the consolidation of Castro's revolution in Cuba, so as to make more palpable the audacity of Mayta's insurrection. No attempt is made to justify the insurrection by providing a detailed account of Peruvian politics in the 1950s. Neither does Vargas Llosa at all go over the failure of democracy in Peru in the late 1960s or the coming to power of the military "revolutionary experiment" at that time. The atmosphere of Peru in the near future of the novel makes us feel that all manner of awfulness has occurred. But issues of the sort that Vargas Llosa will debate in public meetings or in newspaper articles are not a part of the texture of the novel. "We know" as we read that politics in Peru has everything to do with health, malnutrition, terrorism, corruption, military dictatorship, and the relationship between various despots and the United States Marines. But the novel furnishes no way to talk about these issues. They are part of an undifferentiated given, the more or less unarguable facts of life. In the face of such facts, never really subject to rational discussion, the activist impulses of a Mayta can only seem misguided (which is to say, without reasonable hope of success), or inevitable (a necessary expression of a desire for drastic change which cannot be impugned by recalling that it had no reasonable expectation of success). It is the special purpose of Vargas Llosa's novel to make the impulses of a Mayta seem both misguided *and* inevitable. Insofar as his motives seem to us idealistic and he proceeds to act without any taint of self-importance, he will seem to us an embodiment of an inevitable and largely attractive will to change. Insofar as his thinking is revealed as inadequate to the magnitude of the forces arrayed against him, he will seem disappointing. For the reader of Vargas Llosa's novel there is no way to ask whether Mayta might have gone about the business of changing his society in another way, say, by embracing some form of parliamentary democracy and strenuously working towards that ideal. As readers we are only in a position to consider the motives of the character and the palpable consequences of projects like the one he undertakes.

Evaluated simply in terms of consequence, Mayta is undeniably a failure, his revolutionary aspirations clearly hopeless. The insurrection he leads is rapidly broken up, his chief cohort is shot and killed, and Mayta spends many years in prison. What is worse, this first Peruvian Marxist uprising and subsequent small- or large-scale insurrections have inspired nothing but a further cycle of repression and brutality. The Peru of the near future is if anything in worse shape than it was when Mayta was young. The evidence, in other words, suggests not only that Mayta was unable to foresee the consequences of his actions but that motives in isolation from the capacity to think clearly and consequentially are not to be judged as good motives at all. This is not to suggest that the only good motives are those which lead more or less inevitably to the accomplishment of reasonable ends. But Vargas Llosa *would* seem to suggest that idealism and utopianism ought to be susceptible to judgment quite in the way that more ordinary and pragmatic approaches to reality have been.

That such judgments are not easy to arrive at or to trust we discover again and again as we try to get a definitive fix on Mayta. Early in the novel he'd emerged as a genuine priest of revolution, an ascetic with a vocation, obsessed with the sufferings of the poor and "capable of reacting with the same indignation to any injustice." Nothing we hear about him in the various interviews conducted by the author-narrator can quite dislodge from our minds that initial, powerful image of the man. None of his homosexual exploits, for example, can at all tarnish the image of the somewhat juvenile idealist, and it matters little to our ultimate sense of Mayta that the vivid accounts of him as a practicing homosexual are later repudiated. Neither is our sense of his somewhat sophomoric enthusiasm diminished by those passages in which he reflects with a grave sobriety on revolution as "a long act of patience . . . , a thousand and one vile deeds," and so on. For if Mayta is at forty still a naif, he never seems to us a fool or without the capacity to surprise us. If as the novel progresses he seems less and less the intellectual we had perhaps taken him for, he remains in important respects the person we thought we admired earlier, and might still admire at novel's end.

What continually complicates our view of Mayta is what we take to be the inconclusiveness of Vargas Llosa's feelings and intentions. The conflicting accounts of Mayta offered by this person or that we can explain by speaking of their needs or their limited perspectives. But the author-narrator has a perspective that by definition cannot be limited in the same way, encompassing as it does the full range of sentiments and motives expressed in the novel. If we say that he maintains—through all of the changes Mayta's portrait is made to undergo—a consistent affection for Mayta, and that this affection is more than the novelist's love of a creation upon whom he can project anything he likes, then we have still to say what it is he admires. Perhaps it is Mayta's capacity to hope, to defy reality. Perhaps it is the absence of cynicism, the inexplicable intensity of resolution. Is this what the narrator wants us to admire when he gives us Mayta imagining the aftermath of his little insurrection: "the working class would shake off its lethargy, all the reformist deceptions, all its corrupt leaders, all those illusions of being able to coexist with the sell-outs, and would join the struggle." But even in this passage we suspect that Vargas Llosa wants to admire Mayta's optimism more than he can bring himself to do, that the impulse to caricature is as strong as the impulse to celebrate. Eighty pages later, when we read, "He saw them multiplying like the loaves of bread in the Bible, every day recruiting scores of boys as poor and self-denying as themselves," or "the assault on heaven, I thought. We shall bring heaven down from heaven, establish it on earth," we cannot but feel that the gap between Mayta's optimism and the reality he confronts is an essential component of the portrait. What may have seemed simply a portrait of the revolutionary as idealist is also the portrait of a dreamer dangerously yielding to a vision that has taken possession of him utterly. As we confront the futility of Mayta's enterprise and the delusional component in his forward dreaming, we are left with an uneasy sense of not knowing quite what we feel or why we have been taken through Mayta's adventures.

Does it clarify matters to recall that Mayta's delusions are explored again and again in the novel, that the narrator is routinely at pains to remind us that Mayta "let his imagination run wild," and that Mayta's optimism strikes most of his acquaintances as incomprehensible or ludicrous? But this doesn't alter the fact that Mayta remains in many respects an appealing person. Compare him with alternative figures who lucidly criticize his naivete and his gift for defeat. Even those who are most sensible and sophisticated, like the intellectual in charge of a progressive Development Center, have little to offer apart from a knowing disdain for visionary intensity and a capacity to thread their way between partisans of the left and the right. It is Mayta's naivete, after all, that permits him to conclude in his one year at the university "that the professors had lost their love of teaching somewhere along the line"; and it is that same naivete that permits him to summon something like the old intensity when, at age sixty-five, he tells our narrator about the food kiosk he ran with a friend amidst the squalor of the unspeakable Lurigancho prison. " 'We created a genuine revolution,' he assures me with pride. 'We won the respect of the whole place. We boiled the water for making fruit juice, for coffee, for everything. We washed the knives, forks, and spoons, the glasses, and the plates before and after they were used. Hygiene, above all. A revolution, you bet . . . We even set up a kind of bank, because a lot of cons gave us their money for safe keeping.' "

Perhaps naivete is not the word with which to describe the quality of character involved in these passages. One way or the other, is the feeling evoked merely pathetic? Here I think we must answer that it is not. If the mountains of garbage swallowing the landscape of Vargas Llosa's Peru have something to tell us about his vision of the country and its people, then surely Mayta's revolutionary pride cannot be dismissed so easily. It may not provide the key to the political vision of the novel, but it does suggest the kind of thing to which the novel most warmly responds. In fact, as we have already intimated, it is difficult to say that there is a politics in this novel beyond its elaboration of attitudes which in another work might have informed a more focused vision. Mayta, after all, late in the novel remarks not only that he is no longer involved in politics but that "politics gave me up." Is this intended to suggest that he is too good for politics, or, more broadly, that politics cannot finally address what is most real in our lives? Again, it is hard to be sure precisely what Vargas Llosa would want us to feel about this. But he would seem to suggest that those who cannot do justice to Mayta will not know how to think about politics or the future.

If this seems doubtful, a passage near the end of the novel may help to clarify what may be taken to be a proper attitude to Mayta. "Later," we read,

> when there were outbreaks of guerrilla fighting in the mountains and the jungle in 1963, 1964, 1965, and 1966—all inspired by the Cuban Revolution—no newspaper remembered that the forerunner of those attempts to raise up the people in armed struggle to establish socialism in Peru had been that minor episode, rendered ghostlike by the years, which had taken place in Jauja province. Today no one remembers who took part in it.

Here, beyond the prestidigitations of Vargas Llosa's post-modern narrative procedures, is some semblance of the sentiment that unites the author-narrator with his protagonist. For all of the novelist's oft-repeated insistence that "all fictions are lies" and that we can never know anything with certainty, he cannot but affirm that there is something in Mayta which continues to compel and attract. The impulse to honor—with whatever misgivings—whatever is authentic in Mayta's passion for social justice is the center of Vargas Llosa's novel and the substance of the meaning that abides.

Tyranny
and Language

Augusto Roa Bastos, *I the Supreme*, translated by Helen Lane
(New York: Alfred A. Knopf).

For more than a decade the Paraguayan novelist Roa Bastos has
been regarded in Latin America as a major writer. In the years since
the publication of his masterpiece *Yo el Supremo* in 1974 hundreds
of articles examining the novel have appeared, and an authoritative
critical edition of the novel was published in Madrid in 1983. When
Carlos Fuentes recently declared the book "one of the milestones of
the Latin American novel," he was merely confirming what has
long been taken for granted south of our border. Now that a superb
English translation of this dauntingly complex work is at last available, readers in this country will be in a position to see for themselves why readers in Latin America have been moved to invoke
the names of Joyce and Musil, Cervantes and Rabelais to get at the
breadth and ambition of *Yo el Supremo.*

A great many Latin American novels have been haunted by the
idea of the dictator, and several of the most famous of these actually revolve around a dictator figure. One thinks immediately of
García Márquez's *Autumn of the Patriarch*, or Alejo Carpentier's *Reasons of State*, or of an earlier novel like Asturias's *El Señor Presidente*.
Such works sometimes treat the dictator as a principal source of the
misery and destitution endemic in Latin America. Others regard
him as a part of a large and complex bureaucratic apparatus within
which it is difficult to assign blame, even when the likely target is a

From *The New Republic*, June 15, 1987.

person obviously charged with responsibility for much that occurs. Often the dictator in these novels is a composite portrait drawn from various originals, with the consequence that the character seems larger than life, so awesome in the range of his brutalities that he is more a force of nature than a person. Other writers work from a single model, with results that vary from one case to another. If Roa Bastos has written about an actual dictator, a singular historical figure, he has nonetheless attributed to him extraordinary powers, and though he has resisted the mystifications associated with works for which the dictator is a force of nature and therefore unaccountable to any mundane human law, he has made his all too human character an impressively ubiquitous figure about whose virtues and defects we are often in doubt. We may feel, as we study the world dominated by this dictator, that there is no one else to whom blame might reasonably be assigned, but we are loath to apply the categorical judgments to which representations of tyranny usually tempt us. To compare Roa's dictator with other despots portrayed by Latin American writers is to feel that Roa's is distinguished not only by the quantity of detail lavished on him but by his remarkable capacity to seem at one moment a person, at another an embodiment of contradictory elements not usually identified with a single person, let alone a powerful tyrant.

To speak of Roa's dictator as having been drawn from a model is in some sense to misrepresent him, for Roa's character is never really permitted to stand free of the original. In important ways we are dealing here with a historical novel, with all that entails of a work incorporating actual, named personages who have a documented existence outside the pages of the fiction. Roa's dictator is not based on the nineteenth-century Paraguayan despot José Gaspar Rodriguez Francia, who in 1816 brought his country to independence; in many ways he is, palpably and persuasively, Francia himself. So much is this the case that the words lavished upon him are frequently taken verbatim from nineteenth-century accounts of people who knew him. Though much that he is made to say has obviously been invented by Roa, it is difficult to think of him as an invented character subject to the imperial whim of a writer. So consistently does the novel make use of documents well known to students of nineteenth-century Latin American politics that even the most unlikely statements coming from the character inspire us to feel that they might indeed have come from Francia. If Francia probably never said this thing or that, he must surely have said or thought to say something like it, and Roa must somewhere have found a document that authorizes his "invention." It is not often that readers of a novel will suppose that the words spoken by a character require authorization if they are to seem credible. But so assiduous is Roa to support Francia's statements in this novel that it is impossible to ignore such a requirement. A novel containing numerous footnotes and quotations inevitably encourages us to believe that we are dealing with facts, or at least with plausible hypotheses and extrapolations.

Francia is hardly a household name in the English-speaking world, but he was much discussed in the middle of the nineteenth century. Thomas Carlyle's long 1843 essay responds to several books on the leader who ruled his country from 1816 to 1840, and it is fair to say that Roa was deeply influenced by Carlyle's account. By 1843 Carlyle was well into the phase of his career that produced his best work, including the lectures on "Heroes and Hero-Worship" and the superb book known as *Past and Present*. Francia he treats as a man with the stuff of heroes in him, a figure at once impressive and forbidding, alternately foolish and inspired, credulous and cunning. But whatever he is moved to say about Francia, Carlyle knows that in important respects he eludes judgment as he eludes any sort of clear definition. Everywhere the figure is surrounded by "a murk of distracted shadows and rumors." Under such conditions, "who would pretend . . . to decipher the real portraiture of Dr. Francia and his life?" Those who wrote about him during the years of his reign had their own reasons for treating him as they did, and out of their accounts Carlyle could draw "mere intricate inanity," "clouds of confused bluster and jargon," "not facts, but broken shadows of facts," and, not surprisingly, "a running shriek of constitutional denunciation." Carlyle's impressions of the available material would not be so very interesting did they not draw upon much of the commentary on Francia which is incorporated within Roa's book. Nor would Carlyle's tentative encomia to Francia seem more than the predictable expressions of an overheated hero-worshiper did they not inform evaluations of the dictator which Roa would seem, however ambivalently, to support. No more than Carlyle is Roa prepared to overlook the "reign of terror" instituted by Francia in the name of law and order. But no more is he inclined to overlook the beneficent results of that reign when Paraguayan civil society in those years is compared with conditions obtaining in countries like Brazil and Argentina. No doubt, as Carlos Fuentes says, Paraguay under Francia was "a sick utopia," a peaceful place not unlike a graveyard. But—so Carlyle reminds us—Francia was "driven by necessity itself" to what "was properly a reign of rigor" in a society which had neither popular institutions nor a class of citizens equipped to take effective control. In adapting to his own novelistic purposes so many features of Carlyle's equivocal portrait, Roa builds a figure who is richly various, whose strengths of character and intelligence are inseparable from his sense of isolation and his impatience with the decorums of parliamentary and representative democracy.

Having in effect invited us to measure his character against alternative portraits of the dictator, Roa cannot be surprised when readers conclude that there is little new information to be found in the novel. Neither is there much improvement upon Carlyle's complex view of Francia as originally a noble fellow, a republican at heart who led his country to independence only to end by "stealing the constitutional palladiums from their parliament-houses." None of the many thousands of words uttered by Francia in Roa's novel substantially revise or make untenable that complex impression. Just so are standard twentieth-century accounts of Francia's place in Paraguayan history more or less reinforced in the novel. The dictator's decision to seal off the borders of his country to avoid contamination or incursion by its powerful neighbors is presented in the standard way as an awful but probably necessary strategy to preserve independence. Roa allows for sharp expressions of disappointment in Francia, who clearly betrayed his own republican and populist ideals. But Roa is at one with other commentators who typically recall the perpetual wars that kept other countries in turmoil precisely because no leaders arose to prevent the church and other corrupt interest groups from tearing to pieces what there was of a civil fabric.

With no desire, obviously, to rebuke more conventional accounts of Francia's reign, Roa must have wished to accomplish something other than a scrupulously balanced historical portrait or political analysis. Carlos Fuentes's prediction that students of the decolonization process in general "will find much to reflect on in *I the Supreme*" suggests that there are fresh political insights in the novel. There are not. The most audacious political insight Roa generates is the idea that Francia survived his own death in 1840. By having Francia anticipate at various points in the novel events that took place many years later, even going so far as to refer explicitly to a 1930s conflict with Bolivia, Roa in effect shows that Francia is implicated in every postindependence phase of Paraguayan history. To make the case in the way that Roa does is to invest quite literally in the idea, and that is part of Roa's strength. But one has only to consult straightforward accounts of the country since 1816 to note that Francia is routinely accorded great attention. If the shadow he casts in the novel is disproportionately large, that has more to do with the nature of the work as a mostly first-person narrative told by Francia himself. It is not a sign that Roa reads the history of his country in a way that substantially revises other accounts.

To get at the object of Roa's ambition it is perhaps necessary to consider the novel's peculiar organization. Principally the novel is a record of exchanges between the Supreme and his private secretary, or amanuensis, Policarpo Patiño. Patiño speaks so infrequently, however, that the "exchange" is in effect an interminable monologue which contains the interpolated utterances of an entirely marginal figure who exists mainly as a narrative device. In fact, the dictator may be said to "contain" Patiño just as he contains the many other figures whose complaints, encouragements, solicitations he permits them to express as occasional voices trapped within his peremptory monologue. This is not to say that there is but one character in the novel, but it is obvious that others exist largely for Francia and the reflections they provoke.

Roa has no interest in the sort of psychological insight that would conclude from all of this simply that Francia was self-absorbed. The self-absorption here is a given, a device which underwrites or rationalizes narrative procedures. These procedures include the Supreme's recourse to a double persona, a *yo* and an *el*, in terms of which an interior debate is intermittently mounted. Exactly how the one persona is to be distinguished from the other no one has yet definitively established, but it seems clear that the *el* is the more permanent incarnation of the Supreme, that aspect of him which exists in the world and in the minds of others and is destined to have a posterity. The *yo* has more to do with the self for itself, though the notion of a private identity for a Supreme is not always persuasive.

In any case, a description of the novel as a more or less continuous monologue is inadequate. Not only are there the disruptions and internal debates to which we've referred. There are also distinctly separate discourses within the novel, each with a characteristic designation. The sections marked "in the private notebook" ostensibly contain material written by the Supreme entirely for himself. The sections marked "Perpetual Circular" are dictated by the Supreme to Patiño and are intended to give orders and advice to state officials, including minor Paraguayan functionaries in foreign countries and subsequent generations who will one day conduct the affairs of state. Other sections are in the nature of citations or notes, some integrated within the main narrative (though typographically differentiated from it), others printed at the foot of pages and often containing lengthy excerpts from other works. There are also what might be called special discourses: the more or less extended testimony of another character, the transcript of an official document, and so on. These usually play an important role in the text, conveying necessary information or providing a background against which we can measure the reliability of subsequent remarks coming directly from the Supreme.

It is not always clear to the reader that a particular discourse has come to an end. On occasion, what seems to be part of the perpetual circular sounds more like the more intimate ruminations we associate with the private notebook. Elsewhere, the exchanges between the Supreme and Patiño carry over from one discourse to another, so that the separation into distinct discourses seems no more than a self-canceling, transparent artifice enforcing the utter fictionality and arbitrariness of the whole enterprise. Ostensibly put together by a "compiler" who, in a final note, reveals that it was "culled" or "coaxed" "from some twenty thousand dossiers" and all manner of other documents, the novel is best described as a polyphonic discourse with a perspective that is only superficially controlled by a presiding presence. The compiler aims to amass a record that will show what happened and thereby testify to the legacy of Francia. That legacy is Paraguay, and if the ambiguity and discontinuity of the narrative sometimes obscure things, we are never so much in doubt that we feel we have lost our way.

I the Supreme is a polyphonic work in important ways that go beyond the strategy for telling a story or settling historical accounts. It is committed to a plurality of voices and perspectives and judgments because it refuses to acquiesce in certain assumptions. One of these is the assumption that a literary work is the product and therefore the private property of an author who creates and disposes. Roa challenges the very idea of the author, setting in its place the idea of the compiler who draws from various sources and in fact relies upon materials that do not originate in him. To argue that the compiler is a fiction and that Roa is obviously the creator of his novel is to ignore the unmistakable intention of a work which is infinitely various in the sources it employs and relentlessly self-contradictory in its elaboration of insights.

The polyphony of Roa's novel is most obvious in its concept of language. Other contemporary writers, like Roa, employ multiple personae or alternate voices so as to avoid any suggestion that truth is to be identified with a single character or simple idea. But Roa's prose is saturated with the idiom, the rhetoric, the wordplay of other writers and other languages. When the Supreme speaks we hear now Baudelaire or Montaigne, now Blake or Shakespeare or Rabelais. Allusions proliferate, the sources not always clear or important, but the fact of intertextual borrowing, pastiche, and correction unmistakable. Now and then exotic Paraguayan terms or Guaraní (Indian) words (translated in a special appendix) are freely intermingled with sophisticated literary terms or bits and pieces of a Rousseauist philosophical vocabulary. Explicit references to and borrowings from Greek and Latin texts support an ongoing sense of language as anachronistic, capacious, and vigorously opportunistic. We do not infer from this that for Roa all is one, that for him all cultures are exercised by the same dilemmas and all languages more or less interchangeable in their expression of basic ideas and sentiments. We conclude, rather, that language in *I the Supreme* is an instrument for expressing difference and discontinuity, the radical incompatibility of various cultural norms and literary conventions. The novel brings together a wide range of incompatible and flagrantly contradictory idioms and assembles them in a way that is often disorienting and deliberately provocative. This it does persistently because it wishes to subvert the procedures by which facts and otherwise familiar impressions are routinely processed and accommodated. Roa's prose is not a fancy-dress expression of standard historical materials. It reflects the attempt to reorder the familiar so that it will speak to us freshly.

This Roa accomplishes by drawing our attention again and again to words, to the way in which language controls, lies, retards, reverses. When he has Francia speak bluntly of his intentions only to have him order Patiño to "cross out this paragraph," he in effect calls into question the record of Francia's deeds we have inherited. When his compiler quotes a document accusing Francia of plagiarizing "clauses and conceits," "mottoes and maxims," motivated not by a passion for truth but by a wish to impress, he subverts the observation by reminding us that the dictator is a penetrating and scrupulous literary critic with a sharp eye for "living language" and a powerful aversion to the kind of "dead language" which can only lie, whatever its ostensive sincerity. And when he gives to the Supreme some of his most affecting and humanly impressive utterances, he compulsively undermines them by having Francia interrupt himself with "that still sounds like a sermon, an edict, a proclamation" or "How does that sound? Like real horseshit!"

But the most subversive element in the novel is the attempted negation not merely of the orthodox and familiar but of writing itself. Frequently the dictator denies the importance of words and asserts that his investment in writing is intrinsically ridiculous. "When all is said and done," he laments, "what is prodigious, fearful, unknown in the human being has never been put into words or books, and never will be." To write is inevitably to falsify. "When I dictate to you," Francia tells Patiño, "the words have a meaning; when you write them another. So that we speak two different languages." And of course, as Borges has shown us, those different languages may in fact be utterly different even if the words they contain are identical. When in Roa's novel the rumor circulates that Francia wishes to write his own *Quixote*, we cannot but think of Borges's imaginary Pierre Menard, whose desire to rewrite the *Quixote* exactly as Cervantes wrote it expresses a similar obsession with language and the illusion of control. "I am trapped in a tree," Francia laments as he considers what it means to write, to rely on words which always betray. "The tree cries out after its own fashion. Who can know that I am crying out inside of it?"

Ultimately the novel lives most fully in its language and implicitly struggles against the negations intermittently insisted upon by Francia himself. If the Supreme is obsessed with his failure to communicate his own authentic cry and concludes that we understand nothing, we feel nonetheless that a great deal comes through. If to Francia it is "all the better" that no one understands, since then he can feel free to say and write anything he damn well pleases, it is clear to us that he is served by language as much as he is betrayed by it. When he declares "I don't write history. I make it," he announces a distinction which persuades no one, certainly not Francia. For it is the record that he wants desperately to affect, his motives and thoughts to defend from "those rodents" whose "error consists in gnawing holes in documented truth." To make history is for Francia, whatever he sometimes says to the contrary, a matter of "adjusting, stressing, enriching its meaning and truth." Roa's novel affirms the significance of the project even as it ambivalently exposes and undercuts the dictator himself. If the only enduring monument to Francia is an edifice of language known as *I the Supreme*, it is fair to say that his words or the words he inspired are at the heart of that edifice. Francia and Patiño may "disappear in what is read/written," like the rest of us, but always there remains the possibility that language, more properly literature, will accomplish a purpose that warrants the hope and desperate labor invested in it.

That there is more to say of Roa's novel is obvious. To set out the dominant terms, stratagems, and oppositions of such a book is simply to do the preliminary work of criticism. No reader will feel upon first acquaintance with Roa's novel that he has adequately come to grips with it, that he can say how well its eccentric, introspective intensities are balanced by a feeling for the surfaces and conflicts of ordinary life. Edmund Wilson wrote many years ago that even when Joyce or Proust turned their sights upon social or moral life one felt they were giving us an "exercise . . . of the pure intelligence playing luminously all about but not driven by the motor power of any hope and not directed by any creative imagination for the possibilities of human life." It is tempting to think of Roa in these terms. Some have found him a different sort of writer, even going so far as to read his book as a political novel, a critique of Paraguay's current dictator, General Alfredo Stroessner. But though Roa's universe is ventilated by strong winds blowing through the sometimes close and tangled thickets of Francia's mind, it is largely what Wilson calls "the shuttered house" of Roa's imagination that we chiefly feel we inhabit. For all the interest we take in the texture of the prose and the virtuosity of the various narrative devices, we are not always certain that the insight achieved is commensurate with the fantastic energy expended on its behalf. Nor are we certain that there is sufficient dramatic tension and development in a work that has more than its share of verbal energy and schematic brilliance. There is no doubting the extraordinary magnitude of Roa's enterprise, but the precise nature of his achievement will be debated for many years to come.

PART FOUR

Poetic Quests Without Objects

John Ashbery: A Quest Without an Object

John Ashbery, *Houseboat Days* (New York: Viking Press).
Laurence Lieberman, *Unassigned Frequencies: American Poetry in
Review, 1964–77* (Urbana: University of Illinois Press).

John Ashbery has become the most successful poet in America. He
has won the major literary prizes, his books are widely available in
paperback editions, and his work is carefully scrutinized in the
important quarterlies and review columns. Harold Bloom, surely a
central voice in contemporary criticism, thinks him the most distinguished American poet of our time, and the magazines are full of
poems written by younger writers trying to sound very much like
the master. Though other accomplished poets like Howard Nemerov also win the prizes and attract readers, none creates interest
like the interest aroused by Ashbery.

This is a peculiar phenomenon. Some of us have tried, with
small success, to explain Ashbery in the classroom, concluding that
a great many complete poems, and large portions of others, resist
any kind of explanation. Other more gifted interpreters have concluded that, even where ordinary readings work, they discover
nothing of genuine consequence in Ashbery's thought. Now Ashbery has won a great many admirers in recent years, but none
would make of him an easy or routinely accessible poet. For adherents and detractors alike, he remains often puzzling, sometimes
impossibly obscure.

T. S. Eliot more than once recommended that we be tolerant of
genuinely innovative poets who seem difficult, reminding us that

From *London Times Literary Supplement* (*TLS*), September 1, 1978.

Browning was early thought a willfully difficult poet. Somehow, though, it doesn't help to be reminded of Browning when one is trying to come to terms with a sequence of lines like the following:

Uh . . . stupid song . . . that weather bonnet
Is all gone now. But the apothecary biscuits dwindled.
Where a little spectral
Cliffs, teeming over into irony's
Gotten silently inflicted in the passages
Morning undermines, the daughter is.

The lines are taken from a long poem called "The Skaters," and have been identified by other commentators as pointless and enraging. But one finds such passages in recent Ashbery poems as well, and one may not be consoled to discover adjacent passages that communicate something more. Eliot contended that the "seasoned reader" would not "bother about understanding; not, at least, at first," but it is surely reasonable to assume that we shall in time want to make something of what we read. Some readers, apparently, have been willing to accept Ashbery for the fragments that do offer an insight, contemplate an object, represent a particular desire, or evoke a sentiment, no matter how modest or fleeting. Starved for ordinary meaning, such readers have been grateful for the little they could find.

The question of meaning in poetry remains for most of us an open issue, and what convictions we have about it are likely to be threatened by poets like Ashbery who flout conventions without wishing to apologize. If, as Eliot thought, and most of us would now agree, meaning is not what a poem is for, it may be thought to be an option like any other, a device to be resorted to or not as the given project requires. This is not an alarming view so long as you associate meaning with ideas. We accept, gladly, that most poets do not work from formulated ideas or positions which they can proceed to illustrate as vividly and cleanly as they can. But if we take meaning to refer to the possibility of shared discourse in which speaker and auditor may participate more or less equally, then we may be less willing to see it as an option like any other. Eliot wanted meaning "to satisfy one habit of the reader, to keep his mind diverted and quiet, while the poem does its work upon him." But he conceded that it could not operate in just that way for all poets, some of whom would "become impatient of this 'meaning' which seems superfluous, and perceive possibilities of intensity through its elimination. I am not asserting that this situation is ideal," he went on to say, "only that we must write our poetry as we can, and take it as we find it."

Ashbery is an instance of the poet who, through much of his career, eliminates meaning without achieving any special intensity. Always concerned with what to leave in and what to take out, he seems to have generated the anxiety for himself to demonstrate that he can operate without fear of check or censure by canon or convention. It doesn't matter in a typical Ashbery poem what is left out, or what might have linked one thought to another. The poet operates in what is thought to be a mild trance, in which he is relieved of the compulsion to connect. This is no agony of trance, mind you; no visionary fever in which new worlds are discovered. Ashbery's trance discovers nothing but the posssibility of ordinary experience, an experience so disburdened of ordinary sequence and weight in these poems that it ceases to seem entirely familiar. Though he tells us he is on his way to some well-known, half-remembered moment or place, we feel he cares little for the moment or the place, that he likes the sensation of reaching without knowing what it is he's groping for. His defiance of ordinary meaning has less to do with its being superfluous than with its shuttling him too conveniently to places he'd as soon never reach. Committed only to groping, never to seizing or holding, anything he can identify securely is likely to seem superfluous to Ashbery. On a quest without an object, meaning is a too comfortable harbor the skilled mariner will steer around, pretending to be carried by currents created by the unmeasured, intermittent flailings of his own arms rippling the surfaces.

Meaning, then, is often left out of an Ashbery poem not to deprive readers of what they expect but to ensure the continuity of a quest for which ends are necessarily threatening. For the reader to understand more than he does, the poet would have to try to master his materials more completely. Though the poet here and there indicates there are epistemological depths he'd like to plumb, and thereby invites comparison with Wallace Stevens, he is not really interested in what he can know. Aiming instead at a ". . . pure / Affirmation that doesn't affirm anything," he is a modest adventurer who savors the sensation of an experience without determinate content. There are worse things for a poet to aim at, and Ashbery has the virtue of refusing to pretend he's after anything else. To appreciate his restraint one has only to compare his accounts of the project with some of the more inflated claims of friendly critics.

Ashbery has no new meaning to deliver, no apotheosis to portend. His song of himself is resolutely committed to meandering about and proclaiming the small satisfaction of moving without significant impediment. He associates "freely" not because he's discovered a new way to put things together but because where nothing stands still for very long a reflective observer must learn to shift his attention comfortably and without complaint. There is a plangent note in Ashbery, but it's hard to see what he misses when he seems unable to desire anything he can't simply conjure.

Ashbery published several books in the 1950s and 1960s, but the volume *The Double Dream of Spring* (1970) marked a departure. The poems were recognizably his, but the discontinuities and reticences seemed less willful, the occasional bursts of lyricism more rewarding and sustained. And the spiritual ancestry of Auden— who'd selected *Some Trees* as a Yale Poets volume in 1956—seemed for the first time fully apparent. This was one way of coming to terms with Ashbery. If readers felt they could tell what was going on in an Ashbery poem, they could respond to it at last as addressing or failing to address their needs. These needs may be surmised by studying the version of Ashbery offered by the poet Laurence Lieberman in a new book surveying the American poetry scene. Lieberman devotes his longest essay, some sixty pages, to Ashbery's "Self-Portrait in a Convex Mirror" (1975), and though he doesn't make much of the Auden connection, the essay might in part be taken for a gloss on the late poet's best-known projects.

Lieberman's Ashbery has done his best to clear away obscurities. The poet continues to dream, but he has more patience with particulars, more readiness to let a thing or a thought work itself out before displacing it. The displacements, when they occur, are more liquid, less abrupt, as though Ashbery had come to feel some muted affection for the objects and sentiments brought obliquely to the fore. It is not always possible to name the relevant emotion or to make out the function of objects, but one feels that a drama of some moment is taking shape. We sense that Ashbery's is a sensibility for which mundane experience has a value that nothing more terrific or challenging can gainsay. Like Auden, he is moved by the homely brow and by quiet sensations. If he remains still more difficult than Auden, it may be only a matter of his coming to terms reluctantly with a disposition Auden was ever prepared to celebrate.

Lieberman celebrates the disposition for Ashbery, as though he'd been commissioned to do so by the poet himself. This can be an amusing spectacle, the critic making perfectly clear and obvious what is tentative and full of defensive irony in the verse. Thus, Ashbery is made into a "bold and disaffiliated" voice, and given "power to fully embrace the present moment" when he's never more than in doubt about his desire to do so. The poet who speaks an essentially private language is said to be bent on making "changes in the whole fabric of our country's mass sensibility"—as if Ashbery believed such a thing were possible. Committed to surfaces, the play of moods over temperament, Ashbery is turned into a spokesman for "the invisible depths" with a mission to heal long-standing cultural wounds. It's hard to imagine Ashbery in this version of his "Convex Mirror," but then American poets are always turned into seers and culture prophets by the faithful, and it has to be a mark of success for a poet to feel the mantle on his shoulders without ever having asked for it.

But Lieberman can be very good at elucidating the disposition Ashbery shares with Auden. The poet is said to be on the leading edge of momentous changes sweeping the culture. He is, in fact, "ready—as no one else can be—to collaborate with the change, to be its faithful steward." This he manages by being alert to every possibility, so that in time he "catches its scent in the wind." We are never told by poet or critic what comes to pass in this great change, but it is associated with an enlargement of the communal dream-life, a greater willingness to let events happen without forcing or directing them. By affirming a general drift without affirming anything in particular, the poet finds himself in time "accepting everything." What he leaves out of his poems "is mysteriously found to have been put back in—in some other form," so that really nothing is ever slighted, nothing taken to be more vital than anything else. Lieberman is singularly helpful in getting at this tendency in Ashbery to accept everything by totally flattening distinctions and pretending they were never serious distinctions at all. Only Lieberman thinks of it as a heroic enterprise, where Ashbery is altogether more uncertain, and Auden positively amused by the unheroic ironies implicit in such a posture.

Now Ashbery's is no ideological posture, no following up of a conviction he wishes to impose. When Lieberman correctly states that "all moments and events are equalized" and that Ashbery's medium reduces everything to "one uniform substance," he doesn't mention that this is an effect of trance, not the achievement of a program. Like Auden, Ashbery is the more or less comfortable victim of a tendency he has not the power to resist. In projecting his experience as if it were general and familiar, he simply refuses to acknowledge other ways of being in the world. Acquiescing in his own temperament and trancelike disposition, he turns his own law into a law of nature. What seems to Lieberman a "mythic reality" to which we gain access is in fact nothing more than the poet's shadow on the wall, which he takes for the truth itself. Randall Jarrell's 1940 critique of Auden in these terms has much to tell us about Ashbery, who operates in similar ways. What makes the poets finally different is the absence of a moralizing dimension in Ashbery, who is content to pursue his experience without insisting upon its viability for others. Lieberman's emphasis on the political and moral agency in Ashbery reflects an attempt to substitute a definitive "Audenesque visage" for what is an even milder and more limited ambition.

Whatever the very real differences, Ashbery can sound more like Auden than like anyone else, even in poems so playfully oblique that it is hard at first to say what they intend. Consider the opening stanza and concluding fragments of "The Lament upon the Waters," from *Houseboat Days*, a volume that flirts with domestic coziness so persistently as to put one securely in mind of Auden:

> For the disciple nothing had changed. The mood was still
> Gray tolerance, as the road marched along
> Singing its little song of despair. Once, a cry
> Started up out of the hills. That old, puzzling persuasion
>
> Again.
> . . . .
> . . . . . It is all one. It lies
> All around, its new message, guilt, the admission
> Of guilt, your new act. Time buys
>
> The receiver, the onlooker of the earlier system, but cannot
> Buy back the rest . . .

Or look at the opening of the title poem:

> "The skin is broken. The hotel breakfast china
> Poking ahead to the last week in August, not really
> Very much at all, found the land where you began . . ."
> The hills smouldered up blue that day, again
> You walk five feet along the shore, and you duck
> As a common heresy sweeps over. We can botanize
> About this for centuries, and the little dazey
> Blooms again in the cities. The mind

Is so hospitable, taking in everything
Like boarders . . .

The surprising strength of a line like "The hills smouldered up blue that day" won't suffice to distract us from the essential limitation and coziness of this verse in what is the most accessible of Ashbery's books. One doesn't have to be able to identify the second disciple in the first poem, or the common heresy in the second, to see how the poems go. The critic Roger Shattuck recently observed that the poems refuse to identify the "it" they revolve about, but no one may suppose Ashbery has more in mind than circumstance, the way of things to which he is flexibly compliant. The poems bear reluctant witness to an indefinite experience which is intended to awake fleeting instances in our minds. If the poet's images are blurred rather than sharpened by the gropings of memory, they serve nonetheless to stir vague sensations in us which may move to locate ostensively poignant sources. We care, intermittently, for what transpires in Ashbery because the consciousness is so nimble, so adept at skirting the issues that rear their heads only to duck down again. Auden had greater wit, and seems to have felt he had more at stake in getting things down accurately before passing judgment. But Auden could be as unscrupulous as Ashbery in playing at candor without actually coming across with the goods. And no one else but Auden could seem so positively unashamed to pursue his own small pleasures in the face of what others take to be menacing.

It's not just the Auden of the final period we hear in Ashbery, not the poet of *About the House* and *Epistle of a Godson*, handing out his grains of crumby wisdom. More certainly it is the poet of the middle years, of "Nones" and "In Praise of Limestone" and "The Shield of Achilles." For many of us this is the Auden who will stand, and Ashbery does little to compromise our feeling for the refinements of his civilizing measures. To think of Auden, though, as one reads Ashbery on "the admission / Of guilt" is to register how little our poet calls upon himself to work through a thought with care, how easily he glides from every brief encounter. Guilt for what? we may wonder, to no end. In Auden's "Prime," the first poem in "Nones," he also entertains the ordinary guilt to which most of us respond, and suggests at least a perspective in which it might plausibly be regarded. For Ashbery, guilt is but a word, the possibility of a sensation which never peaks but blows off with an air of discreet inconsequence. The hospitable mind is a "little dazey" because it doesn't feel seriously compelled to elect plausible options or focus causes. Practicing a "gray tolerance," it colors its experience gray, resisting differentiation and unseemly urgency. Auden at his best has a feeling for real options, warmer and colder climates. He has the capacity to sustain interest in an idea, to invite genuine response to a thought as he helps it to take shape. For Ashbery, the poet's business is to play, to build what Charles Molesworth calls "a sort of polymorphous perversity of contextuality" in which nothing seems true for very long. If the mood is vaguely elegiac, as it is so often in Auden, it owes its poignance to the uneasy sense that nothing—not even the poet's adroitness—will be effective very long.

In some ways Ashbery is just the poet American literary people have been waiting for. He is intelligent and learned, but unassuming and ironic about his gifts. The lyricism is part of the equipment, but deliberately used as a foil to the deeper strain of denial and abrupt termination, as in these lines from "The Double Dream of Spring":

> Mixed days, the mindless years, perceived
> With half-parted lips
> The way the breath of spring creeps up on you and floors
>   you:
> I had thought of all this years before
> But now it was making no sense. And the song had finished:
> This was the story.

One critic speaks of these lines as attempting "to transform a collage of moments into some cognitive meaning," but one sees at once how limp and halfhearted is the attempt. Ashbery appeals to American readers because he knows the game is hopeless even before it's played, and is too sophisticated to be taken in by the prospect of renewing encounters. What the critic calls "cognitive meaning" is nothing more than surrender to an experience without point or climax. Lieberman similarly speaks of "cyclic progression" and marvels at the way form "slowly accumulates epiphanies"; but he never tells us what is shown forth in those epiphanies, and fails to locate actual positions in the cycle. Ashbery is literary America's favorite poet because the emotional truth he means to convey is entirely resistant to questions of value and substance which contemporary intellectuals take to be tedious and empty.

Lieberman's new collection of essays and reviews represents

some of the best and some of the most self-indulgent thinking to be found in the American poetry community. He is a thoughtful and usually careful critic, but his elaborate misreading of Ashbery is symptomatic of large tendencies. He makes of him, as indicated, a prophet of the new dispensation, a genuine hero whose "interior cosmos" will "provide an antidote to the disease of the culture." Represented here is the prospect of assuming a "role in public life" without taking actual positions or responding in particular to any existing challenge. Ashbery knows better than to promise anything, and he can usually be counted on to deplore nothing but firm thoughts and substantive ideas. For the discourse of worldly types with a stake in palpable arrangements he has a ready attitude of wry condescension. Lieberman, though, likes his poets to keep in touch with reality, and is willing to celebrate a reality that has been reduced to "one / uniform substance." That he can take this reality for an antidote indicates that he has not thought critically about the culture in which nothing is forbidden and each alternative is made to look much like every other. Ashbery is Lieberman's poet because the aura of dream in which he bathes his lyric discourse can promise everything without dismissing any possibility. In Lieberman's radical vision of the future, after all, "supply is always equal to demand": What a pleasure it must be to speak such words and believe one is speaking of reality even as one describes the "economics of the dream." In the American poetry community, the casual glide from one realm to the other, as if they were one, is often the mark of serious accomplishment.

Lieberman's book doesn't purport to cover every corner of the scene, but he considers a good variety of poets in pieces composed over a dozen years. As anticipated, the critic who has an elaborate case to make for Ashbery will have less favorable things to say of Howard Nemerov, whose "obsessive sanity of vision" seems to Lieberman a betrayal of function. He takes James Wright to task for "premature closure," and waxes ecstatic over the "unbroken flow" of meandering music in A. R. Ammons. He is typically suspicious of surface brilliance—say, in Richard Howard or Howard Moss— and far too ready to embrace a body of work that speaks to the "purity of being" in him; thus, his illuminating essay on W. S. Merwin which sadly fails to notice the limpness in standard lines or the maudlin intensities worked up in his other quoted passages. Lieberman has an eye for young talent—witness his enthusiastic review of John Peck's brilliant *Shagbark*—but it's not usually possible to distinguish his praise of one poet from his praise of another.

The critic who thinks Ashbery finally committed to an ethics of "clear-sightedness" is likely to blink a fair proportion of the evidence that passes before him. Lieberman is too close to the pulse of the country to understand completely what it's done to many of its poets.

Ashbery might be thought to go against the grain of popular American verse, to present a challenge to those who want their poetry soft and relatively easy to chew. His "Portrait in a Convex Mirror," though it is not at all what some have tried to make it, is a work of great majesty and inventive daring. In its philosophical rigor it demands a kind of care and seriousness not required by most poetry in our time. And it works closely with a more or less fixed subject which it takes to be interesting not merely for the sensations it may evoke but in itself. Had Ashbery been able to sustain that kind of commitment in his more recent work, we should have no occasion to complain of him. The poems in *Houseboat Days* are not his best, but among them we may find items that repay attention. Among these are "Syringa," "Crazy Weather," "Business Personals," "The Explanation," and "The Gazing Grain." No single poem in the volume may be said to fill us with wonder and gratitude as our favorite poems do, but none seems perverse or willfully "exotic" in the way of the earlier work. The achieved poems may not be terribly different from the others, but we do have, occasionally, the sense that Ashbery's whimsy is in check, and that he wants us to work at something with him, not to be astonished or tamely curious.

The most notable development in *Houseboat Days* is apparent in each of the better poems I've cited. Ashbery has taken to thematizing his material in a way that is bound to seem helpful. One doesn't always grasp the significance of a particular or agree that it is required, but one proceeds with the assurance that the project of the poem is in view. Nor does the explicit thematizing seem a bitter concession. Rather, the poet has come to acknowledge the intellectual dimension of his project, the essentially contemplative cast of his mind, so that he can take pleasure in thinking about experience without insisting it be immediate or translated into memorable insights. He has never seemed more in touch with mundanity, despite the continuing absence of a fully imagined world. When he speaks of removing "today's / Bandage" he accepts his rightful place "In the increasingly convincing darkness" which he creates and supports. In "Business Personals" he tells us that "the song makes no mention of directions," but that we know ourselves to be moving in the shadow of the past we long to inhabit—though we know it never existed. Ashbery's is a poetry of approximation and melancholy. It misses what it never had and intimates a quiet it can almost persuade us to want to share. It invents dimly palpable presences to shadow what it can neither see nor remember, though it is ever in slow pursuit. In what he calls "the clear bluish haze / Of uncertainty" he moves to determine the source of the consolation he has come to take in simply looking about, reflecting, and drawing breath. This may not strike us as finally amounting to much, but it describes an occupation that is serious and compelling. And it is good to feel the poet knows which phantom he is after. Ashbery may not be the poet Americans need, but he's surely better than the others who tell them they're too well endowed, too intuitive and knowing to think on what they haven't got.

Swollen Gates:
The Case for
a Homosexual Tradition

Robert K. Martin, *The Homosexual Tradition in American Poetry*
(Austin: University of Texas Press).

There are at present in the United States several accomplished
poets who have let it be known that they are homosexuals. Some of
them write openly about their personal relationships or explore in
their poems the lives of homosexual precursors with whom—in
one degree or another—they obviously identify. Others are content
to move in homosexual literary circles while creating a poetry that
defies definition as sexual statement. The situation is interesting.
One wonders why so many of the most original writers are homosexual. Since there is no longer any need for these people to conceal their sexual preference, it may not be said that they are *forced* to
be inventive in a way not required of other writers. One's impulse
is to propose that these gifted people just happen to be homosexuals, that the numbers will shift the other way before long, and that
in any case no good can come of classing writers by sexual preference. On the whole I believe this is a salutary impulse, though
there may be more to the matter than I am ready just now to admit.
There are reasons, surely, for the remarkable—some would say
alarming—representation of homosexuals in the American literary
and artistic communities. But it is a long way from acknowledging
and looking into this to deciding that there is a homosexual tradition and a coherent ideology which at once supports and validates
that tradition.

From *London Times Literary Supplement* (*TLS*), May 30, 1980.

Professor Martin's book is more than a work of literary history. It is frankly a political work which advocates positions on a number of important issues. Its focus on poets and poetry never obscures the fact that it is a personal book, that it espouses a reordering of political, cultural, and literary priorities which answers deeply to the needs of Professor Martin himself. There is nothing objectionable in the critic's decision to write out of himself, as it were. Successful critics do so all the time, many without acknowledging the operant personal bias. We tolerate, even welcome, the consequent discourse when we feel that the materials at issue are being handled scrupulously. It is not the pretense of perfect detachment or objectivity that weighs in our sense of the thing, but the communicated intelligence of the critical witness. Martin's book demonstrates certain modest literary skills, but these skills are unfortunately set in the service of an ideology so riddled with contradiction, so arrogant and banal, that one knows not what to make of it all. Were it an isolated case, a merely silly or pretentious or shallow book, one would be content to let it alone. But this is more than a standard academic volume, and it attempts to confer new literary status upon developments which have come more and more to the fore in recent intellectual life. Insofar as the case for homosexuality as a privileged mode of consciousness has come to be made with increasing insistence in our time, and is accorded largely uncritical tolerance by Anglo-American intellectuals, it seems to me essential that we engage the argument wherever we can. Martin's book may not be an intelligent defense of a pernicious ideology, but it is all too characteristic of other efforts lately under way. The focus on American poetry must not obscure the fact that more is at stake than the relation of contemporary writers to Martin's good gay poet, the redoubtable Walter Whitman.

Whitman is of course the pivotal figure for Martin. Though recent studies by Harold Bloom, Hyatt Waggoner, and others identify Emerson as the central influence in American poetry, a book with a homosexual orientation will necessarily select Whitman instead. Without him, in fact, without the example and encouragement he provides, it would not be possible even to think of a homosexual tradition. Whitman serves because he did clearly produce a body of fitfully impressive work, because he represented something like a coherent point of view in his poems and tracts, and because he did exert an influence—for better or worse—on gifted poets like Hart Crane, Theodore Roethke, and Allen Ginsberg. Martin thinks to make a case for Whitman as a model, not for the various heterosexual poets like Roethke who adopted his long line and some of his robust lyricism, but for poets who needed a way to come to terms with their own sexual nature. From this perspective, Whitman is less a poet with various literary strategies to enact than a democratic enthusiast with values to distribute, repressions to overcome, and lovers to attract. The poets who follow in his train may not sound like Whitman, may even deplore the slovenliness of his verses and the affected naivete of his posturings. They are, all the same—so the brief asserts—in his tradition, for where would they be without his having first knocked over the dominant bourgeois conventions? If homosexuals are now permitted to identify themselves as such in their verses, they owe that fact to the poet who first got away with it when the risks were more palpable.

Martin spends a good deal of time ridiculing various "straight" critics who thought years ago that the only way to protect Whitman was to prove he was not sexually "deviant." But the issue is, now as then, a false one. Martin himself concedes that Whitman may not ever have "engaged in genital sex with another man," and the poet was himself so eager to cover his tracks that it seems a pity to nag at him through the documents that survive. Supposing he did have male lovers, was an active participant in homosexual affairs. What does this show? According to Martin, it shows that Whitman's attempts to include women in his poems or to sing the glories of heterosexual love were strategies designed to conceal from the censors what were in fact his real concerns. It shows, moreover, that Whitman was the kind of homosexual truly suited to found and inspire a tradition. Throughout his book Martin argues that Whitman defined himself as a homosexual and did everything he could to fly directly in the face of bourgeois values. But there are fundamental questions he refuses to engage: In what degree is homosexuality essential to the adversary postures Whitman struck? How evident and how useful are the homosexual elements in Whitman's best work? Is there any point—beyond sectarian politics—in translating Whitman's mostly vague homoerotic metaphors and occasional fantasies into explicit terms that make him into a programmatic rebel and a forerunner of contemporary gay-rights activists? Finally, is there a body of work by other poets sufficiently close in form and spirit to Whitman to make us feel that there is indeed a living tradition? Once these questions have been addressed, it is possible to move on to the more crucial issues at stake here.

The adversary postures celebrated by Martin are familiar to almost everyone who has lived through the past twenty-five years. To the positive values of socialism and democracy he adds an opposition to all directed activity and to all "distinctions of age, class, beauty, and gender." The primary enemies are capitalism, aggression, male domination, and ownership. What separates Martin from other social critics is his conviction that these goals and the radical energies that mobilize activity on their behalf are best managed by homosexuals. How so? If it is the case that ordinary heterosexuality is repressive, which is to say, a function of standardized behavioral models systematically imposed upon us by "society," no one comfortable with those models may be said to have arrived at them for himself. The radical temper will be lacking. What is more, participation in heterosexual intercourse is inherently capitalistic, which is to say, it calls into play the "male domination and ownership" which are constant factors in unequal relationships. Only relations between equals—for Martin, between those of the same sex—may produce the kind of democratic satisfactions which alone can generate beneficent social values.

Martin fails to correct his argument by saying the obvious: that there are as many different kinds of relationship possible among heterosexual persons as there are among homosexuals. Only one who sees relationship as the physical position assumed and the depth of genital or anal penetration achieved can imagine that models of human nature can be so neatly described. What is more, since many radical critics in our time and in the time of Whitman have seen no necessary connection between politics and sexual affiliation, and were themselves heterosexual, the case for the one as dependent upon the other would seem untenable. Is this too obvious to say? We do not argue here the relative merits of socialism and capitalism, or the relation between directed activity and the freedom Martin thinks he values. We argue only that there is no clear relation between homosexuality and adversary postures of a political or cultural nature. Whitman is a good test case because he seems to embody the various qualities Martin wishes to exalt as a single posture. Would Whitman have agreed to be made use of in this way? No one who has read his poems with an intelligent sympathy will think so. He was not a subtle man. But he knew that his was a special nature, and that there were different ways of bearing witness to a truth. He did, in *Democratic Vistas*, describe the future as dependent in some way upon a "fervid companionship," a "manly friendship, fond and loving, pure and sweet, strong and life-long, carried to degrees hitherto unknown, not only giving tone to individual character, and making it unprecedentedly emotional, muscular, heroic, and refined, but having the deepest relations to general politics." If Whitman meant thereby to say that only homosexuals would have a proper idea of the good life, and the character to realize democratic ambitions, he was as much of a fool as his detractors routinely claim. I should think he meant rather to say that a revolution on behalf of democratic values could best be undertaken by persons capable of disinterested admiration and unstinting affection, and of behaving without a repertoire of received postures and reticences. The characteristic tendency to vague sentiment and overstatement is to be noted however one reads the passage, but there are good reasons to believe that my reading is the one Whitman would at last have preferred. No one so assiduous as he to celebrate ordinary relations and the lives of heterosexual heroes like Lincoln can have intended to call into being a republic led by a self-promoting homosexual vanguard.

There is enough homoerotic suggestion in Whitman to satisfy even Professor Martin, who is nonetheless at constant pains to discover what is nowhere to be found. What Martin wants, in fact, is an explicit homosexual component which will serve as a rallying point for timid homosexuals who need detailed descriptions of anal intercourse to woo them away from the milder consolations of vague fantasy or sentiment. And since Martin can pass up nothing that comes easily to hand, he is wont to grab hold of any fleshly item in Whitman and wring it for the hard evidence he demands. Throughout the one-half of the book devoted to Whitman one finds examples of the homo-ecstatic gloss: "the fallen penis may rise again" or, better yet, "One must accept the penis beneath the foreskin, the erect penis, and the penis after coitus." What instigation for this transport is provided by Whitman in the poems themselves? Here is one of the more explicit passages cited by Martin:

> Is this then a touch? quivering me to a new identity,
>
> .   .   .   .
> On all sides prurient provokers stiffening my limbs,
> Straining the udder of my heart for its withheld drip,
> Behaving licentious toward me, taking no denial,
> Depriving me of my best as for a purpose,

Unbuttoning my clothes, holding me by the bare waist,
Deluding my confusion with the calm of the sunlight and
pasture fields,
Immodestly sliding the fellow-senses away,
They bribed to swap off with touch and go and graze at the
edges of me,
No consideration, no regard for my draining strength or my
anger,

.   .   .   .

No published poem of Whitman seems to me to go beyond this in sheer erotic cunning, the speaker's confusion and resistance working to intensify the excitement and to make the final submission to the reverie an ambivalent satisfaction. It doesn't matter that some may take the passage for a simple worked-up masturbation fantasy and nothing more. The point is that there is more to *Song of Myself* than this kind of fantasy would suggest. There is variety, a broad responsiveness to all manner of things, from grand opera to bird song. Yes, there is indiscriminate enthusiasm, and yes, the body seems to Whitman more wonderful and satisfactory than it is likely to seem to others who have watched it decline or groaned with the agonies it can inflict. But there is, clearly, more in Whitman than the ejaculatory urgency hopefully ascribed to him by Professor Martin. No wonder, to support his thesis, the determined professor is driven to turn, with apparent relish, to the unpublished manuscript versions of a few Whitman poems. There he finds, among other stimulating details, an explicit description of fellatio. The omitted passages seem to Martin to prove that "Song of Myself," like Whitman's other major works, is a poem with " 'real' sexual content." The trouble is that one can also find, in the same long poems, plenty of heterosexual content, and that in any case the explicit sexual material can in no way be said to constitute the content the poem as a whole was designed to communicate. Consider, in this regard, the concluding sections of "Song of Myself." Why would the poet have displaced the content of his poem at so crucial a point? If he wished to make a case for homosexual experience as the *sine qua non* of everything good and lively and free, why did he choose to lay final emphasis upon other qualities, upon the capacity to speak "honestly," to "contain multitudes," to feel oneself a part of all that nurtures and grows? Once, in his book, Martin confronts the disturbing thought that homosexuals have no viable way of continuing the race, and that even a poet like Allen Ginsberg has considered seriously "the need to embrace some form of heterosexuality." To this Martin responds with the suggestion that there is ample "continuity" in "creativity." No wonder his sympathy for Whitman is so partial.

At various points in his study, Martin cites a clearly heterosexual passage in Whitman, only to remark that "here, as so often in 'Song of Myself' the content appears to be heterosexual, though only in symbolic terms." Elsewhere he will speak confidently of the stallion Whitman evokes as a "symbol of the male lover," suggesting that the signifier is nothing in itself, that only what is signified can properly claim our attention. Like other ideologues, Martin wants to have things both ways: When it serves his purpose, he will derogate the symbolic relation; elsewhere, he will insist upon its primacy. In fact, the stallion does serve as a symbol in Whitman, but like other symbols in poetry, it signifies much more than a particular person or thing. It has the quality of something rich in possibility and extension; it casts shadows. Martin's insistence upon literal translation would deprive the figure of its power to give a various delight and turn it into an obvious device. The critic does even more terrible things to a poem by Hart Crane, so that the words "black swollen gates" are made into "an explicit depiction of a recognizable sexual act: the 'black swollen gates' represent the anus of the lover, which finally admits . . . the poet." To consider Crane's "Voyages, III" as Martin recommends is to see, for a moment, what he wishes us to take for evidence. But just as quickly do we conclude that several key elements in the poem resist any such reading, and that in any case Crane's power throughout resides in his holding meaning just beyond the grasp of any categorical intention. In Whitman too metaphor typically serves to open up rather than to determine meaning, and symbolic references are always elusive and unstable. This is no reason to discount the symbolic dimension, as Martin does when it seems to invoke heterosexual content. Obviously the symbolic or metaphorical equivalences constitute the very heart of most poems, and no willful insistence upon literal or unambiguous statement can distract us from the poet's plural intentions.

The literal translation of metaphor into explicit diagrams of physical encounter has, of course, a political purpose we mean shortly to explore. At its most vulgar, though, it converts the visionary poet into a pamphleteer and an activist. This is not only unseemly, it is a falsification of the biographical record and of the poetry itself. Whitman may have wanted to be taken for an activist, but in fact his poems describe a dreamer whose characteristic mode is fantasy, not rebellion. To turn his impassioned exclamations into political slogans is to suppose that the poetry is itself but a vehicle for a set of ideas, a blueprint for a particular life-style or strategy. Martin's view of poems as tutelary documents and of aesthetics as summary judgments issued, as it were, after the fact has much to do with his inability to read without seeking confirmation for what he already knows.

Whitman's influence has never been exerted uniformly or predictably on any group of poets. Contemporaries treated in Martin's book are as different from one another as they are from the heterosexual poets with whom, nonetheless, they may fruitfully be compared. To say that the poets included "used their texts as ways of announcing and defining their homosexuality" is, on the whole, a barren proposition. Richard Howard's dramatic monologues or dialogues for two voices, whatever the proportion of homosexual characters they include, are not autobiographical statements. In their way as brilliant and resonant with implication as Browning at his best, they enact a strange tension that has nothing to do with the homosexual's need to catalogue his favorite positions. Likewise, James Merrill's elegant ironies have more to do with the carefully arranged surfaces of Richard Wilbur than with the self-assertive posturings of Whitman or Allen Ginsberg. Apparently unable to take no for an answer, Martin blunders confidently from one figure to another, demonstrating in spite of himself that there is no homosexual tradition and that the better poets he selects have better things to do than to boast about their achievements in the bedrooms and steam baths of New York.

But let us turn to the political content of this book. In essence, Martin argues that the "tradition" inaugurated by Whitman has produced an adversary spirit that promises to improve the quality of life among us. He offers no explanation for the failure of this tradition to take hold generally, but is satisfied that conditions are looking up. Homosexuals at least are free to express themselves as they like, and the values they espouse are no longer dismissed so routinely as they were in the past. Martin has no patience with those who think homosexuality "unwholesome," and he concedes that "repressive sexuality" is still the norm. Still, the appearance in America of several accomplished homosexual poets should give reason for hope, and everywhere the "system" is under stress.

Now it is not simply Whitman's attraction to other men, but the very special nature of this attraction that stimulates Martin to celebrate his example. For it is perhaps the central contention of this book that, in order to promote democracy as a spiritual *and* political objective, homosexual experience must be sought and achieved with anonymous partners. "Anonymous sex," Martin argues, "is an important way station on the path to the abolition of distinctions of age, class, beauty, and gender." Homosexuals may find long-term partners, quite in the way that married people do, but always there must remain a readiness to venture beyond the stable relation, to respond ecstatically to the vagrant promise. Interestingly, the word "promiscuity" never appears in this study, and it is clear that Martin would rank it with the word "unwholesome" as an empty and dismissive term signifying pathetic incomprehension. In the brave new world to come, "long-lasting affection between human beings" becomes a secondary goal, yielding pride of place to "instantaneous sexual attraction between two strangers as they pass in the street." Whitman's capacity to embrace multitudes has never before taken on so literal an aspect. "Do you know what it is as you pass to be loved by strangers?" Whitman asks in "Song of the Open Road." "Do you know the talk of those turning eye-balls?" Earlier readers may have thought the sexual feeling suffusing these questions a generalized sort of thing, portending not so much exotic genital refreshments as more mundane comradely excursions. There is, to be sure, "the shuddering, longing ache of contact" in Whitman, but it is evoked in the context of a satisfaction that is only intermittently erotic. Must one really think of anal intercourse in order to follow out the meaning of "those turning eyeballs" or the "large and melodious thoughts" Whitman is brought to entertain? And is it really the case that every reference to the love of woman—as in "What gives me to be free to a woman's and man's good will?"—is an enforced or dishonest reference?

Funny, nothing in Whitman ever seemed to me unwholesome until I agreed to set in place Martin's greasy lenses. It is not the intimation of a vague if potentially promiscuous sex that is offensive, at least not as it appears in Whitman. What offends is the critic's celebration of promiscuity as if it were an achievement worthy to stand beside other exemplary feats. It is also a fact that, in much of the "serious" promotional literature and journalism distributed by contemporary homosexual activists, the same ideological bias is prominent. I have no desire to censor these publications or in any way to punish those who do what they like with other consenting adults. But the deinhibition represented by the campaign on behalf of "anonymous" or promiscuous sex is not a spectre to be idly tolerated. The rhetoric of gay-rights activists and careerist homosexual academics like Professor Martin is dangerous and vile because it pretends to be something that it is not. It parades as a campaign for democracy and equality while promoting a total indifference to actual persons and a reduction of human contact to the grating of organs. One need not defend a repressive sexual morality or the conventions of bourgeois marriage to be appalled at the way in which Martin blithely says of Whitman's encounters that they "could well be repeated in almost any steam bath of a modern large city." Is it, again, too obvious to suggest that the people who frequent those steam baths are not likely to enjoy the robust and equable nature actually celebrated by Whitman? That they are likely to be disturbed, yes, disturbed and crippled persons enacting fantasies of release or liberation that can at best relieve momentarily the fear of impotence they experience when they confront real people capable of making complex emotional demands? Martin devotes not a sentence to the thought—did it never occur to him?—that certain kinds of behavior are neurotic, that they represent, as in the lives of perverts, an interposition of ultimately frustrating fantasies between the subject and those with whom he attempts sexual relations. For those who suffer, only sympathy and assistance are appropriate. For those who are satisfied to do things in their own special way, there is tolerance and, perhaps, respect. For the delusional and often rabid ideologues, nothing less than frontal criticism will do.

Martin chatters routinely in this book about preserving "the integrity of the individual selves," which means, apparently, protecting men from damaging or intimidating contacts with women and children. He claims for Whitman and other homosexuals an intuitive sympathy for the plight of women "in a patriarchal society," though the best he can recommend for them is release from "repressive sexuality" and from child-rearing. The child itself he describes as "a product . . . which will continue to feed the economic system." Homosexuals, he insists, have a responsibility to enjoy themselves and, if possible, to make a spectacle of their sexual proclivities: "If men walk arm and arm in the streets, they are not busy in the factory or begetting children." No doubt it is hopeless to argue with someone like Martin, to propose that the routines of child-rearing may seem utterly rewarding and life-enhancing even to enlightened persons, that many children grow up to do more than "feed the economic system," or that middle-class women suffer today less from repressive sexuality than from an inability to choose among the various temptations indiscriminately set before them. Certainly Martin is entitled to his view of these things, though he does his position a disservice by demonstrating how fully it is a function of simple aversion and conditioned reflex. It is tempting, in preparing to answer Martin's assertions, to come up with comparably insupportable alternative propositions, a procedure legitimized by Martin's avowal, following Whitman, that " 'What we do is right and what we affirm is right.' "

But enough. Is it unfair to say that the case for homosexuality as a privileged mode of consciousness and as a necessary basis for a viable political radicalism has not yet been made? The late Newton Arvin, an American literary critic claimed by Martin for the homosexual fraternity, may have had as little justification for his statement that "homosexuality . . . is only one of the eccentricities or pathologies that may give a particular bias to a writer's work." But it is a much more modest and plausible position; one, moreover, that is willing to be clarified or corrected when the state of knowledge permits a more encouraging description.

PART FIVE

Cinematic Readings and Misreadings

Explanation and Conviction in Godard: *The Married Woman*

Godard has been the subject of extended and sophisticated debate turning not only upon the validity of his films as political statements or as aesthetic objects but upon the very limits of film as an expressive medium. Perhaps the most interesting of the commentaries are two essays by Susan Sontag in which a case is made for Godard as a determinedly unpolitical artist whose treatment of political and social issues is persuasive in formal rather than in ethical or psychological terms. What is more, Sontag argues, it is the character of great art in general that it aims to prove rather than to analyze: Thus, a Godard film ". . . is an exhibit, a demonstration. It shows *that* something happened, not *why* it happened. It exposes the inexorability of an event . . . it does not explain anything."

Now I do not entirely approve a theory so eager to dismiss from works of art the function of explanation, as if the desire to explain were somehow bound to pollute or divert the aesthetic project. Nor am I convinced that Godard cares not at all about psychological motivation and patterns of social interaction. What do we mean, after all, when we speak of explanation in a work of art? In what sense is it possible genuinely to account for something which a reader or viewer knows to be made up, and which, at one level at least, is generated to contribute to a design, rather than to further a program? To show *why* something happened is not, after all, to provide an indisputable account, but to indicate a viable perspective in which it may become part of our experience. To show *that* something happened is not sufficiently to stake a claim to it, and no

From *Georgia Review*, Fall 1976.

event is likely to seem inexorable which has merely formal legitima-
tion. Formal requirements, when they have been satisfied, always
seem inexorable to those who restrict their inquiry to the finished
surfaces of the static object. Those with an interest in creative process will know how many plausible options confront the artist, and
will see in the finished form a provisional response to various
substantive and purely technical problems that are likely to tempt
the artist in other ways as he continues to practice his craft. If the
work proves anything we are to care about, it will prove that even
provisional solutions have a distinctly human content no commitment to formal emperimentation can gainsay: If, as Sontag tells us,
Godard wants us to realize "that things are as they are," we shall
be disposed to such knowledge only if there is something in it for
us. We shall need to feel that the completion of a formal requirement simultaneously enhances our understanding of issues to
which the work of art bears at least intermittent witness. Though
we may be too sophisticated to demand perfect verisimilitude or
massive psychological detail, we shall probably insist that books
and films order insights to suggest that some ways of looking at
things are more appropriate than others.

This is, in fact, the subject of Godard's best film, his ninth, entitled *The Married Woman*. What, Godard asks, can we know about
ourselves, and how do contemporary men and women come to
make choices, to determine priorities? An intensely lucid meditation on contemporaneity, Godard's film explains all sorts of things
while working out an intricate formal pattern of great beauty. The
pattern of the work, the structural relation of parts to whole, is in
this sense available to useful description and evaluation only insofar as we approach the film as a function of specific purposes. To
speak of the fragmentary character of a Godardian image, of the
discontinuous narrative line, or the repetition of various ritual elements, is not in itself to account for the appeal of Godard's film.
Nor is it adequate to suppose that Godard mounted images simply
to display the "inexorability" of events, or that he had no desire to
situate with some sense of cultural and historical particularity the
characters in the film, so as to analyze the necessity wherein they
shape their prospects. Indeed, Godard's purposes are consistently
analytic: The married woman of Godard's film is what she is, no
more and no less, for reasons at least partially indicated in the work
itself. While the elaboration of these reasons is not predominantly
logical or discursive, the film carefully structures a framework in
which plausible attribution is not only permissible but unavoid-

able. Ms. Sontag, in her extraordinary essay on Godard's *Vivre Sa Vie*, quotes the following words of a character in that film: " 'A plate is a plate. A man is a man. Life is . . . life.' " But though the impulse to such a sentiment is clearly present in *The Married Woman*, though the filmmaker himself seems tempted to conclude that we may simply love or leave his figures in their frequently brutish imperfection, he demands of us, and of himself, a more difficult response. For, as we need hardly be reminded, a plate is not always a mute or indifferent object, and there are times when to be a man seems very like being a cow, or worse.

Among Godard's standard theoretical gestures is a kind of fake *cinema-verité* interview in which a character, usually in close-up, answers questions put to him by an off-screen voice, sometimes unidentified. In *The Married Woman* the device is used with considerable freshness, as when Charlotte's young son explains how to do something—we never know what—in exactly ten steps. But the most important and troubling of these interviews is with Charlotte's husband, Pierre, on the subject of memory. Viewers of the film will recall that Pierre has returned to his family with a friend after a sojourn in Auschwitz, where he'd attended the belated trial of German war criminals. Nowhere does Godard force the German question upon us, but it is there throughout the film as a kind of counterpoint to our involvement with Charlotte, and in the interview with Pierre the connections are really as explicit and directive as anything in a work by Godard is apt to be. Even before the interview we are introduced to the issue of memory in an exchange at the airport between Charlotte and the friend. He tells her a little joke about someone's response to the Jewish question: Why *bother* to exterminate them, the response concluded. To which the married woman replies, "yes, why bother," immediately revealing that she does not know what happened at Auschwitz. Shortly afterwards she confides to the friend her impression that the Auschwitz trials had to do with Thalidomide babies. The exchange is so casual, and yields so easily to later events, that one might well conclude it had only marginal importance, were it not for the subsequent interview on memory. There the question of German guilt and responsibility is tentatively engaged by Pierre, who launches into more personal reflections as well.

Pierre opts for a view of memory as an involuntary reflex: We remember, or fail to remember, because of what we are. Memory is not, in this view, an ethical concept or goal. Charlotte had undoubtedly heard, at one time or other, what happened at Auschwitz, but there is no reason why one constituted as she is should remember the unpleasant facts. In these terms, Godard suggests, it is difficult to be confident about the routine distinctions between Germans and other European peoples to which Pierre briefly alludes in his interview—if the Germans have done their best to forget Auschwitz, the rest of us do no less under comparable circumstances. Further, given a world in which Godard's married woman is a familiar, even somewhat appealing type, we may well ask why Germans should bother themselves about the dreadful past. Who is in a position to demand that they continue to suffer guilt, or, for that matter, that Charlotte trouble her pretty head over infamies in which she's not participated?

But the issue is rather more immediate as it's projected in Godard's film, for Charlotte is herself confused about responsibility and memory as these are implicated in her own life. Ought she to think regularly about the pain she caused her husband by having begun an affair with Robert, still her lover as the cinematic narrative unfolds? If she intends only to cultivate an extramarital relation, is she responsible for her husband's having found out, when she'd done her best to keep the truth from him? In his interview Pierre remarks how even the most ordinary kinds of settings frequently turn into concentration camps, and though one ought to be annoyed by the glibness of the observation and the overall glide in the argument, one can't help at the same time being a little serious about it: What sort of people think that ordinary settings have much in common with concentration camps? What emotional advantage does one gain in looking at mundane experience in this way? Leaving a rented apartment with her lover one afternoon, Charlotte thinks "I used to be not here a year ago"—the whispered voice-over creates a chilling effect, and we cannot but feel how anxious Godard is to locate his protagonist, who moves breezily about through much of the film. Clearly, the sort of person for whom the comparison between stable bourgeois life and concentration camps is likely to seem suitable is also apt to observe that most events in life, including pleasurable experiences, come upon us as by an energy and cunning of their own. Only what is random and without compelling content is, in this view, at once natural and good. No wonder Pierre and Charlotte were drawn together, despite obvious differences: Both know, he more articulately than she, that we suffer even modest difficulty with great unease, that it is our duty to be free, to let nothing tie us down. This is why, for Charlotte, the fact that only a year earlier she did not have a lover is so troubling: Since all experience is random, since things "just happen," it is hard to accept that there are consequences. After all, there could as easily be none, or none to trouble us, at least. Why should poor Charlotte need to think of the complication caused by having a lover and a husband at once? Better not to remember how comparatively simple life seemed when there was only the husband to consider.

The focus on memory, then, is a way into the vision of Godard's film, and is itself of considerable importance. To argue that the subject of memory is itself indifferent, that Godard uses it simply to state a case without explaining it, is to argue that he has no attitudes towards the case which he feels compelled to express. No one who sees Godard's film can possibly imagine that he is neutral as regards the figures he portrays. That his feelings include a large measure of ambivalence there is no doubt, but it is possible to have several attitudes towards a person or idea while managing at the same time to take sides. For an artist, of course, taking sides may have nothing to do with hoping that one character wins and another loses, or that capitalism be finally and totally destroyed to make way for socialism. Godard, for example, in his best work takes sides by structuring satisfying explanations for difficult problems. The failure of historical memory explains the incapacity of particular human beings to respond in what are customarily thought to be acceptable ways to dilemmas of their own making. The relation between phenomenon and explanation is never simple, but everything in *The Married Woman* points to the sufficiency of suggested connections. There is, in other words, a vision which serves as warrant for these explanations, which ensures that we respond to various particulars in a relatively consistent way. In part this is a function of Godard's ability to project a unified sensibility such that attitudes are imparted even as the filmmaker might not himself know for certain what he thinks about a given prospect. He takes sides by indicating to us, in the broadest terms, what are and are not legitimate extrapolations from a given body of particulars, what are the parameters of feeling to which we may be appropriately susceptible in observing his figures, and so on. The filmmaker takes sides by structuring our relation to the work of art, to the specifically human material it evokes. He shows us why some things are truer or richer or more beautiful than others, and incidentally explains how it is possible to communicate such things.

Many works of art operate very differently, of course, and it would be foolish to claim that a unified sensibility will always establish a basis of plausible explanation to account for the phenomena it generates. It is obvious that we cannot always know what an artist thinks about this and that. When Wallace Stevens, in "The Idea of Order at Key West," writes, "She sang beyond the genius of the sea" and "For she was the maker of the song she sang," he does not need to tell us who *she* was or why she should have sung. In fact we do not care to know, accepting that a sensibility like Stevens's will not be exercised by such questions, and that we had better learn to watch for other pleasures as we give ourselves to the poem. On the other hand, it is rare that a novelistic sensibility will wholly insist that we suspend our feeling for credible explanation of a more or less mundane kind, and this is true of films as well. The exceptions are generally playful films, which withhold explanation with a kind of wry diffidence, as though coming across with the goods would offend simple good taste and encourage an attitude of pedestrian solemnity. Eric Rohmer's *Claire's Knee* is such a film, and we have only to think how different it is from *The Married Woman* to recognize the hopelessness of any categorical approach to the medium.

At one point in Godard's film Charlotte is driving along with Robert as a sequence of images passes before us, rapidly intercut with shots of the couple in their car. Charlotte's internal monologue, again presented as voice-over, recites the words "Will the relation weather another meeting?" just as we get a drizzly glimpse of statues in the Louvre gardens. This is more than statement of fact, though to say precisely what the juxtaposition of words and images might explain is clearly to violate the implicit premises of the Godardian montage. The key premise intends that every patently serious insight be mounted with astringent disregard. Connections must seem to have been discovered rather than worked out, and nothing is to be painstakingly elaborated. No matter that motivic patterns multiply at every turn in the narrative—so long as they seem to just happen into place, Godard is content. In this sense a viewer may see perfectly well what statues in the Louvre gardens have to do with Charlotte's affair, but is—ideally—so well instructed in the Godardian premise that he will resist any explicit observation. His resistance is nicely encouraged by the rapidity with which one set of images gives way to another, so that there is little time for steady reflection and earnest sentiment.

Charlotte, then, does not remember what happened at Auschwitz, but is capable of being reminded by things around her that there *is* change, erosion, unpleasantness in every human life. It is one of the little glories of Godard's medium, of the way he uses it, that he need never indicate whether it is Charlotte or only the filmmaker who registers the image of the Louvre statues, but either way, something central is explained. The married woman has no dependable way of weathering her own inconstant demands, of setting up viable resistances to this impulse and that. If she has any self-image at all, it is importantly informed not by monumental statuary but by brassiere ads and lascivious record-album covers: *They* provide the image of femininity from which eagerly liberated young women will have to fashion a self. Insistently Godard weaves through his narrative line these debased consumer artifacts and their packaged undifferentiated images. If Charlotte is confused and behaves badly, even by her own lights, it is because she does not know what she ought to be. She wants only to be attractive, and to achieve pleasure, and in these she frequently succeeds. What can she possibly make of monumental statues? Beautiful in their strictly formal properties, they propose as well a vision of the feminine as a typology of pliant solidity, wonderfully poised and burnished, knowing what they are because they can be no other. Their capacity to weather change and inclemency is a function of easy accommodation to the abiding status of the given. By contrast, Charlotte's misfortune is to have grown up in a time for which nothing is unqualifiedly and unashamedly given, in which no one may calmly propose his participation in a condition to which he yields because others like him have so yielded and because life is somehow simpler that way.

But what, a reader may well ask, can all this have to say of Godard, who so eschews this kind of conservative argument and logical piecing together of small details? What is one to make of the undeniable playfulness with which Godard handles his materials, and the affection he persistently shows his married woman, despite her characteristic lack of poise and monumental solidity? About the playfulness, I suppose, one may be grateful, for Godard knows *how* to play, which is to say, knows that play is no permanent obstacle to serious engagement. Though he may use a Beethoven string quartet as accompaniment to a frivolous little sequence, he does so not to debase the music or to wholly diminish the characters but to suggest how entirely dislocation affects everything we touch and recall. That, in our hunger for meaning of any kind, we anxiously impose a consecutive reading upon a veritable anarchy of particulars is a consequence of which Godard had to be aware when he made his film. Such things may make others melan-

choly, but Godard knows how to deal with them, just as he manu-
factures the ponderous solemnities uttered by his characters not
merely to lament or mock. Godard is, in this film at least, an artist
of the first rank precisely in his capacity to love his characters, to
allow them their otherness, even as he toys with them and makes
the viewer uneasy about what he is to think of the spectacle. That is
why Godard's indictment of advanced industrial society and all its
works is devastating in *The Married Woman:* The filmmaker has
many objects, and deliberately plays some of them off against others. He is obsessed by no one idea, no single program or figure he
wishes to score. The primary drive that animates the film is a good
deal more diffuse, and may best be described as a will to respond to
everything in the contemporary environment, a will not to be permanently burdened by any combination of persons, ideas, and
images, no matter how weighty. So fervent a will, to be effectual,
may be realized only by one who remains light on his feet, who, in
cinematic terms, is master of the jump-cut and montage effects of
stunning ingenuity.

Godard, though, does not always present serious insights in so
offhanded a way as he frequently affects. There are sequences in
which he dwells on a figure so insistently that its symbolic function
may not be overlooked. The statues in the Louvre gardens pass by
rapidly, but Charlotte and her lover come back more than once to a
mechanical device, an elaborate belt designed to encourage erect
posture and set off an alarm when the wearer slouches. Near the
end of the film, Charlotte pays her lover $250 for the belt, which
strikes her as simply terrific when she sees it earlier on Robert.
What, specifically, do we see in these belt sequences? Robert wears
the belt, then passes it to Charlotte, who tries it on, looks herself
over, tests the feel of the thing to see whether it may plausibly
affect her posture. She wants one, asks the price, determines to get
the money—presumably from her husband, since she does not
have an income of her own—and subsequently receives her trophy
from Robert during a furtive last meeting at an airport hotel. Both
characters are very much in earnest as they appraise the belt and
ponder its potential effects. And what of the viewer? Surely we are
amused by all this interest in a dubious trifle. Godard, it seems, is
having a good time with his characters. The belt may be silly, but
we cannot help being touched, if also a little incredulous, at their
continued absorption in it.

That the belt must also and at once call to mind a chastity belt
would surely have occurred to Godard, but it is not as clear whether

or not he thereby intended that the belt be compromised as an object in its own right. For if we think of the more ancient device, we may be unable to look squarely at the present object on screen without, as it were, seeing through it to what it is not. The experience of the viewer, then, may involve an emptying of sheer visual presence from objects and from persons to whom they are attached. If the belt on screen comes more and more to assume the status of a visual pun on chastity belts, will not Charlotte and Robert come increasingly to recall—in elaborating a contrast—other figures with a rather different notion of posture and its liabilities? Such figures, it is true, never actually appear in Godard's film, but it is their absence to which everything eventually refers. We come to define Charlotte and her several relationships by learning to penetrate surfaces, by searching out a content which the characters themselves are assiduous to deny. The perspectival thrust of Godard's film consistently reinforces the habit of analysis by making it difficult for us to accept the inexorable presence in the world, the irreducibility of its central figures. We analyze because the multiplication of resemblances, of patterned intentions, is so great that we have no choice but to do so. The mechanical belt may briefly command its own space, may at first draw vision to it as a genuine object rather than as symbol or symptom, but it cannot do so for long. In the same way, we view Charlotte only briefly as a particular individual, resist only so far the inclination to "read" her as a type, as a means to making a point.

In Charlotte's belt we have the idea of correct posture translated to the dimension of a physical mechanism which sets off an alarm not to keep people chaste but to keep their backs erect. For Charlotte the idea of posture has no authoritative content. No agency in the culture officially prescribes that she be concerned with such things, or that consequences will invariably follow from a failure of concern. She does not really know why keeping one's back erect should be preferable to slouching, but senses that the one posture is more attractive than the other. To be attractive, one supposes, means for Charlotte that she will not find herself alone, that she will continue to have people and things around to consume. Godard forces his viewer to ascribe meanings, to interpret and explain, because objects and persons in the universe he examines have no durable content of their own. Charlotte's belt is unreal to her even as sheer physical presence, for she has no genuine commitment to the physical posture it purportedly enables. She will quickly use it up; it is a toy she will grow tired of. We observe as much not by way of moral indictment but as a means of accounting for the addictive explanation to which Godard's film impels us. What emerges is an overdetermination in the marshaling of particulars, so that fragmentary evocations, snatches of song, transient images assume logical coherence for us even as we're intermittently dazed by the mobility of Godard's roving attention.

Of a piece with Godard's treatment of the belt is his use of music and song. At one point, for example, he has Charlotte singing ever so sweetly to herself "Where Have All the Flowers Gone?", a song reasonably familiar to everyone who lived in the United States or in Europe during the antiwar years of the 1960s. Especially resonant are the plaintive repeated words in the refrain, "When will they ever learn." Now it is obvious to the viewer of the film that Godard has Charlotte singing this song, rather than another, for good reason. It is not the case that he might as well have had her sing the theme from *Cabaret,* that a song is a song, that Godard wishes only to state that his character sings when, on another day, she might have been silent. In responding critically, that is to say, with analytic scruple, to Charlotte's song, the viewer recognizes his own resistance to Godard's implicit invitation to admire and enjoy the sweetness of her singing. What business has Charlotte with an antiwar song? She, who does not know Auschwitz from Thalidomide, is literally incapable of registering what the words of her song invoke. Must we then shut our ears to the possible pleasures of her song, and is Godard himself insensible, determined as he is to make use of the song in his overarching scheme? Because the married woman cannot think concretely about anything, because nothing has meaning for her, except as an object of use, we are therefore inordinately engaged in a procedure of restoring vanished meanings. This we may accomplish not by insisting that they be present but by thinking through the phenomena offered us to their functional relations with a domain of experience not available to Charlotte. In this sense, the song she sings calls to mind several things at once: the protest movements of the 1960s from which Charlotte is alienated, the easy assimilation of social consciousness and political conviction to mass entertainment (the conversion of generous sympathies to the "sincerities" of musical tag lines and slogans), the larger brutalities of recent Western experience (Auschwitz), and the general difficulty even sophisticated people may have in formulating reasonable responses to such experience.

Godard's handling of the song does not allow for anything like self-satisfaction on the part of the viewer. Though we listen to it and reflect upon it as Charlotte cannot, we have all we can do to mentally set it alongside the belt and several other symbolic elements in the cinematic discourse before having to engage additional items thrown up by Godard's infernal ingenuity. We have not the leisure to dwell upon easy distinctions between Charlotte and ourselves, on the song as index to our larger awareness. Always what we sense instead is the pull of Godard's restless intention, the abrupt reeling in of each vivid particular, as though Godard had cast it on the water merely to discover how it would affect the ripples created by other castings. Ms. Sontag quotes with some disapproval Godard's description of his own cinematic process: "In short, life filling the screen as a tap fills a bathtub that is simultaneously emptying at the same rate." I do not think this is "disingenuous rhetoric," for the words describe quite accurately the primary effect of Godard's rapid displacement of images. But while nothing in *The Married Woman* seems destined to sustain itself for very long, the viewer grows progressively more secure in the conviction that, by remaining attentive, he will know how to handle the materials given him. If he has no desire to consume materials by allowing himself to be passively tickled—and the film clearly contrives to ensure that he have no such desire—he is likely to be anxious about arranging them. And what is the status of the life that fills the screen only to disappear, often before it's had a chance to register an impact? Is it lifelike? The point is that Godard is interested in meaning at least as much as he is interested in capturing the surfaces of our routine comings and goings. It is not reality as such that informs his art so much as possibility. Bluntly stated, Godard works through his materials without exhaustively using them up because the materials are themselves less important than the vague reaches in the direction of which they compulsively gesture. We, no less than Godard, resist Charlotte's song because of the vacancies in her and in ourselves it reveals. When we listen to the few gentle lines, look at her eager yet uncertain figure lost in some vacuous daydream, we think, perhaps, of an earlier encounter with Charlotte. She has met Robert at a rented apartment. They have made love, and though she seems restless to get up and leave, she lingers; they waste time, chat, not always comfortably. Finally, sitting at the edge of the bed, Charlotte says no, she doesn't want to make love anymore, as the camera shows us the rows of empty shelves on the wall behind the lovers. The camera rises, slowly, searches out the shelves: nothing.

Does Godard wish to indicate simply that the shelves in the apartment are empty because no one really lives there as yet? Or that his characters are, somehow, empty, in the way that we say people who are incapable of genuine feeling for one another are empty? His purposes are, I think, larger and more elusive. For one thing, the dialogue in the apartment scene amply informs us that the arrangement is provisional, pending the outcome of Charlotte's design to leave her husband permanently for Robert. Nor does Godard close himself off from Charlotte, as well he might if he thought her empty in some ultimate way. More likely, Godard wonders why his characters should *feel* empty, why they do not know how to fill themselves up, why they should need to pass with such desperate hunger from one event to another. It is the purpose of his film to extend inquiry, to analyze and propose possible explanations. Charlotte grabs everything in sight because nothing is denied her, because she has never learned to resist desire, because, so it seems, nothing is literally forbidden her. It is not vile perversity, built up in her, that makes her want more, more, no matter how much she devours; not, either, her "nature" to be greedy or insatiable. She wants, and wants, Godard would have us see, not because she is empty but because her transactions with others and with the world lack definable content. There is no contract that binds her compellingly within the various nexal relations she marginally inhabits. Husband? Why *not* dump him? Child? Probably better off without me. Lover? Can't tell me what to do. Songs, gimmicks, identity-images? Too many to handle with care. Assaulted as she is by an unlimited variety of options, lacking instruction in how properly to take any of them seriously, or to think seriously of her own stature as decisively affected by the choices she will make, the married woman feels empty. No wonder, when he intrudes upon their lovemaking, Godard shows us fragments of bodies, arrangements of arms and thighs and navels, rather than whole people in stark embrace. If there is no psychological depth in these characters, no complex of carefully elaborated feelings, it is not because Godard wishes to leave them out, or considers them unimportant, but because the characters themselves lack the words to articulate such depths. Insofar as they might *ever* express an interest in psychological motive, or probe the texture of their feelings, the operant vocabulary would necessarily be a literary vocabulary, the words themselves alienating, already threatening or frivolous in their obvious reference to other discourses imperfectly assimilated. What Sontag calls, in a beautiful passage, "the brutal or lyrical opaqueness of the human condition," in Godard is an opacity the filmmaker is assiduous to counter by offering a film language that penetrates surfaces and resurrects possibility.

If the shelves in Charlotte's temporary apartment are empty, Godard's purpose must be, in some sense, to fill them. Otherwise, why compulsively draw attention to them, and to comparable features of Charlotte's universe? The shelves are not empty in Charlotte's marital apartment, which is filled with the spoils of bourgeois accumulation. The husband, in fact, likes to gloat over his trophies and bric-a-brac, and though Charlotte doesn't take quite the same pleasure in them, it may be only because she is troubled, her loyalties divided, when we observe her. It is clear, however, from what Godard shows us, that what fills up the shelves and clutters the tables in the marital apartment cannot answer to the difficulties posited in the film vision. Again, it is not the fact that they are superficial, mere things, that Godard holds against them, but that they are primarily related to as novelty items, gimmicks, that the characters obviously want more from them than they can possibly give. Charlotte is bored at home, and her problem is not simply that Pierre travels a good deal, or that Pierre's son by a former marriage spends much of the time away at school. When Charlotte looks at things about her she sees what they promise more than what they are—there is always more where *these* present objects come from. To say that she is starved for meaning is to suggest a resemblance between Charlotte and the standard protagonist of a Bergman or Antonioni film, a resemblance which is artificial at best. Charlotte, for one thing, doesn't know what she craves, would no doubt stare with ingenuous wonder at one who told her she was facing the void. Forced momentarily to reflect in this way, she would observe that there were plenty of people around to occupy her, that she was as "into" meaningful relations as anyone else. Just so would she deny that she had a hard time putting things together, that she had been victimized in some mysterious way by all the sensory phenomena pressing in about her: After all, she'd proclaim defiantly, she has options, views, like other normal persons. In one of Godard's self-interviews, entitled The Present, Charlotte feels a little sheepish discussing her own ideas, but persists in expressing them all the same, confident ultimately that she is not only entitled but positively required to do so under the conditions of advanced liberal-democratic society. Only reticence and insecurity are forbidden. Confidence in one's humanity, for people like Charlotte, depends upon the sense that there is always more: more to say, to do, to see, to take in. Nothing is irreplaceable, no utterance but can be altered or improved, no object but can be traded in for better, no relation one cannot do without or idea renounce. This unlimited openness to possibility is what drives Charlotte perpetually to see promise rather than gratifying substance. Her problem is that she is trained to look for more of the same, that she lacks the imagination to seek any *other* kind of promise. For all her openness to possibility, she is confronted by a landscape of undeviating opaqueness. If she has any gift at all, and it is a gift the film affirms as partly ours as well, it is precisely the gift of relating with occasionally lyric abandon to the otherwise harsh and unyielding fixities that continue to promise so much, and so little.

So Charlotte wants more than she knows how to get, and Godard entertains an understandable ambivalence towards her aspirations. What is more, the formal surfaces of *The Married Woman* encourage a sometimes lyrical approach to the film, as if the various sculptural tableaux and ordered disjunctions had no object but to ratify the shrewd waywardness of Godard's invention and to embarrass or intimidate analytic responses. We have seen, of course, that such intimidation is uncalled for, that the film provides its own analytic tools and inducements to explanatory rigor. It is true, as others have previously observed, that Godard likes to mock explanation, his own and others', that every proposed *solution* simultaneously points to its own insufficiency, to the various weightings that compel it without making it authoritative or indisputable. In this sense film language itself constitutes an object of derisive if playful reflection, for it seeks regularly to evoke and explain without satisfactorily capturing the essential qualities of the experience treated. We note how, in the middle of an abbreviated lovemaking sequence, Godard cuts abruptly to a plane roaring overhead, and recall the standard film image employed by a variety of other directors: the bird soaring gracefully above. Neither bird nor plane, Godard would have us consider, aptly evokes the complex experience of liberation and fear involved in sexual consummation. All the same, there is a code vocabulary, a repertoire of gestures, words, and images, which is, finally, all we have to work with. No good pretending it is possible simply to dispense with the code, or to rely entirely on one's own. All language is at some level a shared language, despite impulses to concealment and obliquity built into its very structure. We may not always know how to express something without saying more or less than we mean, but the language code at least allows a measure of simultaneous communication and reticence. If Godard has any claim to innovation in film, it rests upon his mastery of the code peculiar to his medium, the way in which his struggle with film language informs the drama his characters enact.

Godard's married woman is dissatisfied with her life, though she wants only to be happy, because even simple things have become problems. She does not trust what she feels and says any more than she can trust others. All explanation seems to her and her comrades invariably suspect. More and more they think anything is possible, and hence take nothing to be true, no statement of the case a reliable gauge to what is going on. We note, as we observe their struggles, that for all the novelty of Godard's invention, we know what he is about, know what his imagery purports to convey, confidently measure the gap between the filmmaker's reflexive self-awareness and the broken surfaces of the film narrative. No character within that narrative experiences a comfort even vaguely comparable, and Godard's analysis shows us why. During one scene Charlotte demands that Robert tell her persuasively that he loves her: How, she asks, can you know that somebody loves you? A preposterous question finally, but one each of us may have to answer, and it will not be enough to say: Each knows in his own way. Precisely how, and what, do we know? Robert answers confidently at first, almost ingenuous in his reliance upon what he takes to be his own patent sincerity. Meanwhile Charlotte continues to demand yet more transparent certitude, driving the actor to repeat himself in a variety of ways. He explains, offers this warrant and that, and the more he offers, the less certain he seems. Frustration grows; he is dissatisfied, we are dissatisfied for him. What is the operant code-language for expressing something so fundamental? Is it a language of terrible extremity? Must Robert declare that he would gladly lay down his life for Charlotte, bear any indignity on her behalf? It seems, in the universe these people occupy, that nothing will do. Finally, Godard determines that we should test the conditions for ourselves. With Charlotte facing him in profile screen-right, Robert faces the camera and begins to speak. "Je t'aime," he says, three times, the words inaudible, so that we are obliged to watch the lips move. As we watch, anxious not to miss anything, we find ourselves forming the words, imagining more pointedly what it feels like to say "I love you" to the married woman, and responding to the anticipated "I love you, too." The words, of course, can hardly inspire confidence in the truthfulness of sentiments therein expressed, but they do address a terminal insight: namely, that the code is all we have, that we may think to evade or negate it without altering the simple fact. Not perfect efficacy but modest approximation to the common sense of things as known is what we are enjoined to aim at.

For Godard, then, proof is out of the question. If we want to learn that things are as they are, we shall have to accept that the means of establishing truth and falsehood are customarily limited. Every imaginative excursion is bounded by necessity, itself a fiction we maintain to ensure that we have some place to return to when we remember how temporary are the satisfactions of setting out on one's own. It is good to know there is a generally acceptable way of doing or saying something, even as we are encouraged to feel our own way is likely to be better. Charlotte and her friends do not know how to sustain that tension, and it is a great pity no one has taken the trouble to teach them. Godard is no moralist, but there is a moral dimension in his film discourse which we cannot overlook. If he grants his characters the liberty, in the words of Georges Bataille, "to go at some given moment to the limits of one's possibilities," he insists they maintain as well some plausible lucidity about the restraints built into their expressive projects. Godard's respect for his medium explains by inference what his characters fail to achieve in their own melancholy lives. The moral dimension is invoked in the film as a failure of lucidity, without which it is impossible to speak seriously of one's freedom, indeed, of one's status as a responsible moral agent. On the way out of their temporary apartment, Charlotte and Robert remember his having parked his car illegally. She fears he'll get a ticket, but Robert assures her that he knows how to "kill it." She reports her husband's doubts about getting away with such things, but Robert insists that "there are ways." This is more than sociological observation, though less than straightforward moral commentary. The insight, overdetermined by its intersection with many parallel details in the film, suggests quite simply that it is hard to know what to think or to do when violations of ordinary standards become common practice. Ethical conduct is bound to lose its meaning under such conditions. It is not certain therefore that people will be worse than they ever were, only that they will be hard put to judge or to estimate the consequences of what they do. If there is always a way to fix things, we need not take them seriously. Forbidden violations have only to do with failures of self-concern, and the narcissistic preenings of the married woman before mirrors and slick identity come-ons may be said to elaborate a cultural norm. Efforts to obstruct or to compete with these random violations and innocent preenings are likely to seem quixotic, and Godard's camera eye readily attests to the attraction exerted by those, like Charlotte, who don't think they ought ever to pay a fine or study a ticket.

The married woman as ingenue is not, in the abstract, an enticing idea, but Godard can't help smiling in her direction all the same. She may not be a responsible agent, but she has a fine pair of legs and makes her way in the urban landscape with a minimum of complaint and unseemly spiritual malaise. She is in some very fundamental way a naif, and she belongs: These alone may recommend her to Godard. In the face of Charlotte's projected image, her pretty voice, slender body, and coolly willful indifference to all but immediate promise and provocation, the viewer is likely to feel his own knees buckle more than once. It is only the gift of analysis and explanation that enables what resistance we can come by. *The Married Woman* succeeds as a work of art because it provides its own analytic framework and encourages us to resist versions of the truth which propose an idea of reality without any viable means to judge it. Though not a model for every aesthetic project, Godard's film indicates the necessary working out of a vision on the level at which its issues are posited. *The Married Woman* is neither proof nor inexorable demonstration because the conditions for establishing the truth of any case have, in Godard's vision of contemporaneity, to be continuously rediscovered.

Feminism
and Film

The woman's movement in the United States has "arrived" in a
variety of ways it would be foolish to ignore or to condescend to. In
subjecting to severe scrutiny our most stable assumptions about
the life and structure of our institutions, movement spokeswomen
have encouraged us to think seriously about matters many of us
were not anxious to consider. Though we may not always be grateful for such encouragement, most of us will agree that thinking
about sex roles, image management, and the like is not apt to
impoverish our lives. If we grow increasingly self-conscious about
the things we do in our families, about the words we use when we
refer to our spouses or try to describe their professional status, if,
finally, communication with members of the opposite sex becomes
on occasion more difficult than some of us remember it having
been, we feel all the same that there may be good reason for it all.

It is not easy to be so generous about certain feminist critics and
the stuff they've been turning out in recent years. A large number
of literary women in the academy have turned to the writing of
feminist criticism, clearly conceived as a tool of the larger movement which addresses itself to the condition and experience of
women in every corner of the culture. No one seems to be sure just
what feminist criticism is, or may be supposed to accomplish, but it
has attracted sufficient numbers of enthusiasts and willing practitioners as to assume the dimensions of a major cultural industry, with
its own magazines, special-studies programs, and so on. It has, at
the same time, mounted an assault on established literary institu-

From *Partisan Review*, Fall 1976.

tions that is intended to call into question their domination by "male" standards, and to elbow some room for the consideration of issues which more orthodox members of the profession once considered irrelevant or, at best, extra-literary. That feminist criticism has produced a number of important works for which most of us are grateful is not in question. What remains problematic is the claim that we now have a developed feminist aesthetic by means of which we may think seriously about works of art and the kinds of experience art enables. The limitations of works which purport to do the things that a feminist aesthetic should be able to do make many of us wonder whether feminist criticism has the promising future its adherents anticipate.

Feminism proposes to "raise consciousness," alter outworn identity-images, and enlarge the range of life-choices available to women. Feminist criticism proposes to enhance the prospect for these changes by demonstrating new ways in which to approach a text. It is nothing so simple as persistent concern for the lives of women characters that feminist critics urge upon their constituencies—all sorts of conventional critics in this century have focused upon the plight of women in books without in any sense contriving to produce a feminist criticism. What distinguishes ordinary books and articles about women from much feminist writing is the feminist insistence on asking more or less the same questions of every work and demanding ideologically satisfactory answers to those questions as a means of evaluating it. Whether the work at hand be *Paradise Lost* or *Emma* or a Sam Peckinpah western, the essential questions asked will have to do with the status of women characters, the author/director's attitude to these women, and the degree in which role-relations as depicted allow readers/audiences to think of women as the feminists want us to. If the work at hand is an accredited masterpiece, like Milton's poem, it may be possible to make allowances for the poet's barbarous distortions of women, such as they are, without entirely dismissing the poem—the task for the feminist here will be to point out Milton's failures, his ideological retrogressions, and to put up the various warning signs around the body of the text that will permit otherwise innocent readers to penetrate it without being harmed by the ideological contagion. The prevalent attitude in such criticism is a blend of condescension and amused tolerance towards the liabilities of genius.

Where the work at hand is not, or not yet, an accredited masterpiece, the tone of the criticism is likely to be more belligerent. It is little matter to the feminist critic in such circumstances whether the author of the work at hand slandered all women, some women, one woman, or whether the deficiencies of his women are a function of his insight into the dynamics of culture. Whatever the case, the feminist critic is apt to be contemptuous and dismissive of the work in general, casting a derisive glance at the unavoidable felicities of the work as well, as though they constituted proof of the author's attempt to dexterously conceal his attitudes to women, or to make those attitudes seem less important than they are. If, in *The Bostonians*, Henry James drew caricatures of women, he will be subject to the same strenuous disapprobation he would have warranted had his male characters in the book not also been treated as caricatures. The intention and texture of the work are of marginal importance finally for those whose almost exclusive preoccupation is with ideological condemnation and the imperatives of correctness.

A correct work, in the view of many feminist critics, is one which portrays women as potentially independent and creative beings who, despite what the culture has done to them in the name of this and that, will never be satisfied with the role stereotypes typically promoted. Books and films which provide a persuasive representation of what life has been for most women, but which do not suggest how profoundly dissatisfied they have been, are reactionary and, by definition, unrealistic. While feminist critics concede that most women have been all too adaptable to normative conventions which injure them emotionally and unnecessarily limit their growth, they argue that simple, even moving representation of such adaptation falsifies the genuine reality of women's lives by failing to reflect the possibilities they might have realized had they been conscious of the actual choices. Considerably more vicious, in the feminist view, are works in which women characters fail to adapt but, in failing, achieve nothing but unhappiness and more or less permanent disaffection from the stable norms of their culture. No matter that, in fact, only quite exceptional people do manage to feel satisfied and to grow despite their having refused to adapt and to moderate their demands. Correct works may acknowledge the norms, but will stress that there are people in this world who are ready to resist, and who become all the more appealing, to themselves and to us, in the degree that they elude comfortable solutions.

What I am suggesting is not only that much feminist criticism is characterized by ideological inflexibility but that it deliberately encourages and is itself suffused by wishful thinking of a pernicious sort. This has nothing to do with the legitimate, sometimes extravagant demands feminists in general are inclined to make. Their demands may, or may not, in given instances, be viable. Feminist criticism, though, insists that works of art are not entitled to our love and admiration unless they tell us what we want to hear— unless, that is, they serve the cause of liberation. That this has little in common with serious Marxist criticism, for example, should be perfectly clear, though the rhetoric of militant feminist criticism may temporarily obscure the distinction. We know that Walter Benjamin's Marxism could accommodate Proust and Kafka as well as Brecht, and that Lukács, for all his rigidity, could make use of a reactionary like Balzac and of a high bourgeois like Mann without doing violence to the subtlety and texture of their work. In fact Lukács was as militant politically as any of the feminist critics with whom I'm familiar, which is to say that he could not for a moment forget the ideological imperatives to which his Marxism committed him. At the same time, he recognized the futility of laboring to extract from a work what was only marginally present in it, or of elaborating a response based primarily on the conclusive attitudes or opinions attributable to its author. That Balzac's women were types, at least in part, was important to notice, as it was important to consider the various punishments Balzac contrived to visit upon characters who behaved in ways of which he disapproved. One could not, in Lukács's view, go on from such considerations to indict Balzac for failing to draw the proper conclusions, or for failing to paint in vivid colors the utter demise of institutions whose weaknesses he'd indicated, albeit without any hint of an intention to promote revolutionary aspirations. For many feminist critics, the failure of artists like Balzac to arrive at proper conclusions and to explicitly reject the existence of character types functionally required by the male-dominated institutions of advanced capitalism is unforgivable, humanly and aesthetically reactionary. The view of literary creation implicit in all of this is that the best writers necessarily have what current fashion takes to be the best ideas and opinions, that these ideas take hold of writers before they conceive their creative projects, and direct their efforts. Qualities of temperament and will are ignored or entirely discounted.

Many observers in the last fifty years or so have remarked the "scandalous" fact that most great writers since the French Revolution have been conservative. Few, though, have drawn from their observations the necessary conclusion: that there is something about literature, and film as well, that almost demands that this be the case. The argument has been made very well by Fredric Jameson, whose work on Lukács, Benjamin, Sartre, and other Marxian theorists has instructed many of us in the subtleties of dialectic.* In an essay entitled "On Politics and Literature" (*Salmagundi*, no. 7, Spring 1968), Jameson writes:

> But the very source of literature's intensity lies precisely in its contact with Being. To work at all, to have any kind of effect, the literary work has to have a kind of density to it, a kind of solidity and massive quality; whatever else a novel sets out to do, it has to evoke a feeling of permanence and continuity, of place, of stability in its objects. So in this respect, the conservative evidently has the advantage over the radical, for it is precisely his specialty to linger lovingly over things as they are, to delight in their individuality, in even those flaws and blemishes that lend them a certain character and distinctiveness. The conservative is not likely to ignore Being itself, as imperfect as it may be, for a mere abstract idea. His orientation is not toward the future, but towards the present, and particularly towards that kind of cyclical, repetitive present, that kind of recurrence of habit and custom, to which the past lends a supplementary depth. And yet that kind of time is in many ways the privileged time of the novel itself.

Now none of this is to say that writers may not entertain political positions approved by most readers of good books. In our time, for example, a writer may protest American policy in Central America while cultivating the sentiment of Being extolled by Jameson. The writer's views may have nothing or very little to do with what appears in his novel or film, though, if he is politically *engagé*, the work may accurately reflect his political *interests*. Jameson mentions political novels by writers like Dostoyevski, Flaubert, James, and Conrad, and observes that "in these books, over and over again the same point is made: radicals are abstract, they don't know and don't love life, indeed they resent it, they love ideas only, and they tend to do irreparable damage to those around them . . . It is the novel as a form which speaks through this anti-revolutionary passion, and which thus expresses its intolerance for the abstract, for the disembodied, for the pure idea, unless it is turned to ridicule."

*See his *Marxism and Form* (Princeton, 1971).

Feminist criticism typically insists that women are not what they seem, or have seemed, and that works cultivating a sentiment of Being invariably betray a commitment to what is oppressive and unjust. The proper business of the novel or film is to move beyond all received images and convictions, to fashion a profile of human experience in the image of our collective political desire. This desire is of necessity oriented towards a future for which there is no conclusive or generally accepted design. At the same time, thoughtful and enlightened middle-class people are supposed to have a very good idea of what may not be tolerated in this future. Among the primary targets of the common derision will be ambivalence about the goal of liberation itself, or uncertainty about the effects of liberationist politics upon the creation of works of art and the respect for nuance and precision in ordinary discourse. Told, by Jameson or some other predictably "male" theorist, that "it is the novel as a form" which resists a programmatic and largely future-oriented approach to difficult issues, feminist critics may contend that the novel is itself a tool of oppression, and will continue to clamor for a final and unanswerable rebuke to the entire tradition. It will not matter to such critics that they are imposing impossible demands upon works of art. So long as they believe that there are more or less inflexible standards of correctness which apply to works of art, and that these standards have largely to do with ideological content or the inspirational potential of various character types, they will turn a deliberately deaf ear to skeptical reproaches which they take to reflect an elitist or explicitly chauvinist bias.

Nothing more perfectly illustrates the accuracy of Jameson's observations, and the relative impoverishment of much feminist criticism, than recent feminist approaches to the art of film. Everyone knows, of course, that films do not unfold and claim our attention exactly as novels do. Indeed, gifted writers like Siegfried Kracauer and Walter Benjamin were assiduous to suggest that films have their own laws, their own dynamics, and that their emergence to prominence in our time has to do with a great deal more than the technology that facilitates their creation and distribution. Nevertheless, it is clear that films and novels have a great deal in common, and that comparisons of modernist masterpieces like Joyce's *Ulysses* to Godard's experiments in film serve both media exceptionally well.* What is more, most film critics, even those determined to

*See Norman Silverstein, "Movie-going for Lovers of *The Waste Land* and *Ulysses*," *Salmagundi*, no. 1, Fall 1965.

make a case for the uniqueness of film, customarily treat movies as they do novels, that is to say, in terms of plot, theme, characterization, plausibility, point of view, pacing, richness of texture, scope of interest, and so on.

Avowedly feminist film critics are no different in this sense from their less political colleagues in the profession. In fact, they attack films much as elementary critics of the novel do, by isolating for analysis various passages in the text and constructing an argument whose persuasiveness largely depends upon the representativeness of the passages selected and the demonstrated viability of the persisting analytic perspective. The last thing such critics will allow is a playful relation to the text, an approach that takes its critical function as an opportunity to be speculative about a whole range of questions and images without demanding a dismissive or otherwise patently judgmental response. By contrast we have only to think of the best criticism of a Susan Sontag, who writes usually of films or novels or essays she admires, whether or not she approves unequivocally of everything they "say" or of the various uses to which they may be put. Sontag's approach to ideas and works of art dwells always upon their resistance to easy encapsulation of any kind. Where the given work lends itself too readily to the categorical usages of political or ethical opportunists, Sontag becomes suspicious, and works to retrieve from the body of the work that irreducible complexity, that complicated essence which finally cannot be handled in any predictable way. Like the writers Jameson discusses, Sontag's object has been to see the works at hand in their own terms, and to suggest a variety of contexts to reveal what they are.

Feminist film critics typically hold that the vision of the film ought necessarily to encourage audiences to reconceive their lives, and to recommend how this might practicably be arranged. Just so, the feminist film critic will herself tell us what films ought to have done, and how we can make proper use of them once we've determined to say *no* to negative portrayals of women, such as we find in most American and European films. In this view, there is a neat congruence between one's abstract ideas and one's capacity to embody them and direct the course of their unfolding. Genuine dialecticians, like Jameson and Sontag, accordingly, are disappointing to the feminists, for they fail to follow through with the tenacity and single-mindedness of those who are properly committed. That is, they refuse to assert a range of primary political and moral truths which will determine their responses to phenomena of every kind.

Good film criticism, in this view, always knows what it wants the film in question to do, and the critic's capacity to articulate his demands has the special merit of putting him "on the firing line," "up front," where liberated people invariably belong.

Neither Jameson nor Sontag would ever demand that the work of criticism, or the work of art, refuse to express the convictions or personal sentiments of its author. Such expression would be at best a secondary feature or premise of the work, however, and would in no sense strictly control the discourse to ensure the prevention and elimination of ideologically retrogressive elements. Both understand that works of art, and the best works of criticism as well, frequently assume a life and momentum of their own which has very little to do with the particular views or wishes of their authors; also, that we frequently know we are in the presence of a first-rate mind by observing the degree in which it resists its own judgments, and discovers with great difficulty what it hadn't thought to find at all. These are qualities of dialectical thinking which we find in great writers, including some with radical political sentiments, like Stendhal or Brecht. Of such men Jameson observes:

> It seems to me that if we were called upon to pass judgment on the revolutionary quality of these writers, we should tend to be just a little suspicious of them. They describe capitalism with too much gusto; the process of making money fascinates them even more than it disgusts them; and instead of showing the alienation of the human being beneath the capitalist, they tend to lay emphasis on his energy, on his slyness, and cunning . . . they seem to have become a little too mesmerized by the existing order, by Being itself.

What we have, Jameson contends, is a "visceral fascination with what they (radical writers) hold intellectually loathsome."

The work of art, then, is very likely to develop according to laws dictated less by the artist's specific ideas than by his sensibility. In similar ways, the critical discourse, if it has any dialectical subtlety at all, will result from a careful working through of details in the selected texts, in a process which allows for the critic's sympathetic attention to his internal experience of the structures uncovered. The phenomenon that calls itself feminist criticism is too often based upon a misreading of its own function as criticism and a misrepresentation of the dynamics of works of art. The problems are usefully concentrated in a book by Joan Mellen entitled *Women* *and Their Sexuality in the New Film.** I shall say at once that it is an awful book, and that it has done considerable damage. It has been praised by a variety of feminists and academics, and is widely distributed in an inexpensive paperback edition. Moreover, Mellen knows how to write and has read just enough Freud, Marx, and Reich to sound like she knows what she's talking about. Alas, her book indicates that a little learning is as dangerous as some have said it is.

But let us consider what Mellen has to say. Her original object was to discover in contemporary films "a new perception of women which assumes their capacities and value." Disappointed in this goal, she wishes in her book to examine the various "negative" images of women projected in recent films, and to urge upon filmmakers and filmgoers a liberationist discipline that will create a new kind of film informed by "a new perception of women." This is not the place to go into all of the assumptions underlying Mellen's approach, but surely we can pick at one or two. First, and most obviously, there is the theory of "negative" images. In Mellen's view, these include most generally "patronizing and hostile portrayal[s] of women as flawed creatures." What, we may wonder, is a patronizing and hostile portrayal? It may be, in the feminist's judgment, any one of a number of things: the image of a hard-driving and professionally successful career woman who is, as a result of her ambition, denied more intimate satisfactions; or the portrait of an "empty, disintegrated and alienated" young woman, "a part played frequently in recent years by Karen Black," Mellen tells us; or finally, the image of the mildly repressed and cautiously accommodating figure whose attractiveness for men is a function of her posing fewer emotional threats than her liberated sisters. For each of these, and other types of the patronizing and hostile portrayal of women, Mellen has several examples ready to hand. Most of these are drawn from films familiar to people with an interest in cinema, and are therefore easily reevaluated in light of Mellen's analysis. The theory has it that a negative image vividly impressed is not a recognizable portrait of a human being. Any representation of women as flawed or otherwise unhappy people who fail to respond to their situations with anything less than militant *and effectual* rage will tend to enforce acquiescence in that status as a given of the feminine condition itself. Since we know, or

*Horizon, 1973; Dell, 1975.

so the argument runs, that there is nothing in femininity itself which requires that women be unhappy or passive or repressed or alienated, why should filmmakers represent them as such? Why not show them as vital, positive, integrated? To do so will be not only ideologically correct but realistic, for as all decent people know, real human beings may always shape their lives in accordance with conscious desires.

The theory is feeble on many grounds:

(1) It is notoriously imprecise. That is, it makes no distinction between an intention to exalt women, albeit for "incorrect" reasons, and an intention to demean them, for the same reasons. A critical approach to serious films would need to draw such distinctions very carefully indeed to do justice to the complexity and ambivalence of feelings and structures of consciousness illuminated in the film. Consider, briefly, Eric Rohmer's masterpiece *My Night at Maud's*, a film Mellen treats with some tolerance, even grudging admiration. The film's protagonist is a male, but he moves between two life alternatives vividly embodied by women, one Maud, the other Francoise. Mellen wants Jean-Louis to select Maud, but he chooses Francoise instead. What's wrong with Francoise? She is the type of the mildly repressed and cautiously accommodating figure mentioned above. Though pretty, she's in no sense as dazzlingly beautiful as Maud, and her imagination is limited and sluggish by comparison with the older woman's. Where Maud is openly sensual and challenging, Francoise is rather timid and old-fashionedly introspective. Though as a student she can aim at all sorts of professional goals, Francoise has decided to be a lab technician; Maud, by contrast, is a doctor.

Mellen's approach to the film proposes that Rohmer's vision inevitably demeans women by demonstrating that they will remain unhappy, like Maud, unless they are strenuously unimpressive. In her terms, "the cultural ideal, the blonde, coy, mindless coquette is placed beside an intellectual, witty woman, capable of humor and irony, but unappealing to the hero for her very independence and unique sense of self." We shall overlook the simple fact that Rohmer's blonde is neither coy nor a mindless coquette, and that, where coyness and coquetry are concerned, Maud has few equals in recent cinema. The important point is that Rohmer's intention is neither to exalt nor to demean women in general, or the character of Francoise in particular. That his male protagonist should decide to marry her is entirely appropriate given Jean-Louis's temperament and predilections. Had he determined to pursue Maud he'd have discovered in time that he was no match for her, that no matter how carefully she treated him he'd have felt overpowered, pressed beyond his capacities to try to say what he meant and express what he felt. Rohmer's project has nothing to do with the elaboration of a model woman, an entirely positive character type. In the vision of his film, Maud is an appealing and extraordinary person, but her unusual strengths suggest she may have difficulty in personal relations, in the way that extraordinary persons frequently do. To indicate as much is not therefore to recommend we avoid such people, or give up emulating them. Rohmer's sensibility is generous and playful in its willingness to entertain various possibilities and to look at liabilities associated with any given choice or character. His idea of them is no more important to the film than their experience of themselves. Both Maud and Francoise know who they are and have some notion of what they may expect from life. Neither would be pleased to emblematize the hope and future prospects of the sex.

(2) The theory assumes that represented flaws in women characters who are successfully realized cinematically will stand out from the body of the films and draw the viewer to dwell morbidly upon feminine disabilities. Thus Mellen's contempt for "the familiar posture of the delighting pessimist." We are reminded at this point of what Fredric Jameson called the "visceral fascination" artists frequently experience in the presence of the "intellectually loathsome." The question is, what effect does this fascination have on the structure of the work and the experience of the viewer? Take the Karen Black character Rayette in the American film *Five Easy Pieces*. Mellen is offended by her, and clearly feels that no self-respecting, liberated person would bring himself to create such a figure. Now there is no doubt that Rayette is a repellent figure, but her role is drawn with such force and detail, and played with such animation and conviction by Ms. Black, that we do not for a moment want her any other way. Though she allows herself to be abused, discounted, mocked by her lover, though the filmmaker misses no chance to make her a ridiculous working-class piece of ass, she is a successfully realized figure whose presence in the film is essential to its dominant thrust. Does the filmmaker like Rayette? The question is, in this case and most others like it, beside the point. What he has to like about Rayette is the occasion she provides for a display of wit and the elaboration of a striking character profile. He likes too the way Rayette can be played off against other characters, providing comic relief in otherwise tense circumstances, or pointing up by contrast

the relative abstractness of more intellectually impressive figures, the quite different though no less striking ways in which they too are "alienated" from any genuine sense of who they are.

The filmmaker, then, is drawn to Rayette on behalf of the color, variety, and wit she enables. But it is clear that there is also a "visceral fascination" with Rayette as the incarnation of what is "intellectually loathsome." She has no self-respect. She is content to be a sexual object as long as her basic need to have and hold a man is served by her erotic attraction. She is entirely without cultivation, and without that sensitivity to nuance and irony which we moderns consider exemplary in mature adults. Though she knows how to moan and complain, she does so crudely, with conspicuous indecorum. At the same time, Rayette is a recognizable human being, in the brutishness of her stratagems, the earnestness of her entreaties, and the hideous impoverishment of her imagination. She is, for all her repellent qualities, a particular instance of the thing itself, and the filmmaker is taken with her, precisely as we are, for the range of feelings and thoughts she alone can liberate in him. There is an unmistakable pleasure we take in observing Rayette, even when she is grossly mistreated, for there is in each of us an inarticulate conviction that one so defenseless deserves what she gets. All the more strongly, therefore, do we resent her lover when he steps beyond the limits of "reasonable" mistreatment, and feel stirred to take her part when she is condescended to late in the film by people who have no idea what such a person may have seen and felt.

This is not the place to dwell at length on a single film or character, but it seems to me essential that we see what many feminist critics will not, whether in *Five Easy Pieces* or other films. Whatever the represented flaws in a particular character, if the film is worth our attention the visceral fascination we feel for her will not ensure that we acquiesce in her condition. A major object of criticism will be to discover what relation the character bears to other characters in the film, and in what degree she is essential to the structure of the work as a whole. In the case of *Five Easy Pieces*, to deplore the presence of Rayette in the film is to refuse to see how many *different* feelings and thoughts she evokes, and how well the filmmaker has drawn the cultural matrix of which she is an integral part. If Rayette is a pathetic and hopeless figure at whom it is possible to laugh, it is not an unqualified or glib laughter she provokes. We do not, in the end, take her for granted, though we know that serious engagement of issues that affect her is beyond her, and will have to be urged upon more competent individuals. What makes Rayette what she is, is not the simple fact that she is a woman, but that she is a particular *kind* of woman in a culture better equipped to satisfy other kinds. The density of the film's imagined universe is a function of its resistance to the feminist call for willed transcendence, and to other similar demands.

(3) The theory assumes that "a new perception of women" is self-evidently useful and progressive, and that right-thinking people will agree upon an ideological framework in which to structure just such a perception. The issue here is of course much larger than a limited concern with movies and the demands made upon them by feminist critics, but it is not therefore something we ought to neglect. Briefly put, some feminist critics suppose that in the current state of our culture there can be no rational disagreement on key issues, attitudes to which have as a consequence become almost canonically prescriptive. Thus, like most other forward-looking people, Mellen sneers with knowing disdain at "Catholic doctrine itself which values obedience above individual judgment and the appeal to spontaneous emotion." Old-fashioned characters, in this view, have nothing to teach us, and simplicity of conviction is mere simplemindedness.

Feminist critics usually find most deplorable any work of art which promotes, no matter how complexly and ambivalently, an idea of women as biologically rooted and therefore limited creatures. This is not surprising, since, if we are to have "a new perception of women," we shall need to believe that there is nothing unalterable, nothing biologically inherent in them, aside from their capacity to carry children. Film directors who suggest that women may suffer because of instinctual drives which at the same time it may not be in their interests to resist or refuse to acknowledge become enemies of enlightenment, of the emergent brave new world. That is why the great Swedish filmmaker Ingmar Bergman has become anathema to so many feminists, including Mellen, who devotes a large part of her book to an attack on his work. Bergman is far from a biological or Freudian reductionist, but he does insist upon the significance, *not the primacy*, of instinct and of various intransigent fixations which no amount of cultural engineering and consciousness raising will inevitably affect. An apologist for no ideological position explicitly demeaning to women, Bergman's portraits of confused, anxious, sometimes self-consuming women nonetheless make him a target for those who see in these portraits what Mellen calls "a repellent biological frailty."

What, we may justly ask, is the particular status of the feminist objection to the idea of biology, or of instinctual disposition? Insofar as it is founded upon nothing but the will to deny the validity of explanations that depend upon such factors, it may be said to fly in the face of ordinary experience itself. Sontag and a number of other writers have taken up this point, and descried the attempt to dismiss the concrete stuff of historical and present-day experience as if it were so much "epiphenomenal trash."* It is true enough that women may usefully be encouraged to undertake projects ordinarily restricted in previous times to men, but it is ridiculous to deny that there may be special consequences owing to this recent encouragement, or that these consequences will have something to do with the organic, instinctual, chemical dispositions of women. Elizabeth Hardwick laid out the terms of the argument with impeccable clarity and wit long before the current feminist movement took definitive shape: ". . . a woman's physical inferiority to a man is a limiting reality every moment of her life. Because of it women are 'doomed' to situations that promise reasonable safety against the more hazardous possibilities of nature . . . and against the stronger man. Any woman who has ever had her wrist twisted by a man recognizes a fact of nature as humbling as a cyclone to a frail tree branch. How can *anything* be more important than this?"† Similarly, Hardwick goes on to argue, though it is stupid to claim that their sexual appetites are the same as men's in intensity or persistence, women " 'fight very hard' to get the amount of sexual satisfaction they want—and even harder to keep men from forcing a superabundance their way. It is difficult to see how anyone can be sure that it is only man's voracious appetite for conquest which has created, as its contrary, this reluctant, passive being who has to be wooed, raped, bribed, begged, threatened, married and supported. Perhaps she really has to be." Just as likely, of course, women will differ among themselves as to what constitutes satisfactory levels

---

*See Adrienne Rich and Susan Sontag, "Feminism and Fascism: An Exchange," *The New York Review of Books,* March 30, 1975.

†See "The Subjection of Women" in Hardwick's *A View of My Own* (Farrar, Straus & Cudahy, 1962).

of accommodation to the surrounding "male" reality, but it is clear that feminist criticism will need to establish a less willful and dismissive relation to the idea of inherited disposition if it is to make any sense of our shared experience.

Where an artist like Bergman is concerned, of course, any one-dimensional political approach is likely to do grave violence to the textured complexity of the work. Thus a feminist critic like Molly Haskell* can tell us that "any criticism of Bergman must be prefaced with the understanding that he, more than any other director . . . , took women seriously . . . , never thought of them as second-class citizens . . . and watched over the film-birth and blossoming and development of one extraordinary woman after another," only to devalue most of Bergman's efforts in favor of the most embarrassing and insipid film he ever made, *The Touch*. Why? Because the film is ideologically acceptable within the terms of a feminist perspective. Its heroine, a role played with customary artistry by Bibi Andersson, is in every sense an active, thoroughly modern woman. Better yet, she is not one of those standard middle-aged, middle-class wives whose husbands leave them, but a standard middle-aged, middle-class wife who leaves her husband for a wild sexual fling with—god forbid—a Jewish intellectual manqué played with no distinction at all by Elliot Gould. Good for her, Haskell wants to shout—anything but a "wholesome, antiseptic, normal married life" involving the unnatural suppression of "rude and bloody passions." It is not that Haskell has no right to her opinions, but that she has insisted upon looking at Bergman's film as a text holding a brief for a particular view of women. Had she looked at the film as an aesthetic structure with a range of plural intentions she'd have seen that it is unable to elaborate its own images and insights satisfactorily, precisely because Bergman does not believe in his central female figure. It is not merely that he doesn't entirely approve of her behavior, but that she moves in a universe alien to his, in a hollow, insubstantial ethical dimension with none of the terrible density and weight we associate with Bergman's work. The film reflects what Haskell's ideology prevents her from observing: the filmmaker's attempt to come to terms with the progressivist, liberationist milieu of the leisure-time audiences who writhe in delighted ecstasies of vicarious pleasure-pain before each of his films. Bergman's film is no simple examination of

*See *From Reverence to Rape* (Holt, Rinehart & Winston, 1974; Penguin, 1974).

mass culture and its insatiable hungers; it is a deliberate and largely unsuccessful capitulation to it. Bergman will not, surely, make another film of this sort.

What Haskell does with Bergman's poorest film is modest indeed by comparison with Mellen's treatment of his work in general. But the point here is not to suggest that any one feminist critic can represent all of the things that feminist critics have done. It is to suggest, rather, that feminist criticism is too often disfigured by the kinds of assumptions and procedures we have examined. If we are to have a credible feminist aesthetic that can compete with other serious theoretical and critical perspectives, the feminist critics will themselves have to address the objections I have cited with a rigor few have demonstrated thus far in their transactions with works of art or in their debates with opponents.

Bergman
and Women

In 1968 I published in the pages of *Salmagundi* (issue no. 8) my own essay on Ingmar Bergman's film *Persona*. Subtitled "An Essay on Tragedy," the piece took a rather special, some would say resolutely uncinematic, approach to Bergman's film. In fact, though I'd write a rather different piece if I had it to do again, I think it stands up well enough, and that recent studies of the film don't do much better in accounting for its unusual power and mysterious fascination.

At the same time, I have been approached by several feminist friends and colleagues, especially in the last year or so, and taken to task for my failure in the essay to think even a little about the implications of *Persona* for a feminist consciousness. Indeed, this failure has been described as symptomatic of a larger failure on my part to face up to Bergman's troubling attitudes toward women in general, so that in my various lectures and courses on Bergman I tend to dismiss out of hand suggestions that such attitudes may compromise the integrity of his art. I don't think I have had a bad conscience about all this, but I have been for some time plotting a response that would do justice at once to Bergman, to my feminist friends, and to my own sense of critical probity. What follows is a brief attempt to go on record on an issue that has not yet received proper scrutiny, though large claims have been made and critical abuses have been meanly tolerated. If I speak in the first person, I do so merely for the sake of convenience, and as I move steadily away from my earlier essay's focus on *Persona*, the reader is invited to apply my remarks, where legitimate, to any number of other works and artists who have been badly treated by feminist critics.

From *Salmagundi*, Winter 1978.

In my essay on *Persona* I speak frequently of "Oedipus, Lear, Hamlet, and Bergman's nurse," as though in describing any one of them one inevitably described the others. To a certain extent this remains a valid assumption. So long as one's object is to establish *Persona* as a modern instance of classical tragedy by associating it with distinguished predecessors in the tradition, the methodology would seem unassailable. But if one wishes also to consider a variety of other possible responses to the film, whatever their relative merits, one discovers things that may have seemed unimaginable. Perhaps connections are less clear than one supposed when the idea of tragedy dominated one's thoughts. It never occurred to me to take seriously the suggestion that Bergman was interested specifically in *women* when he made *Persona;* that, for example, he made the psychiatrist in the film a woman because he wanted to present a series of feminine typologies. Nor did I think much about the erotic component in *Persona* as a commentary on female sexuality or the shifting self-images of women; in fact, I paid such notions no more heed than I would have had the focus of my study been *Electra* rather than *Persona.*

It isn't easy to defend certain decisions of this order. If a student in a film course insists that there is an unmistakable erotic impact in *Persona,* that eroticism plays a strong part in several episodes, I must respond with my sense of how particular episodes work. First, I have to concede that it matters if the erotic component is as developed as my young student insists. After all, if Alma's attraction to Elisabeth Vogler is fundamentally erotic, we shall have to explain all sorts of things differently. A crude Freudian reading, for example, would claim that Alma becomes brutal towards Mrs. Vogler to mask from herself the overwhelming, and forbidden, erotic attraction. If there is any truth at all in this insight, though, it is clear to me that Bergman is not at all interested in it, that he has done nothing to make it important. Alma is no Dora, and Mrs. Vogler is hardly a Frau K., though the Freudian case does superficially suggest a possible paradigm. Such associationism is little better than inspired daydreaming.

But where are the erotic components in *Persona* to be found? If you're looking you can find them almost anywhere. One of the images projected in the film's opening sequence is a close-up of a vagina, but it is succeeded so rapidly by a title and a very different image that the eye only minimally registers what it has seen. Joan Mellen locates the eroticism elsewhere: "In their first encounter Mrs. Vogler grabs Alma's arm: the gesture describes their future relationship."* In fact it describes nothing of the sort. The actress desperately grabs Alma's arm to get her to turn off the radio which is broadcasting a play the lines of which remind Mrs. Vogler of her own terrible circumstances.

Later in the film, of course, Mrs. Vogler's letter speculates that Alma is perhaps a little bit in love with her, in a "charming" way, but the insight as such is less than definitive, and may be said to indicate the actress's refusal to acknowledge a rather more important, more enduring mode of influence she has come to exert on her nurse. A number of visual impressions would perhaps seem to contradict my view, and there is no point in simply ignoring them. Alma does become very wrapped up in her tale of late adolescent orgy, and the recitation of the details does inevitably *involve* the viewer in an almost physical if also somewhat uncomfortable way. The actress, though, is totally unmoved by the tale, though she listens attentively to it as to virtually everything else Alma tells her. She expresses emotion only when Alma breaks down and weeps over the perversity of human appetite and clings to Mrs. Vogler for comfort. In that same extended episode Alma tells her companion that she's never felt quite this way before, and looks at Elisabeth with an obvious affection that confuses her more than she can say. None of this quite prepares us for the dream that follows, in which Mrs. Vogler enters Alma's room, a room taken over by fog and weirdly illuminated as by some unearthly light. It is this scene in particular that confuses viewers of the film, who do not know any better than Alma whether it is dream or reality. Since the two women are scantly attired in silken nightgowns, since Elisabeth puts one arm around Alma and Alma's head comes to rest on Elisabeth's shoulder, many have assumed they were witness to erotic embrace. In fact, though, there is nothing like culmination to this embrace, at any point in the film. The photography itself, the grainy texture of the image, indicates that we are looking at a dream. The figures themselves do not kiss or collapse onto Alma's bed. They turn towards the camera lens in an almost stately way and together move towards us. The gesture in which Elisabeth gently lifts Alma's hair back off her forehead to reveal a brow remarkably resembling her own seems directed more towards the viewer, or to Bergman himself, than to either of the women. The

---

*See Joan Mellen, *Women and Their Sexuality in the New Film* (Horizon, 1973; Dell, 1975).

women, almost in trance, are showing us something, opening up a possibility which the film will go on to examine. Later, when Alma remembers the gesture, it is clearly instructive: Alma may not pretend that she is the same person originally assigned to care for the actress. She knows now that she "looks like" Elisabeth Vogler, that the two are not as different as it was once convenient to suppose they were. Neither of the two remembrances of that original dream encounter is suffused by the slightest trace of erotic feeling. Surely, as Alma prepares to put on her plain nurse's hat and to resume her role in the world near the film's conclusion, she is less than excited or titillated by the remembrance of her connection with Mrs. Vogler. It is affecting purely as an object of reflection.

There is more to this, of course, including part of a later dream in which Alma first encourages Elisabeth to suck her blood, then strikes avidly and repeatedly at Elisabeth's off-screen face until the sequence dissolves and another emerges to take its place. Some feminists have made a good deal of this and of other bloodlettings in *Persona*. The reliable Ms. Mellen again: "An oral sadism develops in Elisabeth's attraction to Alma. In one scene she hits Alma across the face making her nose bleed." I'm not actually sure what sort of oral sadism might be involved in making someone's nose bleed, but I do know that nothing of the sort is involved in *Persona*. Mrs. Vogler slaps Alma only in a moment of terrible extremity, when Alma has physically attacked her. The slap is a gesture of self-defense, not a rich psychosexual manifestation.

If, as I've suggested, it is not terribly difficult to discover what Bergman intended in *Persona*, and if sexual readings fail to account for the structure and detail of the film as a whole, why should feminist critics especially hold to their line? Perhaps because Bergman challenges, in an exemplary way, what many in the woman's movement have come to take for granted: (1) the idea that male artists rooted in paternalist cultures and generally resistant to liberationist enthusiasms are unlikely to produce satisfactory portraits of autonomous and biologically un-enslaved women; (2) the idea that in film it is necessary to define and delimit issues in a relatively explicit way in order to avoid the vague submission to generalized stereotypes which, in commercial films at least, is achieved without anyone's being able to call it by its rightful name. Thus, or so that argument usually goes, if Bergman didn't intend us to see erotic relationship in *Persona*, he should not have permitted anyone to think, even for a moment, that he had one in mind. Similarly, if Bergman wanted us to admire his woman characters, at least for what they might potentially become, he should not have drawn them as clinging, vulnerable, dependent, and susceptible to the ravages of sexual guilt and its ensuing repression. The arguments are as usual most vividly embodied in Joan Mellen's book. Consider: "Bergman's women are soiled by their animal needs and invariably hate themselves." The word "invariably" is bound to be confusing when we think of Bergman's many "positive" women who are neither "soiled" by their animal needs—which they gladly acknowledge—nor given to self-mortification. But the debate requires rather more elaborate commentary.

For a good many years Bergman had come to attract viewers of both sexes. Women responded to his films as intensely as men—or so it would seem from the various books and articles devoted to his work by woman critics. Some, like Marianne Hook,* asserted that Bergman understood women as types, that he forced them into schematic postures at once dramatically effective and humanly dubious. A well-known Swedish interviewer, a man obviously much influenced by Hook and incapable of looking at the films for himself, recently accused Bergman of "depicting the intellectual woman, the modern emancipated female, as cold and frigid and neurotic." Other critics, like Carol Brightman, saw this as nonsense, and defended even so frigid a figure as Ester in *The Silence* as a courageous portrait with no hint of sexist implication.† In *Bergman on Bergman*‡ we learn that in his original draft, "Ester was a man. Ester and Anna were man and woman. So you can't find anything there about the emancipated woman being in any way more neurotic or frigid or wrong-headed, or anything of that sort." Neither the enlightened reflections of Brightman nor the passionate denials of Bergman himself are likely to stem the tide of criticism that's been building now for several years. In the face of an ever-growing, ever more distinguished list of critical books on Bergman, the feminist attacks keep coming.

The rallying point is the stunning color film *Cries and Whispers*, which had its Swedish premiere in December 1972. A brutal and, in some ways, a disgusting film, it is also visually gorgeous in a way that would seem to belie its content. With *Cries and Whispers*

*In *Ingmar Bergman* (Stockholm, 1962).

†In *Film Quarterly*, Summer 1964.

‡Simon & Schuster, 1973.

Bergman finally made a film his detractors hoped he'd make, not glib or pretentious like one or two of the others, but cruel and coldly manipulative. Here at last were Bergman's women, several of his premiere actresses—Harriet Andersson, Ingrid Thulin, Liv Ullmann—each a grim and disturbing spectacle: one diseased and dying, another blackly malevolent and venomous, the last stupidly manipulative and, in her own ingratiating way, perfectly deadly. No need here to go too far into the film. Though no one but Bergman could have written and directed it, though it is absolutely brilliant and scathing, it does in itself seem to warrant claims that Bergman dislikes women, that he works with beautiful actresses only to mock or dissect them, that the motor energy in his vision is supplied by a species of sexual rage bordering on the pathological.

There is, it seems to me, no reason to be so categorical with an artist like Bergman, who has made many outstanding films, and has used his actors in many different roles calling for varying kinds of audience identification or disapproval. It is probably true that he needed to make *Cries and Whispers*, but Bergman can hardly be faulted for wanting to work through a long-standing problem in his relation with women in general and with his own actress-characters in particular. Briefly, what Bergman does in this very special and provoking film is to subject to ruthless scrutiny his own extravagant identification with various feminine characters. By coldly exposing them, by forcing them to have at one another and to acquiesce in the process of their own relentless humiliation, Bergman calls into question his own boundless attraction to them. For one who knows Bergman's work, who has been awed by his insistent tendency to undermine his own best sympathies and insights, to turn things on their heads when they might more easily have been left alone, *Cries and Whispers* comes as no surprise. That it is unseemly and ungenerous there can be no doubt, but Bergman has never been squeamish, and after thirty-odd films he had a right to expect more tolerance and insight from an audience he'd been assiduous to cultivate. Why should anyone have supposed Bergman would be consistently encouraging to female or male aspirations? He'd never been before, and if *Cries and Whispers* went somewhat further than previous films in scraping at the marrow of human relationships, there was no reason to assume that Bergman was taking a position on women, any more than he had in obviously "humanistic" works like *Wild Strawberries* or religious films like *The Virgin Spring*.

It is obvious to most of us that a film is more than a series of verbal structures or pictorial images, that it is as well a relation it establishes with viewers; similarly, a body of work, a whole collection of films by a single artist, is more than specific attitudes or ideas taken up in one or more of them. When we think of Bergman we must think necessarily of intonation, the timbre and range of the voice which persists through the changing focus and altogether unstable manipulation of ideas. In Bergman, after all, as with many great artists, vision is not a matter of firm positions or standing or falling on particular ideas. There is a vision, of course, and it has to do with the putting of various questions in a way that suggests they are literally matters of life and death. Not the answers to those questions but the voice that articulates and insists upon their preeminence is what constitutes the signature. Just as it is foolish to draw permanent conclusions about Bergman's convictions on the basis of a single film when there are dozens to consider, it is a mistake to probe the complex structure of an ambitious film like *Cries and Whispers* with a simple question: "How does Bergman feel about his women?" There are, believe it or not, more important questions, more important insofar as they more regularly inform the corpus as a whole and more consistently command our attention. With Bergman we are more likely to worry over the problematic relation between feeling and intellect, an issue made fresh and interesting because in the way it's projected it is obviously more than a matter of idle curiosity or a mechanism for thematizing otherwise inchoate materials. We shall be interested as well in the human status of animal need, not as a means of assigning value-points to particular characters or entire sexes, but as a means of understanding the images by which people come to know themselves and imagine their transactions with others.

A feminist concerned with Bergman's view of women and with the effects of his films on viewers of either sex may well wish to begin with an examination of animal need as it's developed in his earliest films. The inquiry may more fruitfully begin with the mature works of the mid-1950s, when Bergman had found at least some of his standard subjects and was working with a confidence previously unknown to him. Among the films to be considered are *Smiles of a Summer Night* (1955) and *Wild Strawberries* (1957), surely two enduring favorites. Both contain a variety of male and female types, and both may be said to elaborate a sustained critique of egoism, a malady in which the personality is arrested at the level of excessive preoccupation with an exclusive aspect of its own development. In both films the malady is centrally focused in a male character: Fredrik Egerman (Gunnar Björnstrand) in *Smiles*, Isak Borg (Victor Sjöström) in *Wild Strawberries*, though there are other figures who betray similar problems, including Egerman's "rival," the Count, and Borg's mother and son. Each film lovingly develops an alternative to the egoism and the attendant dislocations of function which afflict the egoists. Though one would never guess as much from the writings of Bergman's feminist critics, the corrective to the vision is in each film supplied by the presence of a remarkable, highly intelligent, and highly visible woman character: Desiree in *Smiles*, Marianne in *Wild Strawberries*. Had Mellen seen either film when she wrote that Bergman's women "invariably hate themselves"? No doubt she had, but was determined to score points with or without substantiation. Not surprisingly, male critics of Bergman with other axes to grind conveniently ignore Desiree or Marianne as well. Vernon Young's *Cinema Borealis*,* for example, discusses *Wild Strawberries* as though Marianne (Ingrid Thulin) were an insignificant walk-on, worth no more than a passing mention, when in fact she is on screen almost as much as Isak Borg and has a disproportionately large share of the film's best speeches, and draws Bergman's camera to her for one reaction shot after another.

Neither Desiree nor Marianne is soiled by animal needs. If anything, Desiree has an immoderate though never unbecoming sexual appetite which she does nothing to conceal, and Marianne's determination to have a child, to be a mother, is proudly maintained though it compromises her marriage and raises painful questions about her future in general. In fact, no one who sees these films with a discerning eye will imagine that for either woman animal need and its satisfaction are ends in themselves, any more than Bergman's need in a film like *Cries and Whispers* is a definitive put-down of women. Always in Bergman the vision of the film as a whole signals the continuing difficulty of large-scale and enduring integration, the difficulty we have in maintaining proportion, in expressing at once what we need, what we think we need, and think we ought to need. Though Desiree is without the paralyzing self-consciousness of Ester in *The Silence*, she knows that some things are more important than others, that confident decisions are likely to be rescinded at any moment for good or bad reasons, and that, if there are needs, there is also a reasonably appealing world

*Avon, 1971.

and intractable others with whom to deal, decently if at all possible. Bergman adores Desiree not because she has especially good ideas or because she is an especially kind or noble person but because she has some clear notion of what she wants, how to get it, and how far one may legitimately go in pursuit of one's desires; also because she is a beautiful woman whose carriage and demeanor bespeak a clarity of intention and relative harmony of impulse. She is, so to say, at one with herself, and though that self is capable of mischief and worse, it knows its limits; more, the satisfaction of its animals needs is plausibly related to the expression of ordinary affections and the assumption of worldly responsibilities, including the care of children.

I do not think that Bergman has ever created a more admirable character than Marianne in *Wild Strawberries*. With her we move from the limited consideration of animal need to the potential stature of women as autonomous human beings. The figure of Desiree perhaps too easily provides substance for a rejoinder to various feminist claims. With Marianne we are happily forced to develop a more refined argument, for the character is herself a good deal more complex than Desiree. Mellen claims that Bergman is "completely out of sympathy with the impulse toward liberation and autonomy." To counter the contention with Desiree is perhaps to be told that Bergman liberated her only because she has inordinate appetites and a corresponding *chutzpah* which only famous actresses and other "personalities" may conventionally command. Or perhaps Desiree succeeds in being on her own because she doesn't know better, because she doesn't seriously reflect on what it means to be the kind of woman others take her to be. With Marianne no such argument will even temporarily suffice; in her we have a woman capable of sustained reflection, of agonizing self-appraisal, and of sympathetic and only tenuous detachment from the dangerously involving problems of others. For Marianne, liberation and autonomy have nothing to do with an impulse to escape from immoderately entangling relations. She knows what she deserves—as a person and as a woman—but knows as well that it is not always fruitful to demand a full share unless you're ready to put up with the loneliness and conflict that sometimes come of such demands.

In *Wild Strawberries*, then, Bergman develops an attractive character who manages to steer a middle course between, on one hand, the outright narcissism and escapist self-assertion too frequently urged upon women by feminist militants, and a more traditional accommodation to an ongoing "male" reality. The film has so often been discussed and praised that it is not for me to treat it here in detail. I want only to argue that, though Bergman has developed as an artist in the course of more than thirty years, he is no less taken with autonomous women than he ever was, and no less likely to note the psychological and emotional dangers implicit in too great an insistence upon liberation. Always his films ask not only "liberation from what?" but "liberation to what?" In *Wild Strawberries* Marianne likes to smoke cigarettes, though her crusty old father-in-law thinks the habit unbecoming. It's a small point, and though Marianne can be irritated by small things like the rest of us, she lets this point pass in the interests of a rapprochement which is apt to require major concessions from both parties to the mounting conflict. By film's end, Isak Borg tells her to go ahead and smoke if she likes, not because she has effectively leveled demands or put the old fellow in his place, but because she has persisted in relating to Isak as one finally capable of responding to a simple, human appeal. Marianne is not interested in wringing small concessions to enhance her pride and show that she can be as tough as anybody else. As a person she has passed largely beyond the formal requirements of heady self-assertion, and stands firm only on fundamentals. She *will* have the child she carries because she is ready to *be* a mother and to pass on what she knows in a reasonably confident and optimistic way. She will *not* pretend that she is perfectly satisfied with the level of human exchange when she feels herself willfully misunderstood and disparaged for no good reason. And finally, she will not pretend to be indifferent to the husband who has been callously insensitive to her needs, because she is convinced he should get what he deserves: Responsive or not, he remains her husband, and she continues to love him and nourish hopes for his growth.

Bergman's autonomous women do not always succeed in making satisfactory lives for themselves, and there are times when insistence upon one's own truth, or *the* truth, or justice, goes against the grain of one's real interests. In *Through a Glass Darkly* Karin is a defeated and psychotic woman whose recovery is inhibited by her inability to live with the partial truths that others in her family require. Though her husband loves and cares for her, and puts up with her "episodes" and delusions, she regularly accuses him of insensitivity, as though if he only tried harder he'd be able to divine the needs which she herself can hardly identify. Bergman admires Karin for her fanatical determination to get at the truth of her feelings and to resist the easy pretenses of others who love her, but he knows that she's not likely to find satisfaction in her refusal to "let up." If ultimately the character is "soiled" by her sexual needs, the reason has much to do with her failure to integrate sexual need and mundane attachment. She turns her back on her husband's sexual advances not because he is repulsive or demanding but because she refuses to yield to one who has less than perfect and intuitive understanding of her condition. Surely, as the film indicates, that is her prerogative, as it is her likely fate to turn her guilts and confusions against herself and yield to a perverse sexuality which puts the seal to her specialness and detaches her still further from others.

Bergman also admires the psychotic determination of Elisabeth Vogler in *Persona*, as my earlier paper suggests, but he sees as well the suffering and coldness of spirit required to purchase extreme autonomy. Does Bergman willfully punish women who resist families, husbands, children, who turn their backs on the biological calling? No more so than he punishes men who are cold and all but indifferent to their functions as integrated human beings. We have only to think of Bergman's male artist figures, with whom he so obviously though only partially identifies, to discern the pattern: David in *Through a Glass Darkly*, Jan Rosenberg in *Shame* are two excellent examples. And as for punishing genuinely liberated women, or denying their ability to change, think of Liv Ullmann's Marianne in the recent *Scenes From a Marriage*. Does Bergman humiliate her or allow her to wallow indefinitely in anxious perplexity? To the contrary, he permits her to grow in the face of devastation, to acquire an entirely more sufficient and adult view of her prospects than she'd had before her crisis. Though there are no solutions to the problems opened up by her life, by the split in her marriage and the wrecking of her plans, she emerges as a likable person capable of holding her own with ex-husband Johan and anyone else. Mellen and others have for long contended that "the personalities of Bergman's women are fixed and pre-conceived; they exist beyond change and development." Surely *Scenes From a Marriage* should put to rest such contentions, though they might as well have been served by the portrait of Sister Alma in *Persona*.

To conclude all this, may we say, simply, that Bergman is not guilty as charged with respect to his treatment of women; more, that his films ask to be treated with a grave caution which respects the plurality of his intentions and the scruple with which he examines states of feeling. No literate filmgoer can afford to shut himself, or herself, to the rigorous probings of Bergman's camera eye. No more can we afford the pretense that it doesn't matter in what spirit, or with what questions, we approach a given film. If my original approach to *Persona* as tragedy largely prevented consideration of issues intrinsic to the film experience as a whole, it failed Bergman and failed my own experience as viewer. Did the failure to raise feminist questions in the original essay inhibit a proper appreciation of the film? I hope the present "apologia" has, in its circuitous way, shown that it did not.

Secular Vision, Transcendental Style: The Art of Yasujiro Ozu

The works of the Japanese director Yasujiro Ozu have been said to exemplify a "spiritual" or "transcendental" style chiefly familiar to Western audiences in the films of Robert Bresson and, to a less obvious extent, Carl Dreyer and Michelangelo Antonioni. Though an immensely popular and influential artist in his own country in the years before his death in 1963, Ozu was first introduced to American and British viewers only in recent years, and it seems unlikely that his films will achieve anything like a sizeable following despite extended and favorable critical attention. What an American critic of Ozu described as "the virtues of mannered simplicity" are eminently resistable in a society for which spontaneity, self-expression, and stunning prestidigitation have become the cardinal virtues. If only because his work represents a serious challenge to our sense of the significant, of the meaningful and beautiful, Ozu would be worth our scrutiny. But there is another reason we must study him: His best films allow us to cultivate a mode of pleasure we have largely forgotten or ignored. Ozu reminds us, teaches us, that in art economy of means and reduction of expressive potential often yield the richest results.

But what exactly is a "spiritual" or "transcendental" style? Perhaps it is only fair to say at once that such a style is ordinarily apprehended negatively, in terms of what it is not. It is not the style we are accustomed to in films, or in the other arts either. It is not, in essence, a style we associate with religious works as such, whether by Bergman or Pasolini or Cecil B. deMille. It is not, finally, a style

From *Georgia Review*, Spring 1978.

which seeks to generate for the spectator a quietly dramatic experience in which he feels his life somehow transformed, burdens lifted, eyes heavy with fatigue opened at last. Though the films of Ozu and of others we loosely associate with his work may be said to speak authoritatively for themselves, they cannot entirely be prevented, or so it seems, from falling into categories created by the popular culture. It is difficult to explain to one's students in a film course, for example, that, though Ozu works in a tradition initiated long ago by Zen masters in painting and the other arts, he is not himself adequately described as a Zen master. Though there is an unmistakable, lucid core of unrationalized insight in Ozu's better films, attempts to appreciate them invariably proceed by assimilating them to comfortably familiar perspectives.

The so-called transcendental style has been examined in some detail in a recent book by Paul Schrader.* It is a careful book, perhaps excessively so, and though it doesn't get much beyond the positing of definitions and some fairly elementary distinctions, it does convincingly establish the parameters within which discussion of certain artists can fruitfully proceed. For Schrader, following theorists like M. Eliade, A. Hauser, and G. Van Der Leeuw, the object of a transcendental style in art is "to express the Holy." Such a project is credible, Schrader argues, largely because it does not seek to "*inform* one about the Transcendent," but to "be *expressive* of the Transcendent." Nor in this view is it the business of transcendental art "to express or illustrate holy feelings," which have to do with an aspect of human experience that necessarily impedes proper attention to the culminant object in this tradition: Insofar as a given work draws our attention to the development and waning of particular emotions, and invites empathetic identification with the tribulations of various subject individuals, it necessarily encourages a feeling for life as process, for understanding or wisdom as but a potential modality of experience. By contrast, works in the transcendental style aim, in Schrader's words, "to transcend culture and personality" by attaching us to images of stasis which embody a remote, somewhat abstract, and finally inarticulate quiescence. In the end, according to formulations that suggest a good deal more than they can say, while pretending to say it all, "the mountain has become a mountain again," and "man is again one with nature." I think it is possible to have an appetite for transcen-

---

Transcendental Style in Film: Ozu, Bresson, Dreyer (University of California Press, 1972).

dental style without any equivalent capacity to swallow anything so vaguely submissive as Schrader's resonant platitudes would indicate. For the moment, I suppose, that is neither here nor there. What matters is that we see quite clearly the phenomenon we wish to examine and evaluate.

Schrader describes, in a key passage, one of those special culminations to which an Ozu film, and by extension other works in the transcendental mode, persistently tend. The account is worth quoting at length:

> Perhaps the finest image of stasis in Ozu's films is the lengthy shot of the vase in a darkened room near the end of *Late Spring*. The father and daughter are preparing to spend their last night under the same roof; she will soon be married. They calmly talk about what a nice day they had, as if it were any other day. The room is dark; the daughter asks a question of the father, but gets no answer. There is a shot of the vase in the alcove and over it the sound of the father snoring. Then there is a shot of the daughter looking at him, and a shot of the vase in the alcove. Then there is a shot of the daughter half-smiling, then a lengthy, ten-second shot of the vase again, and a return to the daughter now almost in tears, and a final return to the vase. The vase is stasis, a form which can accept deep, contradictory emotion and transform it into an expression of something unified, permanent, transcendent.
>
> The decisive action, the miracle of tears, has little meaning in itself but serves to prove the strength of the form. The transcendental style, like the vase, is a form which expresses something deeper than itself, the inner unity of all things. This is a difficult but absolutely crucial point; transcendental style is a form, not an experience. The purpose of transcendental style is not to get the viewer to share Hirayama's tears, but to purge those tears and to integrate them into a larger form. This form, like the mass, can encompass many emotions, but it is expressive of something greater than those emotions.

What Schrader calls "the inner unity of all things" is bound to be something more elusive even than a form, and if it is anything but an *idea* of a form adequate to express such unity, I have failed to see clearly what Ozu intends. In what sense, after all, can a static form like the vase be said to "encompass many emotions"? In the most fundamental cinematic terms, the concluding sequence of *Late Spring* contains shots of human beings in the grip of deeply ambivalent feelings; these shots are intercut with shots of a vase, a recurrent form which stands in something like a contrapuntal relation to the characters struggling with their emotions. Is it too obvious to say that the vase is of a different order than the characters, in that it manages to be self-contained only because it is a finished object? To suggest that the vase "can accept" the emotions of characters is to attribute to the vase more than it deserves, more certainly than it can express in Ozu's film. Schrader's account goes wrong in placing undue emphasis on the image of the vase itself, as though it were possible for the vase in a film like *Late Spring* to absorb all surrounding human emotions and to make us feel they are as nothing next to the solidity of the vase. This is no more than wishful thinking, I'm afraid. If the vase is intended to emblematize something like "the inner unity of all things," and if it does even vaguely impose something like the sensation of a stasis, a quiescent accommodation, it achieves these effects at best momentarily. It may well be accurate to say that one purpose of a transcendental style is to "encompass many emotions" in order to get at "something greater than those emotions," but it is not therefore legitimate to attribute special potency in this regard to the agency of any single image—least of all to a static emblem. If the vase is to figure prominently at all, as it should, it must figure as an aspect of an abiding tension in the transcendental work, and is itself encompassed by that tension. Ozu's vase emblematizes not the achievement of transcendence but the will to accommodate a larger tension in which it inevitably participates. As an object, it cannot resist the uses to which a certain kind of imagination will be tempted to put it. It expresses at once the longing of the filmmaker for some ultimate lucidity beyond the tensings of his own ambivalent intelligence, and poignant intuitive awareness of the insufficiency of the static image to comprehend or to resolve the abiding tensions.

There are further difficulties in Schrader's account of the transcendental form. Though he is himself rightly skeptical of too easily yielding to ineffability as an end in itself, he never fully addresses the fundamental questions raised by his own reflections: Why, we are anxious to learn, should viewers accept that there is "something greater than those emotions" that so assault characters in whom we've developed an interest? And why must the "something greater" be figured as a static form or landscape? Why not, for example, some apocalyptic emotion, some utterly ravishing expression to burn off the surfaces of modest restraint and controlled anguish which define Ozu's characters? There is no necessary relation between a transcendental mode, abstractly conceived, and a variety of static objects to embody it. Ideas of transcendence and of apocalypse are a good deal closer to one another in our culture than Schrader wishes to suggest. If the object of Ozu's films is, at least in part, to "undermine the viewer's customarily rock-solid faith in his feelings," what is there in the films to seduce the viewer to a quiescence which has little but an aura of conventional and largely discredited sanctity to recommend it? There is no use in pretending that "sensitive" persons will inevitably be tempted to lonely rigors on behalf of a "something greater" for which they can feel at best a grudging skepticism.

Perhaps it would be well to respond more bluntly than Schrader thinks necessary to the concluding sequence of shots in *Late Spring*, and to see what trophies plain candor can purchase. By the end of the film we have, presumably, discovered some sort of fellow-feeling for both the father and daughter, whatever the peculiar disciplines and restraints to which we've tentatively agreed to submit. We understand that both are subject to a formal convention which has as much to do with the aesthetic and spiritual requirements of Ozu's project as with their individual personalities. We accept, moreover, that it is possible to express one's humanity while refusing to communicate specific feelings such as Western theories of interpersonal relations and mature psychological comportment typically mandate. Still, we ask, why should father and daughter pretend—is there any word but "pretend" to say this?—that the present day is like "any other day"? We look about for suitable explanations, and find all too many we might use. In contemporary psychoanalytic discourse, for example, the word "collusion" is sometimes used to describe a situation in which persons pretend not to notice something they could easily see if they wished, but which, if acknowledged, would compel serious adjustments in their customary self-images and in their manner of getting along together. The "collusion" frequently has the advantage of implicitly bonding persons who are privy to its benefits and capable in maintaining the particular network of pretense, while excluding others who one way or another threaten the collusive bond or warrant its continued importance. Since it is surely likely that a Western viewer of *Late Spring* will be familiar with such an idea, it is not absurd to suggest he may have to deal with it, to accommodate and to banish it, if he is to look at the film in an appropriate way. Why must he banish the idea of collusion? Because there is nothing unnatural or particularly disturbing in the pretense that the day in *Late Spring* is like "any other day." At most the viewer is permitted to register a mild unease: There is a disparity between the occasion as handled by Ozu's characters and observed by the mildly watchful camera eye. Such a disparity is not terribly unusual, of course, and everyone has one time or other tried to hold off powerful feelings by going through the motions of the everyday as though time stood still and nothing were about to change.

We banish the idea of collusion also, and more significantly, because it introduces a mode of reasoning which is nowhere invited by Ozu's film. Since the film accepts the relative sanity of its characters as patently beyond question, since they belong in their world as "naturally" as they belong in the tonally and visually integrated universe of Ozu's film, we have no right to theorize about their behavior as though it were a symptomatology of psychic disorder. None of this resistance to psychoanalytic theorizing will tell us why the father and daughter pretend as they do, but it may enforce a more radical retreat from the question. Perhaps it is sufficient to say that father and daughter pretend because they cannot do otherwise. That they cannot do otherwise because they are who they are. That they are who they are because they are characters in a work of art which requires that certain confrontations fail to occur, that particular acknowledgments remain forever unspoken. Does this help? I think it does, in that whatever the ultimate validity of such speculations, whatever the limited satisfaction they may grant our desire to explain and to know what we witness, we do by their agency gradually discover the actual center of our interest in the film. That center has to do with the discovery of form as at once the very ground of emotion and the vehicle of its articulation. It is not the vase as a form in itself that compels interest but the way in which the vase informs and affirms the rendered inarticulateness of emotions dimly expressed in *Late Spring*. Ozu's film does not undermine our faith in feelings but in the idea of their necessary expression. In encouraging what is for most of us a new appreciation of form in its relation to feeling, Ozu generates in a most generous and uninsistent way a sensation of gratitude in the face of irreducible human complexity.

What then is to be made of the notion of transcendence and of transcendental style with which we confidently began? Clearly, if we are to make any progress at all in addressing the issue, we must dismiss the idea of stasis as the primary object to which a transcendental work would attach us. In fact, as previously indicated, the very presence of the static image in a developing narrative structure ensures the playing out of tensions which no idea of absolute quiescence can fully accommodate. If we are to know what we mean when we speak of transcendental style, we must distinguish the proper objects of such a style from the typical objects of secular art. We have already established that a major achievement of this style is the discovery of particular forms which, on one hand, embody or affirm feelings and, on the other hand, certify the insufficiency of expressive means. Some of these forms are, in the work of Ozu, typically static, and in themselves evoke an encompassing passivity. But passivity is not the predominating experience of Ozu's films. They aim instead at the sustaining of significant tensions which include the call both to a passive, self-surrendering quiescence and to a more active participation in the unfolding of one's fate. In this way the films require the discovery of other forms which we may suitably describe as conventions or motifs. These forms resist the inducements of the static image to succumb to perfect quiescence, and attach the viewer to a process of imagination which is singular, rigorous, and necessary. The hallmark of a transcendental style is its success in imagining or generating an idea of mystic oneness. This idea is sustained by an imagination which is by turns restrained and intuitive, an imagination for which sentimental affirmations of universal brotherhood are not likely to seem persuasive. Transcendental style consists in the continuous unfolding of forms capable of bringing to a temporary rest the various subjective experiences of characters and of spectators, gesturing towards a sentiment of oneness which it knows to be partial and largely inarticulable.

It is difficult to speak of these things, not alone because there are ultimately no words to express the inexpressible. Given limits, built into the very fabric of our speech, we have learned to live with, or to go around. More immediately intimidating are the many formulations of mystic oneness which have seemed persuasive for so long that we forget how or when they originally took hold. These are best dealt with by confronting them head-on or by insistently banishing them as irrelevant to our purposes. In this sense nothing is a better corrective to empty abstraction or willful mysticism than careful consideration of a single film by Ozu, and I can think of no more coherent and affecting film than his *Tokyo Story* (1953). A work that fairly epitomizes transcendental style, it may be said to succeed in attaching us to a variety of forms which, in turn, express a sentiment of oneness without capitulating entirely to it. It is, moreover, an instance of a secular art whose connection with the traditions of transcendental vision is largely formal: It is not the religious content long associated with transcendental style in which Ozu is primarily interested, but the formal properties of the style and their adaptation to the urgencies of the present.

Tokyo Story introduces us to a contemporary Japanese family, elaborating a plot outline of exceeding simplicity. Briefly, in the synopsis provided by the critic Stanley Kauffmann, "An elderly couple who live in the South of Japan, with their unmarried schoolteacher daughter, go to visit their married children and their grandchildren in Tokyo. During their visit they also see their widowed daughter-in-law, whose husband was killed in the war eight years before. Then the old couple return home, and the old lady sickens, badly. The children gather at her deathbed. After her death, they go home, and the old man is alone." Further, "In Tokyo the old couple learn that their doctor son is not quite the success, nor quite the man, they imagined; and that their married daughter has been coarsened into a penny-biting, suspicious shop-keeper. The breath of love they did not expect is from the daughter-in-law, who is still bound to her dead husband's memory, although both she and his parents know that he wasn't the most admirable of men. In responsive concern, it is they . . . who urge her to remarry." Finally, in Kauffmann's splendidly compacted account, the film is importantly structured in balanced sequences: "At the beginning, the parents travel to the children; at the end, the children travel to the parents. In Tokyo the old woman and the daughter-in-law have a scene alone together, a very moving one in which the old woman spends the night in the younger woman's small apartment while the old man is out drinking with some pals. At the end it is the old man who has a scene with the daughter-in-law, after his wife's death. He tells her that his wife said her night in the apartment was her happiest time in Tokyo, and he gives the girl the old woman's watch as a keepsake."

To describe *Tokyo Story* as a secular work is to communicate nothing of its texture or tone. Similarly, to think of the elderly couple as the protagonist figures in the film is to think of it in familiar Western terms. That the film is structured around their trip to Tokyo and its aftermath there is no doubt. But *Tokyo Story* is a transcendental work, which requires that viewers adopt a rather more tentative perspective on its structure and purpose. If it is the business of a transcendental style to discover forms which gesture in the direction of oneness while sustaining a variety of tensions and powerful feelings, and if this is in fact the achievement of Ozu's film, we are forced to ask what is chiefly responsible for this achievement. Conducting an inquiry along these lines, we cannot help but discover that the daughter-in-law, Noriko, is the primary agent in the film, the source of its most compelling and enduring moments. She is, in fact, in her formal constraint and capacity for decisive action, the very ground of emotion and the vehicle of its severely limited articulation. If *Tokyo Story* is more than a "secular film," if it is a visionary work whose roots go deep into a religious tradition it remembers imperfectly—in its blood rather than in its head—it gets its strength by elaborating a narrative structure which at every point prepares the way for Noriko's steady emergence. Though other characters in the film fill the screen through most of *Tokyo Story*, it is Noriko with whom we are chiefly taken: She is the partial but sufficient resolution of an encompassing tension which the film persistently maintains.

We have described the tension in a transcendental work as a conflict between the willed sufficiency of static emblems and their human/behavioral counterparts, and the imagining of alternate forms at once less stable and more immediate. On one side in *Tokyo Story* there are the various interpolated emblem-shots: the utter stillness of a railroad station, tracks without motion spreading nowhere; an empty corridor in a house; a ship in almost frozen passage on a tranquil waterway. Related as behavioral counterparts are hundreds of minimalist gestures, mute glances, greetings without apparent warmth, stoic countenances in the face of death, unyielding fixities: The very type of these fixities is the "Ozu shot," in which persons are viewed inevitably from the eye level of one seated on a floor mat, or *tatami*. With little variation action is viewed from this level, whether characters are sitting or standing. What is more, characters frequently remain seated on the *tatami* even when our experience tells us they must stand, move about, embrace a loved one. The old folks barely turn their heads in acknowledgment of the grandson who is introduced to them for the first time. This might be more readily understood if we felt they were indifferent to the event, but we know that they are deeply affected by everything they witness in Tokyo, and we must work to account for what we observe. There is, of course, the larger tension. In the context of this tension the various fixities are posited and encouraged so as to prepare the ground for the emergence of those alternate forms we associate with Noriko.

But what, precisely, are these alternate forms, and what legitimizes our speaking of a person or character in formal terms? We are perfectly aware, of course, that characters in a work of art are not persons, but it is often appropriate that we should discuss their behavior, their motives and prospects, as if they were. Most often a literary work or narrative film invites us to "read" characters in ways familiar to us from daily intercourse with actual persons. The "reading" is, of course, to be a limited operation, a procedure consistent with the various conventions set in motion by the structure of the work and by its presentation of *selected* aspects of a presumptive reality which literally excludes other aspects easily furnished by viewers with a taste for total verisimilitude. In *Tokyo Story* the various conventions set in motion deliberately enforce a perspective in which *presence* is a function of restraint. Through most of the film, staying power is invariably associated with the capacity to look at things and events impassively. Containment as a fundamental discipline is established as a norm. Characters who permit themselves to be needlessly angry, to rebel—no matter how ineffectually—against the given, are unmistakably cast as foils to a larger and steadier vision. The anxious doctor son, the coarsened shopkeeper daughter, even the more likable railroad employee son Keizo, are drawn as irritant, unlovely, and finally irrelevant features of a universe to which they do not fully deserve to belong. Not that containment and impassivity are value-terms in Ozu; they describe at most an informing condition with which one comes to terms. A character whose very being is encompassed in the idea of containment, who is nothing but passive, has assumed the static posture of an object. By contrast we have the alternate form represented by Noriko, a form whose primary shape is a mode of containment but which continues to move and, occasionally, to surprise even itself. We speak of Noriko in these formal terms because the character has what in an Ozu film amounts to *presence*, and because we know her by the interaction of that particular fluid presence with other more static forms in the film.

Western commentators have tended to dwell excessively on the decorous, undemonstrative simplicity of the old folks in *Tokyo Story*. Though it is true that they establish the pervasive tone of the film, and hold our attention as we watch it unfold, neither is suited to live comfortably in the universe the film describes. The industrial landscape is to them menacing and alien, and they give no indication of a capacity to sustain their vaunted simplicity indefinitely under such conditions. Their return home from Tokyo is a retreat, and we cannot but feel how little prepared they are to withstand the steady assaults of a culture in disorder. Though there is something beautiful in their turnings inward, in their brave imperturbability, we sense that the quiescent postures are largely defensive in nature; that they do not wish to acknowledge what they see; that, in the course of the film, suffering a variety of small but intense disappointments, they discover that they are more dead than alive. It is not merely as an elementary foreshadowing device that Ozu has the old mother speak to the children of impending death as she and her husband prepare to board the train for home. We've seen you—she wants to tell them. We've seen Tokyo. We understand what is what. And you have seen us. No need to bother to come for the funeral when you learn of our passing. We are no more, even as we sit with you watching the clock hands revolve, waiting for the inevitable train.

By this point in the film, of course, Ozu's intentions have been largely realized. The static forms and utterly controlled gestures have been patterned to support an enveloping tonal quality which will need to be relieved, compromised, even as it had been, briefly, in the bedtime encounter between Noriko and the old mother when tears fell and more than pleasantries were exchanged. The dominant tonal quality, then, which suggests continuously that something ephemeral has been, as it were, transcended, comes itself to seem untrustworthy as the film progresses. To focus on the old couple as emblems of transcendental achievement is to miss entirely the developmental thrust of the film, to mistake the beauty of pathos for a more bracing and elusive vision. It is possible to like the old couple in Ozu's film without for a moment feeling that they are the primary vehicles for the expression of his vision. What we get in the impressive formality of their customary reserve is the embodiment of a finished style. As such, it may be said to accomplish what the critic Meyer Schapiro has attributed to other dominant styles: It "reflects or projects the 'inner form' of collective feeling and thinking" within a culture. At the same time, as Schapiro goes on to note, "the content of a work of art often belongs to another region of experience than the one in which both the period style and dominant mode of thinking have been formed." Just so is it necessary to argue that the dominant style associated with the old couple in *Tokyo Story* is at odds with the encompassing vision of the film; that the cultural inflection we take to be typically Japa-

nese, with roots deep in Zen tradition and the emotional dispositions of countless generations, cannot adequately reflect the experience of a contemporary Japanese filmmaker anxious to keep at least
one foot in that tradition.

But how, more precisely, are we instructed to respond to the old
couple? The only certain thing about them, so far as we can tell, is
their suffering and their virtually limitless capacity to turn towards
the void for solace. Their mistrust of verbal and gestural communication is not an intellectual conviction but a settled habit. Though
they do not court suffering, or celebrate the futility of attempts to
"connect" with others, they come increasingly to feel that loss and
hopelessness are constitutive elements of enlightened experience.
This experience they are unable, or unwilling, to confront with
transformative gaiety. Their ancient eyes are neither glittering nor
gay. They see themselves as the eternal victims of a fate they yield
to at every turn. If they console themselves at all, they do so with
the thought that they have preserved a saving decorum in the face
of dire provocation.

Ozu orchestrates our emotional responses to the old couple with
consummate tact, working his will through a variety of carefully
plotted shots which remain in the memory like iconic tableaux.
Particularly noteworthy are moments in the sequence describing
the old couple's visit to a seaside hotel resort, and their premature
return to the city. Unable to entertain their parents in Tokyo while
pursuing their customary routines, the children determine to send
them away on vacation, to do them a favor. The parents take the
"suggestion" well enough, but cannot help seeing what has happened: For their children they have become a nuisance, an occasion
for guilt, and must be "generously" removed. Once or twice in the
film the meaning of this "insight" is underlined and deliberately
extended to refer to a universal process of generational displacement and disaffection, but because the generalizations nowhere
seem warranted, the failure of the parents to resist what is happening to them is especially disturbing. How strongly we must feel
that a well-chosen word or two would turn the process around, get
parents and children talking modestly with one another about their
genuine distress. This is not to be, of course, and the parents
shuffle off mildly.

At the spa our senses are briefly confused, in part because Ozu
sketches the vacation so economically that, to Western eyes at least,
the signals seem somewhat opaque. The establishment seems respectable enough, the corridors polished and orderly, the rooms

reasonably comfortable. If the old couple grow very quickly un-happy with their surroundings, it is difficult to know what is at fault. One observer of the film has written that "they decide to leave because of homesickness and the vulgarity of the other persons at the spa, which appears to be a hotel for newlyweds of the lower orders." Now it is true that they later speak to the shopkeeper daugh-ter of homesickness, but we are asked only to believe that they are offering a convenient explanation which will cut off any possibility of recrimination or unhappy speculation. As to "the vulgarity of the other persons at the spa," I think it is fair to observe that they do and say nothing extraordinary, nothing of which the old man himself would be incapable at an earlier time in his life. Indeed, his drunken one-night spree with two old cronies later in the film adequately demonstrates that "vulgarity" is not the crucial problem in the expe-rience at the spa. A better indication is the old couple's anxious tossing about in bed early one evening while merrymaking is taking place in another quarter of the hotel. It is no Japanese equivalent of acid rock that penetrates their bedroom, but occasional vagrant musi-cal sounds to which they respond with grave annoyance. As we watch them in their distress, we must feel uncomfortable too: We pity them; we are even a little angry at them that they should be in that room, cooperative prisoners in a situation they resent but will do nothing to oppose. If our senses are, as stated, briefly confused, it is because nothing in their present circumstances seems excessively provoking by comparison with the demeaning time they have spent with their own children in Tokyo, and we wonder why they should not graciously—rather than bitterly—resign themselves, as they had before.

Among the most memorable shot-sequences in the film is an outdoor sequence immediately following a restless night. In fact, this sequence creates a substantive visual impression that clarifies everything we've wondered about and points toward develop-ments in the film which, as a consequence, we are fully prepared to receive. The old couple have come out on the beach for an early-morning walk. The screen is suffused with a still and grainy brightness, of a kind that makes the viewer want to squint. The old people are dressed in exquisite checkered kimonos, the cam-era watching them patiently from the rear in a medium-shot as they sit atop a stone wall curving along the shoreline. Everything in the setting is so arranged that an impression of perfect, simple beauty is unmistakably evoked. And yet, as we ease back in a moment of silent gratitude, we note the curvature of the old man's spine, the slump of his shoulders, the tired folding of the old woman upon herself as she sits with eyes down and hands clasped upon her lap. Within the mood of vast stillness, of what might have been a grateful and unanxious waiting for nothing in particular, we see developing a melancholic mood of utter defeat. The posture of stoic resignation will not inspire; the brave auster- ity has dwindled to inarticulate despair. Determined to leave the spa at once, the old people stand on the stone wall and walk, slowly, towards the hotel. Once the old woman seems to stumble and fall forward, and the old man turns to ask what is wrong as she hangs precariously atop the wall on hands and knees. It is a terrible moment, made more terrible for Western viewers, I sus- pect, by the old man's inability to embrace his wife there, to lift and support her for the journey back. Eventually—not very much time has actually passed—she gets to her feet and they continue along the wall. I cannot imagine anything more beautiful and hopeless than this sequence, emblems of a perfect futility moun- ted against an immensity awesome in its indifference. In retro- spect, looking over the film as a whole, we think of the old man as we leave him, widowed and lonely, and remember that at the spa they had each other. Be grateful for small blessings. But grati- tude could not have been the primary emotion generated on the beach.

There are other important shot-sequences that hold in the mem- ory and stir us to recapture even minor details we hadn't thought to recover. Back in Tokyo at the daughter's shop the old folks try to explain why they've returned so soon. They try one or two breezy exchanges, the daughter clearly put out and trying to be under- standing, until, exhausted by it all, the mother comes up with "Kyoko [the schoolteacher daughter] may be lonesome." As she utters these words, so forlorn, so without the strength to make them sound convincing, she looks down, away, and we feel that everything she has is concentrated in this effort to restrain any possible expression of her disappointment. Moments later, the two parents sit alone upstairs, opening packages, deciding what to do. Unable to stay even this one night with the daughter, afraid to leave too abruptly, their thoughts are focused in the plaintive ac- cents of the old man's "Now we're really homeless." No brave transcendental urgency in this, no reflection of a will to strip away inessentials and place oneself in the eye of the gathering storm. Sunk as we are in the mood of sombre devastation that covers everything here, we are further stirred by the unanticipated stately movement of the camera along the pitted exterior wall. Panning right ever so slowly, it discovers after several seconds the old people seated on the ground, apart, displaced, silent. Gravely, but purposefully, he looks at his pocket watch, and speculates that Noriko may by this time be home from work. Together they rise once more to seek shelter, she with Noriko—upon whose benevolence they feel they've already presumed too far—he with friends of his young manhood. As they move off together their figures are virtually swallowed against the dense background of a looming cityscape. They continue to move away from the camera, out into the surrounding darkness, only their heads clear against the light horizon of sky and cloud. Clusters of children briefly appear and scatter quickly in the foreground of the image. Taking places beside one another before definitively parting for the night, the old man says to his wife, "If we get lost we may never meet again." At no previous time in the film have we so clearly understood that these people require more than love, more than simple protection. They represent an order of being which, in its austerity and practiced restraint, has lost touch with what is living and capable in itself. They are sleepwalkers, believers without a living faith to sustain the ardor of their devotions.

Why, then, should Ozu have so permitted them to dominate this film, to impose their constricted, disciplined stylization upon it? In part because the reduction of expressive potential they embody is itself the dominant principle of Ozu's art. The stylization of the film, its authoritative simplifying of cinematic rhetoric to relatively few devices and modest variation, requires a behavioral texture of comparable stylistic reserve. This is not, though, an example of the fallacy of expressive form, for *Tokyo Story* is more than its stylization, and draws on reserves of expressive energy which are nowhere explicit in the narrow emotional range of the old people. Ozu has them dominate the film's surfaces because they represent qualities which he wishes to examine and work through, qualities essential to—though not identical with—any transcendental vision. A secular artist like Ozu may not aim to express the Holy, but there is an important sense in which he must aim, in Schrader's terms, to get at "the inner unity of all things." This unity may best be suggested, if not adequately grasped, by images of a containment almost beyond the reach of political, cultural, or familial ephemera, whatever their immediacy. *Tokyo Story*, however, as we have shown, also describes an implicit critique of the particular mode of containment associated with the old couple: By demonstrating that the unity they represent is a form of death-in-life, Ozu calls into question the especial fascination they exert, and opens up the possibility of their gradual displacement within a still orderly and traditionally ceremonious universe.

That the displacement Ozu cares about is not a simple matter of generational conflict is perfectly clear. Neither the doctor son nor the shopkeeper daughter is for a moment capable of attracting us or of suggesting that they represent a serious option. Theirs is a violent fall into the quotidian, from which no recovery is conceivable. If they were any less human, less recognizable as familiar *contemporary* types, we should simply dismiss them as products of a deeply cynical and embittered intelligence. In fact, though we cannot begin to like them, they are really quite ordinary, intermittently decent; we may even wonder why, after a while, they do not in their banal ordinariness furnish some sense of relief from the suffocating decorousness of their parents. At this level, confirming the unlovely truth of common experience, they may in fact move some viewers to gratitude. At least there is no pretense in their mediocre comings and goings, their shabby connivances. This is "democratic" value with a vengeance, and I cannot believe Ozu had any intention of assisting its entrenchment. A more suitable transition figure in the scheme of the film is Keizo, the son who works for the railroad somewhere on the line between Tokyo and the parents' home village of Onomichi. He is *between* the parents and the Tokyo children in a variety of ways, most typically in his easy capitulation to "modern" sentiments—parents are a frightful nuisance—and his similarly easy but more deeply felt reflection on the saying, "No one can serve his parents beyond the grave." It is fitting that, as he utters those words, he should laugh, for though the old sayings continue to have meaning for him, he experiences them even in his maturity as lessons learned, words repeated, willfully self-imposed ordinances. Keizo is a rather likable young man, but he will not save anyone or restore anything. He arrives too late in Onomichi to be at his mother's side in her final hours. Deeply moved at the funeral, he retreats outside the temple, confused, wanting to assert some conviction, sorry but without redemptive authority.

The sentiment of oneness, then, the felt inner unity on which the transcendental work must set its sights, is to be located in Ozu's film elsewhere than in the containment of the parents or the well-meaning decencies of a Keizo. In this sense it is well that we bear in mind the still eminently useful writings of Daisetz Suzuki on the spirit of Zen. Though hardly a traditional Zen performance, *Tokyo Story* lends itself to many of the misconstructions countless Western commentators have visited upon Oriental art, and Suzuki's warnings to "the Western mind trying to solve the mystery in its own way" are fully pertinent. In *Zen and Japanese Culture* (1938; rev. ed. 1959), he writes: "Plainly speaking, Zen does not acknowledge 'one spirit' permeating all Nature, nor does it attempt to realize identity by purging its mind of 'egotistic commotions.' " Further, and yet more useful, "It is not a sense of identity nor of tranquility that Zen sees and loves in Nature. Nature is always in motion, never at a standstill; if Nature is to be loved, it must be caught while moving and in this way its aesthetic value must be appraised. To seek tranquility is to kill nature, to stop its pulsation, and to embrace the dead corpse that is left behind. Advocates of tranquility are worshipers of abstraction and death. There is nothing in this to love. Identity is also a static condition and decidedly associated with death." It is a genuine advantage to have Suzuki's confirmation of various insights we have been able to generate for ourselves in examining Ozu's work, and surely no writer has been better equipped than Suzuki to mediate the Zen vision to Western readers and filmgoers. But there are problems we do not want to blink. If it is clear that perfect tranquility is not a viable goal for the Zen artist, what of Suzuki's contention that "Zen does not acknowledge 'one spirit' permeating all Nature"? The reader may recall that, earlier in this paper, we remarked that "the 'inner unity of all things' is bound to be something more elusive even than a form," that it is "but an *idea* of a form adequate to express such unity." The formulation seems to me perfectly consistent with Suzuki's argument: To speak of oneness in a Zen work is to describe an idea of something we can never quite hold on to or contain. To speak of a form adequate to express this oneness is to describe a principled motion which, in its gentle matter-of-factness, seems never to have had to learn even the elementary forms of reverence for order and devotion to propriety. Suzuki instructs us very well in his chapter on "Zen and the Art of Tea," where he writes: "While Zen teaching consists in grasping the spirit by transcending form, it unfailingly reminds us of the fact that the world in which we live is a world of particular forms and that the spirit expresses itself only by means of form." Zen is known also, according to Suzuki, in its rigorous ceremonial formalities—of which the tea ceremony is a fitting example—the spirit of which "is to be sought in the avoidance of complicated ritual and mere ostentation."

But Ozu is not, strictly speaking, a contemporary Zen master, and *Tokyo Story* is not a masterpiece of the Zen tradition, fruitful though it is to consider it in part in the language of that tradition. To think of the various cultural manifestations of Zen as treated in Suzuki's book is to see at once how secular, how very mundane are Ozu's evocations by contrast. It is one thing to celebrate the practical aspects of a first-century Chinese Zen brotherhood committed to monastic disciplines, and quite another to celebrate the irremediably worldly gentleness of a Noriko. Suzuki's chapters on haiku, on swordsmanship, and on the art of tea clearly indicate a formally ceremonial perspective quite different from anything we find in *Tokyo Story*. Insofar as there is ceremony in Ozu at all, it takes the form of a much more generalized constraint and attention to moderate decorums that have little to do with the details of a cultivated craft or institutional discipline. Suzuki is most helpful in warning us away from an emphasis on the exemplary characteristics of the old couple in *Tokyo Story*, an emphasis all too likely given the conventional Western misreading of Oriental traditions generally. Similarly instructive is Suzuki's insistence upon the paradoxical qualities inherent in Oriental transcendental vision: On one hand we have the attempt to grasp spirit "by transcending form," on the other an acknowledgment of "particular forms" and the necessity of expression "by means of form." Just so do we have "rigorous cermonial formality" simultaneous with "the avoidance of complicated ritual." This is the heart of the matter, and Ozu has mastered the expression and celebration of these paradoxical imperatives better than any artist of our time. As intimated frequently before, the primary vehicle for the expression of these paradoxical imperatives in *Tokyo Story* is the character Noriko, and though we have examined the structure and tension out of which the character steadily emerges, we've not yet established the specific purpose she is created to realize.

Perhaps the key to an understanding of Noriko is to be located in an exchange between her and the family's youngest daughter, Kyoko. It takes place late in the film, after the mother's passing, after the return to Tokyo of the other children, and shortly before Noriko's intended departure. She has stayed on at Onomichi for some time, helping to put things in order and to comfort the old man. Kyoko speaks rather harshly, though not unfairly, of her brother and sister, of their coldness and relative indifference to everything but their own schedules and settled pursuits. Clearly she anticipates support from Noriko, so tender, so thoughtful. But Noriko disappoints the young woman, assures her that she sees nothing particularly distressing in the behavior of the others, that it is possible to lose interest in one's parents as in other distant persons as one grows into one's own responsibilities and concerns. This is not exactly a startling revelation for the viewer, but we are deeply impressed all the same by the effect produced on Kyoko. She is at once deeply upset by Noriko's equanimity and excessive generosity and, at the same time, strangely acquiescent. Kyoko cries, protests, but she listens all the same to something she already knows, and had almost come, we feel, to acknowledge for herself. What occurs in the exchange with Noriko is not a conversion but a demonstration of a felt unanimity of spirit. Beneath a seeming disunity is an understanding held very much in common. Thus we find in Ozu a reconciliation to a unity which in the course of the film had been called in question by a variety of tensions, formal and otherwise, but which had never been fundamentally threatened at all. The unity has very little to do with the standard humanistic bonds or contracts or fidelities which constitute the substance of conventional *ethical* imperatives. It is, instead, a felt unity which the visionary enterprise may seek to evoke purely because it is a fundamental modality of experience that so often eludes articulation. Ozu manages, quite as the philosopher Owen Barfield recommended in *Romanticism Comes of Age*, "not merely to say sentimentally 'we are all brothers,' but to explain just *how* we are brothers . . ." His explanation is anything but discursive, of course, but wonderfully precise for all its suggestiveness.

Noriko has several memorable exchanges in *Tokyo Story*, each a crucial sequence in determining the culminant effect of the film as a whole. Again each of these encounters must be examined against the pervasive background of patterned restraint and largely implicit tension no viewer can fail to register. In one sequence Noriko entertains the old woman in her small Tokyo apartment, while the old man is out carousing with his friends and later, in an intercut sequence, coming home to his angry shopkeeper daughter. Preparing to lie down alongside Noriko, the old woman says, "What a treat to sleep on my dead son's bed," an utterance that has drawn considerable attention. Even now, as I look at the words on the page, I wonder why they seemed anything but funny when I saw the film. Probably because there is nothing even vaguely morbid in the atmosphere of Noriko's apartment or in their immediately preceding exchange. Possibly also because the old woman's customary reserve is such that we cannot imagine her yielding to maudlin sentimentality. Nonetheless, and quite wonderfully, Ozu has the old woman say, "Forgive me if I seem rude," and go on to speak of the eight years since her son's death. She is painfully tentative, but resolves to speak her thoughts at all costs. She is sorry to see her son's picture on display in the apartment. These are new times, she assures Noriko, nothing like the old days when a widow was forbidden to marry. She presses, holds back, unsure really of what she wants to say, knowing only that there is something unpleasant in Noriko's steadfastness to which she must refer. Noriko listens to all this without evident discomfort, and convincingly assures the old woman that she is quite happy, that she likes her life as it is. She smiles, even as she reminds her companion that she is no longer young, that marriage may not be so lively a possibility as some suspect, even were she anxious to find a man. Ozu's camera is, as always, quietly attentive, letting us watch the facial expressions without unnecessary disturbance, keeping just enough distance to ensure that no private self is needlessly violated. As the brief, softly intense exchange concludes, the women lie in relative darkness side by side; a modest light illumines Noriko's recumbent profile, and we hear the old woman sniffling in the recesses of the sound track.

It would be easy, on the basis of the encounter just described, to speak of the transcendence of earthly lusts and ordinary feminine desire, but this is not what Ozu wishes to exalt or to examine. Though we may not share the old woman's sadness, may even admire the modest gaiety with which Noriko conducts an independent life, the structure of the film does not instruct us to look at such consideration as primary to its larger intention. Instead we focus on the special quality of Noriko's relation to her guest, as to other persons with whom she comes in contact. Ceremony is very much a part of this relation, but it is a ceremony stripped of pretension and undue self-constraint. It is fully appropriate that, as we enter Noriko's apartment, we should observe her warmly massaging her mother-in-law's back, and that she should assure her it is no trouble for her to continue the massage. Similarly it is no trouble for her, later in the film, to attend to the old man, and to speak to Kyoko with a mixture of firmness and tender regard that would seem to reflect a habit of courtesy that is deeply felt just because it is habitual. This habit extends not merely to old people in need of support, but to everyone more or less equally. If Noriko seems at peace with her life, it is because she lives an active life informed by the various courtesies which are given her to perform. These courtesies she does not need to weigh, to evaluate, or to work at deliberately as though they constituted a series of formal constraints to which she was forcibly subject. She experiences the formal proprieties as given, as positive values precisely insofar as they cement relationships without demanding of the individual that he perpetually contrive ingenious ways to make them work.

All of which is to say that Noriko transcends neither particular feminine desires nor anything else we take to be "normal" in the West. If her mother-in-law, and later the old man, urge her to remarry, they do so only because they misapprehend the source of her quiet strength and sanity. Like more than one critic of *Tokyo Story*, they feel that she is self-sacrificing only because she is afraid to be selfish. The point, of course, is that she is neither self-sacrificing nor unduly generous. She knows, in a sense, how to get what she wants because she wants only what is *hers* to possess and enjoy. This we cannot see if, like Schrader, we insist upon a deathly stasis as the object of Ozu's vision, in light of which a "sudden expression of overwhelming compassion"—usually in the form of tears—becomes a miraculous intervention to be gratefully reabsorbed into the unbroken, monotonous regularity. We are moved by Noriko's tears, for example, in the famous scene she shares with the old man in Onomichi, because the entire scene expresses what we have felt to be implicit in the relationship all along. Noriko weeps because the old man does not understand the nature of her transcendental self-possession, because he cares for her without imagining that she may not relate to her prospects as he relates to his. Like his wife before him, the old man urges Noriko to remarry, warns against cutting herself off, but the viewer can only wonder here what these people can be thinking. No one, in the course of the film, has been so fully and comfortably connected to the life around her as Noriko. No one has so flexibly accommodated the unusual demands put upon her, or has managed so well to keep her customary routines in perspective. The tears shed by Noriko near the end of Ozu's film are no miraculous manifestation but a simple expression of gratitude for the reciprocated concern of an old man, and an inarticulate if momentary surrender to the fact of their difference from one another. Significantly, this difference does not compromise the felt unity we discerned in the encounter with Kyoko. Noriko's tears at once confirm relation and establish the precise nature of the underlying unity we feel throughout the unfolding of the film's many tensions.

To get at the "precise nature" of this "underlying unity" is to approach, at last, the transcendental focus of Ozu's vision. In making the approach we must, I think, entirely disclaim any intention to discover miracles, no matter how limited, and dwell instead upon the steady culmination to which the film progressively tends. Not the traditional Japanese *satori*, described by Schrader as "a single flash of awareness," but a slow growth and fulfillment of implicit knowledge are what we aim to study. In this sense attention must be directed to what the philosopher Husserl called transcendental intersubjectivity, not to a private experience of transcendence which insulates the individual against the demands of others and seals him in a kind of solipsistic tranquility. The first Zen principle or *koan*, known as *mu*, a word for negation or emptiness, does not at all describe the transcendental culmination of Ozu's vision. The old man in *Tokyo Story* may, more than any other character, know how to "sit quietly doing nothing," in Schrader's words, but we have already argued that there is nothing especially commendable in this achievement. Indeed, the transcendental experience to which Ozu's film is directed progressively attaches us to the character of Noriko because she is an active presence in a setting filled with deathly stasis. The object of the habitual courtesies and practiced decencies that so distinguish Noriko is not the freeing of the mind from all thought or care but the support of a sensation of felt unity with others which ordinary experience often conspires to obstruct. How is this sensation distinguished from blithely sentimental affirmations of universal brotherhood? It is distinguished by the difficulty with which it is apprehended by most persons, even very intelligent persons, and by the representation in Ozu's film of the many temptations to abandon the sensation for a more commonsensical and opaque relation to one's experience of others.

The achievement of transcendental intersubjectivity is succinctly described in a recent book by the Polish philosopher Leszek Kolakowski on *Husserl and the Search for Certitude.** Skeptical of the largely intuitive basis of Husserl's phenomenology, Kolakowski is nonetheless deeply attracted to his central schema, and expounds the theory with great care. If, in Kolakowski's terms, transcendental intersubjectivity "has the basic features of a mystical experience and is just as incommunicable," it may yet be the case that *Tokyo Story* enables us to discover a more precise *content* for the experience than

*Yale, 1975.

Husserl's meditations may allow. But what, for Kolakowski, is at the heart of the transcendental? The Husserlian question is, " 'How can we go beyond the island of consciousness?' " Which is to say, how can we avoid the solipsistic posture of one who knows him*self* to be the origin of every potential inquiry into the transcending of that self? Since " 'transcendence' itself is a meaning constituted in the Ego," it is unlikely that I will successfully imagine an otherness apart from that Ego and its consequent image or self. The transcendental problem, then, is to "overcome solipsism while rejecting the naive metaphysics of things in themselves." We want, moreover, to constitute an experience of continuous relation among persons and their environments without mystifying the customary perspectives in which all things are apprehended. To begin to manage such experiences we must not fall prey to the easy or "naive metaphysics" to which Kolakowski compulsively alludes, and which he usefully dismisses as follows: "Whatever we can talk about meaningfully, is meaningful (a possible object of an utterance), and therefore to say that a certain object is independent of the possibility of uttering a judgment on it, amounts to saying that we are talking about something we are not talking about—an obvious contradiction." Conclusion: " 'Realism' is self-contradictory, and if we cancel consciousness, we cancel the world."

These as yet fragmentary formulations leave relatively intact the problem of solipsism, and make ever more pressing the question of transcendental experience. In *Tokyo Story* we are confronted with an apparent paradox: As tensions accumulate and emerge to the foreground of consciousness, as the fact of irreversible difference is impressed upon us as upon characters in the film, a corresponding awareness of underlying unity is simultaneously acknowledged and impressed. In deeply affecting encounters with Kyoko, with the old woman, and, finally, with the old man, Noriko leads us firmly to the discovery of our common participation in a reality we can know at best partially, and know at all only in the degree that we imagine the related experience of others working at participation in their own similar ways. In this sense, the goal of vision in Ozu's film is not to discount difference but to accommodate it, to register it as an aspect of one's own *certain* participation in a real world which is real only as it is shared. The procedure involved is not a function of tranquil acquiescence in nature or in things as they are in themselves. It is at once a graceful and moderately strenuous enterprise, habitual without becoming *merely* habitual, a ceremony of innocence which refuses to be passive in resigning itself to the unlovely contradictions none can fully alter. What is transcended is the solipsistic self, the given, self-constituting self—that self which, though it is affirmatively transcended, refuses ever to disappear. And this is the special distinction of the transcendental vision informing *Tokyo Story*, a vision generated far from the precincts of Husserlian philosophy, but wonderfully illumined there all the same. Extended quotation from Kolakowski's presentation of the relevant argument should provide exactly what we need:

> Within the transcendental experience I separate what is particularly *mine* from phenomena which are related to other egos as subjects, for example, cultural predicates that imply a community of many subjects. What remains after this exclusion is "Nature" . . . including my own body and my empirical ego as an object. And so it appears that I, human ego, am constituted as a part of the world and at the same time I am constituting all objects, which is, he [Husserl] says, a paradox . . . In constituting the world, I give it the sense of being accessible to others' consciousness and therefore . . . the first non-ego I deal with is the alter ego, another subject. This is the community of monads, which makes objective Nature possible. This transcendental intersubjectivity has its correlate in the common world of experience. The alter ego is "given" in my experience personally, though not originally (which means, apparently, simply that I do not participate directly in his experience) . . . The transcendental intersubjectivity of separated monads is formed *in me*, but as a community that is constituted in every other monad as well.* My ego can know the world only in community with other egos, and only one monadologic community is possible (there cannot be many mutually opaque sets of monads, because when I think about them,† they are not entirely opaque anymore, I constitute them as a community). Consequently only one world and one time are possible, and this world is bound to exist . . . explaining the necessity of alter ego as a constituted meaning . . .

---

*In applying the Husserlian schema to Ozu's vision, I should have to say that for the filmmaker the ideal constitution of community within each monad is not often fully realized.

†Again, in Ozu the issue may be quite simply that not all will think about such things.

The ethical implications of such a system are, of course, considerable, insofar as it is possible in these terms to structure human communities of thinking though separate egos without pretending that it is generally possible to "participate directly" in the experiences of alter egos in one's own community. The fact of consciousness and its corollary—the potential for reflective appropriation of a world—guarantees an unmistakable world and time as givens which no single consciousness can legitimately refuse to acknowledge. Only the utter subjection of imagination to brute matter, to things as they are as matter, can wholly prevent the individual's participation in the shared experience of a unity never fully compromised by particular differences. In this sense the exclusion of the doctor son and shopkeeper daughter of *Tokyo Story* from a genuine feeling of community with others is a function of an imaginative impoverishment so great that only the special imaginative gift of a Noriko can reclaim them for the community of spirits all are asked to share in Ozu's film. Just so, the old parents of *Tokyo Story* must remain disappointed in their older children because they have not themselves properly imagined the standard relation between self and other indicated in the passage from Kolakowski; they have failed, in fact, to constitute themselves as particular selves, to "separate what is particularly theirs from phenomena which are related to other egos as subjects . . ." Thus they cannot establish for themselves that feeling of community, of unity in difference, which would reconcile them less passively to their condition and to the changes they observe in their children. Unlike Noriko, they are incapable of the paradox that lies at the heart of transcendental achievement: The old people, in achieving a kind of encompassing negation, in learning to sit quietly staring into the void, refuse the burden of difficult selfhood, and can accommodate no contrary because they can *have* none. Negation *has* no meaningful contrary, and the self which cannot constitute itself as object cannot properly apprehend a unity with other comparable, though different, living selves.

In working through the vision of Ozu's film, then, we have discovered a notion of transcendental style appropriate to the active concerns of a secular age. If, as argued earlier, we know a transcendental style by its generation of an "idea of mystic oneness," we are progressively attached to that idea by the simultaneous elaboration of obstacles to the achievement of that oneness. Refusing the gesture of magical incantation, the transcendental style of our age aims at a sentiment of oneness which it knows to be partial and which is never fully or perfectly achieved. Eschewing static form, it works toward a vision of living form that is harmonious, fluid, and confident in its necessary relation to other living forms. But the formal properties of a transcendental style may not be readily appreciated apart from the content of such a style, for the work of an Ozu aims at nothing less than a statement of what is fundamental to human experience. In Noriko we have the embodiment of a simplicity, constraint, and imaginative reaching out we take to be central to Ozu's vision. Significantly, such virtues, with all the paradox they collectively entail, are finally unimaginable together but for the suggestive understatement of a style which is content to evoke the idea of a sufficient resolution without proclaiming the completion of its ongoing quest. Implicit in Ozu's art, in the transcendental project of our age, is the requirement of a vision which is always renewing the event of unification, moving on to the next stage of that imaginative task which is always *to be* performed.

Politics and History:
Pathways in European Film

European filmmakers have demonstrated an interest in political subjects ever since the medium really took hold in the period after the First World War. Accordingly, a growing body of criticism has addressed issues associated with political reality and political commitment in a whole range of films, some of which seem not to have been made with deliberate political intentions of any kind. Indeed, it is fair to say that film theory itself, particularly in its formative stages, was often indistinguishable from political advocacy or, at least, political history. In the writings of Sergei Eisenstein, in Siegfried Kracauer's *From Caligari to Hitler,* we find attempts to understand the film medium and the historic occasion of its rise to prominence in what are essentially political terms. And though other critical works have lately achieved greater eminence—I am thinking especially of the works of André Bazin and of Christian Metz—the original impact of the early theories has not been seriously compromised. Because films have been taken to express "reality" more immediately and recognizably than any other art, and because political events are thought to embody "reality" more convincingly than other events, there still exists a lively interest in film as a means of political expression and as a gauge of historical truth.

Two of the more widely debated documents of recent commentary on film address particular movies as political phenomena which may best be understood by looking beyond the conscious intentions of filmmakers. One document—by the French philosopher Michel Foucault*—takes its shape and direction within a still

*Michel Foucault, "Anti-Retro," *L'Cahiers du Cinema,* July 1974; I wish to thank James O'Higgins and Mary Helen Wood for translating the text for me and for pointing out some of its merits and deficiencies.

From *Salmagundi,* Summer 1977.

developing tradition of Marxist analysis; the other document—by the psychologist Bruno Bettelheim*—is a relatively straightforward piece of humanistic argument, liberally peppered with bits of personal experience and moral misgiving. Though both documents "correct" perspectives elaborated in contemporary European films, they fail in a variety of ways to look at these films as the films themselves ask us to examine them. Though Foucault and Bettelheim are gifted interpreters and—on other subjects— subtle theorists, neither seems to have much respect for the peculiar imaginative relation a good film establishes with its viewers. Both Foucault and Bettelheim think that even the best films have "messages" and that, the better or more skillfully made the film, the more totally the "messages" will be impressed. For Foucault it is a bourgeois delusion to believe that a good film invites a variety of responses which are suitably discriminating, dependent as they are on careful attention to details in the given film discourse. For Bettelheim, if there *are* a variety of responses to a film, they will fail in discrimination—the intellect will fall prey to confusion, emotion will swamp accurate evaluation, and a disastrous "message" will take hold of us as surely as it would if the film were an undisguised piece of one-dimensional propaganda and we were its witting dupes.

Foucault's "Anti-Retro" is the edited text of an interview conducted by the film journal *L'Cahiers du Cinema*. The stated object of the interview is to look at a number of French films which have undertaken to "re-create" history, more particularly the history of France and its people during the Nazi period; also, to discover why so many of these recent films should be devoted to what is, by now, an "old" subject; and, finally, to rescue from these films and from other political accounts of the past a ". . . popular memory of all forms of struggle which has never really been able to speak"—in other words, also taken from the introductory remarks of the interviewers, "to uncover that which the official text suppresses, and lies forgotten in the accursed archives of the dominant class." One does not have to like the hysterical and imprecise rhetoric—"accursed archives of the dominant class"—to recognize in the stated intentions of the interview a number of important goals. There *have* been a great many recent films devoted to the Nazi period, not only in France, but in Italy and in other countries as well. Though Foucault

---

*Bruno Bettelheim, "Reflections: Survivors," *The New Yorker*, August 2, 1976.

is primarily interested in Louis Malle's *Lacombe, Lucien*—certainly the most accomplished and memorable of these films—and in Cavani's *Nightporter*, he might as fruitfully have turned his attention to Vittorio De Sica's *Garden of the Finzi-Continis*, Michel Drach's *Les Violons du Bal*, and to other films distributed after the interview took place. The most interesting of these later items is surely Lina Wertmuller's notorious *Seven Beauties*, the subject of Bettelheim's *New Yorker* essay. Why does Foucault largely limit his attention to French "re-creations"? By deliberately restricting his analytic focus in this way, Foucault believes he can elaborate a "context" for these films and explain how they are "inscribed in a history" which the filmmakers are not anxious to call by its rightful name. He can demonstrate how a number of films emerging from a particular political and cultural climate can implicitly elaborate a critique of previous historical myths and succumb at the same time to a variety of other myths no less dangerous. To accomplish this Foucault must insist that French re-creations of the Nazi period invariably reflect France's official explanatory myths, either by serving them up again with minimal adjustment or by positing countermyths which are presumed to be more appropriate under present political circumstances. Whatever the inspiration of the individual filmmaker, if he is French, he has to do the work of a Frenchman. He will do this work badly, however, unless he is equipped to perform a rigorous Marxist analysis of his materials and to move beyond the historical truth. Though Louis Malle may have thought to show the French people "what they have been," he presents instead "what he thinks they should believe they have been."

It is not entirely clear, of course, that Malle's object—or Cavani's or De Sica's or Drach's—was to show anybody what actually happened during the Nazi period. Nor is it certain that anyone comes away from these films with a clear view of their national experience as ratified by particular moral or political imperatives. Foucault insists because he does not wish to look at the films themselves. He is interested in a phenomenon which began to take definitive shape with the appearance of Marcel Ophüls's long documentary film *The Sorrow and the Pity* (1972). Here was a film whose object was, quite clearly, to adjust the historical record, to set things straight. If it had a lesson to teach, a message to impart, it was not a personal "reading" viewers felt they were getting but a portion of "the truth." A plural "truth" it was, no doubt, but no less realistic or historically valid for being so. Foucault and his friends at *L'Cahiers* speak of the film as having opened up certain "floodgates," and it is indisputable that Ophüls persuasively accounted for the Nazi period in France in a way that no one had confidently embraced before. Grant that Malle and the others were stirred by *The Sorrow and the Pity*, that their films would not have been entirely possible without it; does this mean that their films attempt to do the same thing Ophüls did, to set the record straight and shape the historical memory of Frenchmen? Foucault, apparently, cannot imagine an alternative possibility, namely, that Malle and the others wished to formulate a number of questions and to try out various responses without limiting themselves to documentary fact or tracing indelible patterns on the memory of Frenchmen.

The Foucault interview dwells, to the point of monotony, on what the philosopher takes to be a crucial deficiency in Malle's film and others like it: "The theme, roughly speaking, is that there have not been any popular struggles in the twentieth century. This affirmation has been formulated successively in two ways. The first time, soon after the war, by simply saying, 'The 20th century, what a century of heroes! There were Churchill, De Gaulle, there were the paratroopers and the squadrons, etc.' Which is another way of saying: 'There was no popular struggle, the real battle was that one.' . . . The other way, more recent, skeptical or cynical, if you like, consists of affirming purely and simply: 'Look at what in fact did happen. Where did you see struggles? Where do you see people rebelling, taking up arms?' " The consequence of which, according to Foucault and his friends, is that "the people" are asked to believe that the French nation "collaborated with the Germans," that "they swallowed everything," and that there is no other way to "remember" what happened. If Louis Malle made a film about collaboration, and it seems to confirm what Ophüls presented in a documentary format, Malle must have intended to show that no optimism is possible for those who think realistically about ordinary people and their relation to contemporary political systems. Though Malle may have thought to make an "honest" film, to correct the Resistance myths and inflated legends of popular struggle, he succeeded only in proving that neither he nor the rest of us can take seriously the idea of principled political resistance among ordinary men. "Is it actually possible to make a positive film about the struggles of the Resistance?" Foucault asks, and concludes that it is not. "One has the impression that that would make people laugh, or simply, that the film would not be seen."

Several questions present themselves at this point: (1) If people would laugh at any positive cinematic representation of popular resistance, would they do so because we have been ideologically conditioned to be skeptical of ordinary decency and simple courage? (2) Is it plausible tht films have played a major role in this conditioning? (3) How likely is it that a complex and beautiful film like *Lacombe, Lucien* will convey and implant ideological messages? Would it not be more likely to open up possibilities than to close them off, to make viewers as potentially receptive to the idea of principled resistance as to the idea of perfect complicity in Nazi brutality? (4) Might we not be skeptical about popular struggle—especially in the context of the Nazi period—for good reason? Haven't we been given enough of the historical record to know what may no longer be supposed? Perhaps it is difficult to imagine an entire film about "the struggles of the Resistance" because such a film would probably suggest that we take positive hope on the basis of what had to be—in view of the historical record—a marginal response to Hitler?

Foucault believes that re-creations of the Nazi period in France falsify the fact of an objective possibility which the historical record cannot wholly compromise. It does not matter that most Frenchmen collaborated, or shut their eyes, or refused to lift a finger. What matters is that a significant number of Frenchmen did resist the Nazis, that many others would have resisted had they been able to imagine some means of effectually organizing themselves against the occupying forces. More, if Frenchmen are ever to imagine a means of popular resistance to whatever happens to be the dominant reality of the moment, they will have to be encouraged to think of themselves in a "positive" way. This will not come to pass if the most accomplished artists tell people they are collaborators at heart, that they have nothing to remember but a tradition of dishonor, and that courage consists in the ability to face up to these sorry facts. What Malle and others take to be the facts of life are no more than reflections of a contemporary French political climate in which a deflationary ideological "realism" has come to replace Gaullist "grandeur" in the hearts of citizens. For Foucault, Malle is as much involved in the contemporary French situation as any French citizen. *Lacombe, Lucien* must be viewed as part of the political and cultural climate of its time—which is not 1944, when the action of the film is set, but 1973, when the film was shot.

Foucault's thesis rests upon an assumption that works of art are responsible to the constituencies they affect, that they may not "innocently" address issues as if they were to be held accountable only in terms directly recommended by the works themselves. If

Malle's film does not pass beyond the demythologizing functions assigned to it by Malle, if it is essentially nothing but a "negative" representation, it needs to be "corrected" in terms of what it might have been. This is not, in Foucault's understanding, a violation of the film but an attempt to place it, to retrieve for it a representative status which it seems not to have wanted. In proportion as Malle's film is directed to particular historical occasions and to the delineation of individual characters or agents, Foucault suspects that it may not be able to see what general understanding it will effect. By treating everything, including decisive local events and small heroic culminations, "in passing," as Foucault says, "without *capitalizing anything*" as especially important or broadly symptomatic, the film argues implicitly "that there is nothing worth remembering." If every detail has equal importance, if life is nothing but life, if to be ordinary is to be without significant redemptive prospect, then wisdom lies in cynical resignation. This Foucault cannot accept. Malle and the other filmmakers, like the rest of us, must be instructed in what is really at stake in recent re-creations of the past.

The trouble with all of this is that *Lacombe, Lucien* does not affect us as Foucault thinks it would have to, given the political climate of France in recent years. For one thing, it is not a *French* film in the sense that Foucault suggests. It is so very close in spirit to other national re-creations that it must be said to express a European rather than a French sentiment. Nor is this sentiment what Foucault thinks it is. Its function is not, broadly speaking, demythologizing. No one watching the film in a properly responsive way will feel that Malle wishes to debunk particular inherited attitudes or to prove a point. What Foucault calls "popular struggles" are not at issue, one way or the other. To be attentive to the film is to understand throughout that there must have been struggles in Europe during the period of the Occupation; with so many people affected—for better or worse—some at least would have had to resist simply to protect their personal interests. Foucault cannot mean to suggest that he believes in popular struggles that have no relation to the concrete personal interests of individual citizens. There will always be a minority, of course, who act largely on the basis of political or moral conviction, but these are likely always to be the special cases, the heroes, if you will. If Malle refuses to underline their participation in the conflict, to celebrate their courage, we cannot fail all the same to think of them. Though they hover at the margins of our attention, never threaten really to displace the focus on Lucien Lacombe and his friends, they demand to be acknowledged, intermittently. Does

Malle falsify anything when he has the district Resistance leader brought into Gestapo headquarters to be tortured, and refuses to let us dwell on the event, drawing us off with Lucien to other "business"? We do not forget the image of the Resistance leader, his head fiercely dunked again and again in a tub of water, his captors standing by or participating dispassionately. Nor do we overlook the way Malle structures the event, framing it in a partially open doorway into which Lucien can peer, with the rest of us, only long enough to register what has happened before retreating downstairs to less immediately terrible pastimes.

Malle's film does not attempt to demythologize, because there was nothing left to debunk by the time the film was made. Very few persons—French or otherwise—can have believed by 1974 that political resistance to the Nazi occupation took the form of a principled popular movement. Resentment may well have run high in occupied territories, but there is a considerable difference between resentment and resistance. A wide range of popular historical works and of speculative philosophical inquiries into the Nazi phenomenon had surely indicated—if nothing else—the failure of European populations to take effectual steps to protect the Jewish minority* and to deny the Nazis a foothold. Not even the French—and Foucault seems to think they are among those who cannot yet have heard the news—can have escaped the impact of such influential studies as Adorno's *The Authoritarian Personality*, Fromm's *Escape From Freedom*, Arendt's *Eichmann in Jerusalem*, or Sartre's *Anti-Semite and Jew*. Surely they cannot have missed the more serious novels and plays devoted to the combined issues of Nazism and Occupation, the international debates roused by European productions of Rolf Hochhuth's *The Deputy* ten years earlier, or by Peter Weiss's *The Investigation*. Foucault comes to Malle's film, and to the others, with a mistaken idea, and finds in the works he examines only what he expects to find.

Lacombe, Lucien is, in part, a film about collaboration, but it does not presume therefore to encompass the European experience of Fascism and Nazi occupation. There were, after all, many different kinds of collaboration, the most usual being collaboration from fear. This kind of collaboration we do not hear much about in Malle's film, which dwells instead on such factors as simple stupidity and power

---

*The well-known Scandinavian exceptions only serve to underline the unpleasant facts of the matter.

lust. No record is falsified because no one is given to understand that the entire historical record is at issue. Malle is proposing for himself, and for us, certain basic questions, to which he provides *possible* responses: Not, what were the kinds of collaboration by which the French people dishonored themselves, but what is the meaning of collaboration and how do we make sense of it? Not, collaboration represented the erosion of popular belief in particular democratic values or a collective failure of nerve in France, but collaboration cannot be understood apart from the experiences of the individual human beings whose prospects for one sort of behavior or another are shaped by the concrete circumstances of their lives. In this sense the cool, relatively detached, seeming "objectivity" of Malle's presentation consorts very well with his ultimate purposes. The film critic Pauline Kael observes, with characteristic shrewdness, that Malle's ". . . technique is to let the story seem to tell itself while he searches and observes. His gamble is that the camera will discover what the artist's imagination can't, and steadily, startlingly, the gamble pays off." There is no mystification of the medium and its magic powers here, but an attempt to get at a phenomenon that resists easy attribution or summary. Malle's film leaves us with no message of any kind because he respects the intransigent particularity and terrible complexity of the materials he treats. To say that the camera discovers what we can't think hard enough or well enough to discover without it is to say that, in *Lacombe, Lucien,* we take something away that is not reducible to formulaic explanation. The European experience as such is at once larger and narrower than Malle's intention: larger, in the sense that it would have to involve a synthesis of diverse phenomena rather than unabashed conviction in the persuasive meaningfulness of a singular character or event; narrower, in the sense that it would involve only what we could give a name and relate to other comparably "domesticated" historical experiences.

Ms. Kael also writes that "the movie is the boy's face. The magic is in the intense curiosity and intelligence behind the film—in Malle's perception that the answers to our questions about how people with no interest in politics become active participants in brutal torture are to be found in Lucien's plump-cheeked, narrow-eyed face." Foucault would no doubt respond that this is to capitulate with a vengeance to the ideology of the film, according to which particular images are ever so "convincing" by virtue of their pure visual intensity; an intensity, moreover, fully resistant to verbal translation and its consequent "reduction." I do not think Ms. Kael's evocation need yield to the charge. It is neither ideological nor evasive. She says, quite simply, what the film inevitably impresses upon us: that it is possible to collaborate, to do terrible things, without knowing what one is doing or why one should cease. It is possible, that is, if one is Lucien, and if circumstances invite one to become comfortably involved without having to feel that anything to which one has genuinely belonged will be betrayed. I cannot agree with Ms. Kael that "the movie is the boy's face," because I do not think the questions are limited to collaboration and the participation in torture. But insofar as these are primary questions in the film, Ms. Kael is certainly instructive in telling us what kind of answers Malle is willing to provide.

Foucault does not think it is possible to make "a positive film about the struggles of the Resistance," and perhaps, in a special sense, he is right. If Lucien's face tells us as much as Ms. Kael thinks it does, one will have to wonder what sort of "positive" organization may be expected to deal with it. How will such an organization lure him in? Will it promise him the sort of immediate gratification awarded by his participation in Gestapo activities? What will it substitute for the pleasure Lucien takes in expressing his rage towards the socially "privileged" classes by sleeping with their daughters, sadistically forcing his way into their privacy, casually destroying their material supports—as Lucien breaks to pieces the model ship owned by the adolescent son of a Resistance doctor? Clearly, it would seem, if one is to make a "positive" film such as Foucault recommends, and to be true to what most of us take our recent experience to be, one will have to select an alternative focus. Lucien will not do. This may mean, of course, that, though one wishes to make a film about popular struggle, "the people" will have to be rigorously excluded from one's persisting focus. Lucien's face, or faces like it, will create problems that no determinedly "positive" film will be able to solve. The best one can do is to develop a range of Resistance figures who stand somewhere between "the people" and the larger-than-life heroes who typically compromise any belief in popular struggle.* This Malle did not

---

*The best example of a moderately "positive" film made along the lines I have indicated is Alain Resnais's *La Guerre Est Finie* (1966). Here the principal figure is an aging Spanish revolutionary named Diego who has been working for twenty-five years with a cadre of "professionals" to overthrow the Franco regime. A text by Sartre used as an epigraph in the published film script describes very well the arduous, frequently disheartening "activist" Resistance enterprise: "As for the action itself, it must be called an undertaking, for it is a slow tenacious work of enlightenment which lasts indefinitely." This we feel, and admire, as we watch

wish to do, because, one supposes, he was interested in something else—not in a positive or negative film, but in a series of problems in the domain of imaginative re-creation which required the face of Lucien and of his principal antagonist, the Jewish tailor Albert Horn.

It is curious that Foucault should not have mentioned Horn at all. For though he does not occupy our attention as insistently as Lucien, Horn is an imposing presence throughout the film, as much for the boy as for us. There is much to be said for Lucien's face, for the open depths of its relative imperturbability. But there is more to be said, and fruitfully remembered, about the face of Albert Horn. His is the face of Western civilization itself, and of the ravages wrought by the modern barbarism. One doesn't want to make too much of this representative status, and it is fair to say that Malle resists at every point the temptation to underline it. In fact, we understand Horn rather well in the first two or three minutes of our acquaintance with him—we know him in his erect posture, his carriage, his poise, the restrained sorrow etched in the lines of the face, the worry and sleeplessness contained in and around the eyes. We recognize too the underlying softness in the slightly overfull pucker of the mouth, the promise of "tasteful" compromise which is all he'll have to show for the impulse to resist what others wish to do with him. In every look and gesture, in the terrible restraint of his utterance and the easy elegance of his continuously muffled disapprovals, he is a stone in the path of any possible popular resistance struggle. It is not that he lacks courage or conviction, but that he is tired and does not understand what exactly he would have to fight against to put up an active resistance. He seems as genuinely incapable of hating Lucien as we, obviously, are meant to be. For it is Horn's fate to see what there is

---

Resnais's film. Though we know, in studying it, that the anticipated popular struggle in Spain may be as far from coming to pass as it was twenty-five years earlier, the positive thrust of the action cannot be denied. Probably this is because its focus is mostly limited to Diego and his associates, who, for all their misgivings and increasing weariness, continue to believe that they are doing what must be done. Though they do occasionally lose touch with the meaning of their actions, they demonstrate a considerable measure of what Diego calls "patience and irony." Most telling, I think, in the context of our larger argument, is that Resnais never gives us a glimpse of Lucien, which is to say, of his Spanish equivalent. Though there is much talk of popular resistance, of workers' movements and the like, the film never takes us inside Spain, to the workers themselves and their stubborn, casual limitations. Had it done so, it is unlikely that Resnais could have managed as much as he does in the way of hopeful anticipation.

in Lucien that makes him attractive. Even as Lucien's victim he has to acknowledge the impressive "reality" of unabashed animal vitality. There is even something fatherly in the way Horn observes the boy's adolescent preenings and absurd self-assertions—clearly disapproving, but fatherly all the same. The will to struggle, especially against those who feel no guilt and have no way of responding to a civil appeal, is all but extinct in Horn, and it will not do to complain that he is nothing but a bourgeois shopkeeper, not fit to embody the will to struggle Foucault thinks to find in the working classes. If he is no salvational figure—if he would seem to have no future at all—Horn is yet a moving representation of human qualities we shall need to draw upon if we are to construct a liveable future. I cannot imagine that Malle thought any less of Horn than that, or thought that we should somehow take him for less.

There are a variety of other figures in Malle's film, but its essential resonance is to be located in the steady opposition of Lucien Lacombe and Albert Horn. Malle's object was to bring one face right up close to the other, to see what effects might thereby be produced. In contriving to do this, Malle had to know that nothing "positive" or fundamentally uplifting could possibly be made to emerge. He wanted to discover what it feels like to work upon a fragment of the recent past, what are and are not appropriate sensations in the face of horror and the small paradoxes of history. In the two central faces of his film he could watch the fine registration of states of feeling too fleeting and unsure to fix in words. It is a measure of his achievement that, though there are words in the film, though Malle will not foolishly give up the attempt to articulate some of the things his characters must feel, he lets the faces say most of what matters. This they can do not only because they belong to fine actors but because Malle has played them against one another in a consistently interesting though unemphatic way. We take a great deal from our encounters with Albert Horn because we are permitted to see with him what must be dealt with in the person of Lucien; in the same way we can follow the notable increase in Lucien's avidity as a result of his regular intercourse with Horn—Lucien cannot say, really, what he wants, what moves or excites him, but we know, when we look with his eyes at the slightly rumpled and increasingly forlorn figure of his Jewish antagonist. It is not that he wishes literally to be like Horn, or to have what he has—Lucien can in any case take what he wants. What he envies is the demeanor of control, of grace under pressure, the air of one who has lived and cannot pretend in the interest of pride that he does not miss what he was. Lucien envies, perhaps most of all, the ability to assume the role of victim and suppliant without any corresponding inclination to grovel or whine—as though it might be possible to have one's way after all, if only the right heartstring were plucked. There are limitations in this sort of "strength," and Horn deteriorates badly in the course of the film, letting himself and his appearance go to pieces more even than we'd quite been able to anticipate. But Lucien doesn't care for those limitations as we should. He can admire Horn, "play" to him, just as much as he needs to while tormenting him. It is all very strange, and utterly believable.

To a point, Foucault admires what Malle has done, but he wishes that the French people might have been given a more accurate account of their experience. To accomplish this, he believes, Malle would have had to face up to the inscribing of his account in a history to which the film bears witness. This is the history of recent attempts to understand the phenomenon of collaboration and occupation. Had Malle faced up to the role of his film in "writing" this history, he would have had to conceive and execute it along other lines. Though Foucault does not elaborate the prospect of an alternative development, it is clear from what he says that the character of Horn would have had to be drawn differently, and Lucien as well. As they stand, these characters demand a development which has little to do with politics. Politics has to do with power, with the desire for power and the consequences of its exercise. In *Lacombe, Lucien,* Foucault believes, the issue of power is displaced and evaded. The desire for power is converted to sexual desire, and the necessary resolution takes place at the level of erotic culmination rather than in the realization of political objectives.

Though Horn is not himself an erotic figure, he assists in the process of displacement whereby political conflict is turned to personal difference and the drama of character. But Foucault's indictment has more to do with Lucien. The boy had become involved in politics as a means of asserting a will to power which unmistakably answered to his needs. In the context of the film these needs are presumed to speak for the needs of other persons similarly unable to think through their desires and make sense of their meagre experience. Foucault and his associates resist the suggestion that popular needs are invariably reducible to erotic equivalents. Their conviction is that a genuine politics is possible even for people, like Lucien, who can be diverted all too easily from their attraction to popular movements. This can hardly be persuasive to anyone not already disposed to believe in the idea of popular struggle, but Foucault is nonetheless disarming in the concessions he makes to his antagonists. He sees as clearly as anyone might hope that Lucien is not a likely candidate for participation in resistance movements—though in the course of things, Malle suggests, he might accidentally have fallen in with resistance fighters as easily as he fell in with the Gestapo. For Foucault it is all a matter of potential: One must not close off a possibility by suggesting it could never have been realized, even when circumstances seemed to require that it come to pass. The artist's responsibility, at the very least, is not to confuse matters, not to pretend to be talking about politics while actually collapsing distinctions and displacing one progress for another. At issue are the artist's honesty and clarity of intention. These qualities it is possible to realize even when the complexity of the materials at hand is such as to daunt all confident projections.

"I wonder," Foucault says at one point, "if Marxist analyses are not to a certain extent victims of the abstract character of the notion of liberty. Under a regime like the Nazis', it is clear that one doesn't have liberty. But not to have liberty does not mean that one doesn't have power." What power does Lucien have? The power to exert some control over other lives, to be a factor where before he'd been a cipher. And the Nazis themselves? "We have to ask ourselves," Foucault suggests, "if that regime was nothing but a bloody dictatorship, how is it that on the third of May, 1945 there were still Germans ready to fight to the last drop of blood—if there was no mode of attachment of these people to power?" With liberty one thing and power, decidedly, another, Foucault is bound to be better in the course of these formulations at posing questions than at giving answers. This is all to the good, though the suggestion persists throughout the interview that Foucault is operating from a stable foundation on the basis of which Malle and the other directors come in for disapproval. It has to be taken as a little unreasonable that Foucault should expect a particular kind of clarity from Malle when he is himself so very free to poke and probe, to give out and take back in his own reflections on the subject. Why, after all, should Lucien be any less vulnerable to manipulation and to displacement of affect than he is? And where did Malle really go wrong in permitting Horn to "personalize" the terms of the conflict for Lucien? Foucault's various concessions to the difficulty of it all indicate beyond a doubt that the idea of political liberty is likely to have but marginal importance for most people, and that any filmmaker who thought it irresistible would fail to see its peculiarly inverse relation to the satisfactions of power. Malle, at the very

least, must be given credit for seeing such things, and for demonstrating that it is possible to mount a political action without capitulating to the abstract dynamics of a purely political mechanism.
Lucien and Albert Horn serve Malle so well because they require
that he allow them to grow and to interact in accordance with the
principles of their character. Had they been less coherently realized
as characters, more susceptible to Malle's ulterior purposes in moving them about, the politics of the film would emerge as a mode of
authorial calculation. Foucault doesn't address the problem from
this point of view, but he should.

Bruno Bettelheim, in his long essay on *Seven Beauties*, has more
in common with Foucault than either would be likely to admit.
That their opinions clearly differ on important issues is less important for our purposes than the fact that they approach works of art
with comparable expectations. The most interesting of these expectations is that works of art will answer to particular historical requirements even when the artists have indicated an intention to
make use of history rather than to confirm or establish a historical
record. Foucault wanted Louis Malle to resist the inscription of his
film in a certain kind of "revisionist" historical enterprise currently
taking shape in France. Why? Not because he might thereby have
made a better or more enduringly persuasive film, but because the
cause of a parochial notion of popular struggle might thereby have
been better served. Bettelheim wanted Lina Wertmuller to let us
see the concentration camp experience as an experience different
not only in degree but in kind from any other; also, to project the
will to survive as consistent with the will to retain one's essential
humanity—not with the will to get by at any price. Bettelheim's
demands have more to do with the given world of *Seven Beauties*
than Foucault's have with *Lacombe, Lucien*, but Bettelheim does not
therefore serve our understanding any better. By coming to *Seven
Beauties* with fixed expectations, by "reading" the film with the
eyes of one who feels he knows in advance all that may be truly
said of the concentration camp experience, he denies the viewer's
actual experience of surprise, provocation, and a special kind of
disinterested contemplation.

Important distinctions must be made if Bettelheim's argument is
to be properly answered. The contemporary historian John Lukacs
has had enormously useful things to say about these distinctions.
In an essay on E. L. Doctorow's novel *Ragtime*,* Lukacs contrasts a

*See "Doctorwurlitzer or History in *Ragtime*," *Salmagundi*, no. 31–32, Fall 1975–
Winter 1976.

nineteenth-century genre, "the historical novel," with a twentieth-century form, uneasily labeled "novelized history." Lukacs does not think his categories as flexible as I do, and he would no doubt resist my suggestion that "cinematized history" would serve the basic point of his distinction as well as "novelized history." My reader will, however, follow my advice, for the moment at least, and substitute the one term for the other in pursuing Lukacs's argument: "The new genre is the converse of the historical novel. In *War and Peace* or in *Gone With the Wind* history is the background. In the [novelized history, like *Ragtime,* or Solzhenitsyn's *August Nineteen-Fourteen*] history is the foreground. In the classic historical novel the great events of history are painted on a large canvas in order to lend depth to the story, to give an added dimension to the main characters. In the [novelized history] the reverse: the main characters serve for the purpose of illuminating the history of certain events, of a certain time. In this historical novel the author's principal interest is *the novel.* In [novelized history] the author's principal interest is *history*—perhaps a new kind of history, but history nonetheless." Though recent popular works of novelized history may distort the historical record, at their best they do represent, in Lukacs's view, an advance in historical consciousness. Bettelheim does not think that cinematized history (my term, not his) can represent a fruitful advance in any kind of consciousness unless it registers historical events with documentary accuracy and rests upon a sound humanistic foundation. Though he does not make use of Lukacs's distinction, does not argue the necessary relation between fact and fiction, individual and collective, in the conception of a film like *Seven Beauties,* his paper everywhere cries out for just that sort of theoretical underpinning.

But let us look at Lukacs's distinction more closely. The novelized history is said to use characters and portray particular encounters "for the purpose of illuminating the history of certain events, of a certain time." Illumination—the truth of the historical record—is the goal. Works of art typically propose to illuminate the truth, of course, but it is not always easy to say what kind of truth is available to a given novel or film. When Lukacs writes that in the older genre—the historical novel—"the author's principal interest is *the novel,*" he means to identify a certain kind of truth to which such works are principally suited. This is the truth of human feeling, a truth which is ratified by the accumulated experience of each reader or filmgoer. Insofar as such works are persuasive, they appeal to our intuitive sense of things. If they present extraordinary persons involved in unusual exploits, they will develop their behavior and join events in such a way that our sense of the probable is tested no more than it may be without our turning from the spectacle in dismay. The truth to which we respond is, again, a truth of experience: We sense that, given a certain kind of extraordinary personage placed in very special circumstances, this is the way he would very likely behave; these are the likely consequences of initiating events; these are the sensations and thoughts an alert and intelligent observer ought to be permitted to have when confronted with such materials. This is the kind of truth we want and expect from most works of art.

Lukacs's notion of novelized history proposes to alter this expectation, to explain why it is we may be satisfied with another kind of truth when confronted by a book like *Ragtime*. It is the passion for historical truth which determines our response to these newer works, which have been created to answer to a demand earlier readers were not as likely to make as we: namely, the demand that no truth we are meant to accept be presented without the support of detailed context and place in time. Since all truth is presumed to be relative to particular circumstances and characterological disposition—itself a historical phenomenon which varies from one era to another—even a truth of feeling must be located in respect to time and general probability. Reader interest will tend to be less involved in the truth of human nature than *a* truth of human nature in a given period. This is not to deny that general truths may emerge from the concentration on individual, specifically conditioned truths in their context, only that the terms of extrapolation will be differently weighted than they used to be. The issue is one of emphasis: As Lukacs writes, in the newer genre "the author's principal interest is *history*"—it is not the author's only interest, but his *principal* interest.

Bruno Bettelheim, in refusing to think through such distinctions, never really discovers what Wertmuller's *Seven Beauties* achieves. The issue here is not so much the success or failure of the film, but the expectations and responses it may be said to generate. Bettelheim assumes that Wertmuller's principal interest is history, that the film is an example of what we have called, following Lukacs, cinematized history. He assumes, moreover, that the filmgoer cannot but be misled by the film, since what he is bound to find in it is a particular version of the historical truth which takes unforgivable liberties with the actual historical record it presumes to enlarge upon. The actual record in this case is, of course, something with which Bruno Bettelheim is singularly familiar. As a concentration-camp survivor, as a scholarly authority in the field of holocaust studies, as author of several important works on terror and survivorship, he has at once a very large claim on our respect and attention. The problem is that his primary assumption is mistaken. No one believes while watching *Seven Beauties* that the historical record has been significantly clarified or enlarged. No one need feel that the actual experience of survivors has been betrayed, or demeaned. To argue the case as Bettelheim does is to mistake one kind of truth for another. There are more serious errors in Bettelheim's analysis, but the first one is crucial in directing the course of the others.

Bettelheim remembers the opening of the film—like the other parts—very well indeed, and what he makes of it may be said to stand for his response to the entire film:

> Before the film's story begins, we are shown a series of newsreels of Fascism: demonstrations, marches, Mussolini exhorting the masses, Mussolini shaking Hitler's hand; war, the bombing and destruction of cities, the killing and maiming of people. Though all this is presented as horrible, we are entertained by an amusing, mocking cabaret song accompanying the newsreel scenes. And Mussolini and Hitler are also presented partly as comic figures—an approach that is supported by the song, in which all the contradictions of life are accepted at the same time. The song says "Oh yeah" equally to "the ones who have never had a fatal accident" and to "the ones who have had one." And though most of the lyrics and the singing bitingly reject the world of Fascism we see on the screen, they are also funny, and this quality simultaneously adds to the rejection and takes the sting of true seriousness out of it.
>
> . . . The newsreels and the song accompanying them in *Seven Beauties* take us back to the period when we thought that we did not need to take Hitler and Mussolini seriously. But the war scenes show us at the same time what happened because we didn't take these men seriously. This is a contradiction that runs all through the film.

So, a combination of newsreel footage and "mocking cabaret song" frames Wertmuller's film and instructs us in Wertmuller's approach to her materials. She works, according to Bettelheim, on a principle of contradiction and alternation: The ludicrous and the obscene mingle freely in her imagination with the terrible, the good with the bad, the playful with the serious. The result, in Bettelheim's view, is confusion and irrelevance. If viewers cannot confidently tell an appropriate response from an intolerable impropriety, if they are asked to laugh when they should cover their eyes in shame and horror, they may decide that one thing is much like another, that truth is in vividness of presentation and the power to evoke feeling—not in the substance of the vision. When audiences are so manipulated, Bettelheim argues, they will come to feel that they may not trust their responses at all—including decent and once reliable responses to cruelty and torture. They will find ways to deny that they have such responses at all, or that such responses are more legitimate, more worthy of their humanity, than others.

The opening of Wertmuller's film is no doubt full of incongruity and confusion, as Bettelheim rightly argues. What is its ostensible purpose and the effect it may be said to produce? As the frame for the film, rather than a part of the story, it may be said both to stand apart and to support or establish the central action. It stands apart in presenting what appears to be actual newsreel footage, while the central action is clearly fictional. No matter whether we take the story line to reflect some accurate semblance of what actually took place in concentration camps. Insofar as the story is enacted; as it involves patently "private" or "exclusive" insights into very special characters; as it persistently juxtaposes the improbable and the probable with no trace of apology or regret—the audience knows that it watches the unfolding of a fiction. But what does it think as it labors to follow the opening sequence? Fact, or fiction? The distinction is not usually put so crudely when we speak of a film like *Seven Beauties*, but here there is no alternative. Bettelheim forces the issue in such a way that we cannot but go back to "first" questions. If we take the newsreel footage to be authentic, which is to say, part of the documentary record—no matter how fragmentary—must we therefore suppose that Wertmuller's intention was to prepare us for the unfolding of a cinematized history? The supposition might have been justified had the director not put in the accompanying cabaret song. As it is, the opening sequence undercuts any possible inference that Wertmuller is primarily interested in settling the historical record. If the song presents contradiction, if one interpretation of the holocaust experience vies with another—with no apparent means of reconciling them—the audience must see at once that it is not in for a definitive accounting. It is being asked to assimilate the frightening images on the screen to the shifting perspectives offered by the all-too-knowing lyrics mounted on the sound track. Though the audience may try to manage this at first, it must recoil from the task with some unease after the opening minute or two of the film. Since there is no reliable way of adopting a single perspective on the imagery—not on the basis of the deliberately elusive cabaret lyrics, at any rate—the audience can do nothing but take in what is given, and wait for further "instructions." The unease we feel does not reflect the disappointed expectation that the definitive historical truth is about to be delivered. It reflects some feeling that we may have to work very hard to make sense of the film we are to see; also, that we shall be asked to focus not so much on what happened as on what the imagination is wont to make of the holocaust experience.

This is not an insignificant distinction, and the intelligence that registers the distinction in the opening minutes of the film will find its anticipations throughout unusually tense and uncertain. The film asks us to do several things at once: to compare and contrast what we know of the holocaust with the images projected on the screen—images which are patently fictional but which nonetheless refer unmistakably to real events we are not likely to forget; to think of the intrinsic dynamics of the imagination that contrives to move characters about and arrange events as peculiarly as it does in this film; to set up resistances to our own queasy impulses to reject what we are shown on the grounds that it violates a sombre decorum we take to be appropriate under the circumstances. In thinking about the way we perform these functions—here, as in our responses to many other works of art—we are required to differentiate between the way we ought to perform them, and the way we do perform them. Bettelheim thinks we ought to hold up the given images against the reality of the concentration camps and therefore to reject Wertmuller's images as specious and arbitrary— if *Seven Beauties* wanted to be taken as sheer fiction, it should not have suggested even for a moment that it was telling the historical truth. Also he thinks we ought not to be seriously interested in an imagination for which stacked corpses can as readily stimulate gallows humor as evoke revulsion. Finally, Bettelheim feels that, far from resisting impulses to reject, we ought to dismiss *Seven Beauties* as a film which degrades and confuses—whatever the aesthetic discriminations we may feel tempted to introduce.

Alas, we do not in general respond as we should. Wertmuller's images have a terrible authority which makes it difficult indeed to dismiss them as specious or arbitrary. Even in the opening minutes of the film we are gripped by a central fact of human experience which is imposed upon us with ferocious authenticity: the fact that imagination can put to so many uses events which had seemed singular and astonishing almost to the point of numbing the senses which had long before engaged to deal with them. In witnessing *Seven Beauties*, though we may wish to turn away in horror or to cry out, we are persuaded by Wertmuller's invention to hang on, to watch for the trophies that persistent attention can win. Is it possible to laugh at stacked corpses and do justice to the dead? The question here is almost beside the point. The film makes no pretense to do justice to the dead. Its business is another kind of remembering that has more to do with the dynamics of survival. Perhaps we ought always to think of the dead when we think of the Nazi period. Perhaps some of us are prone to think of little else, and may be blessed for so persisting. But it is a mistake to assume that everyone will be so disposed, or that *Seven Beauties* violates a mode of remembering to which it makes no claim, and to which it is obviously inadequate. If we resist impulses to reject what we are shown, we do so because those impulses are sometimes inflexible and unreliable, because they may inhibit the growth of our humanity as surely as Bettelheim thinks they will preserve and strengthen it.

But what exactly do we mean when we speak of this resistance? The film contains many sequences in which it is called into play. Not much resistance is required in the opening minutes because the presentation of materials there is so very tentative, the tension between image and cabaret song so deliberate that no "statement" may be adduced, one way or another. If we are disposed to be sickened even by the newsreel footage and the "improper" uses to which it is put, we shall not be able to attend to the rest of the film in a satisfactory way, and there will be no more to consider. But resistance of the sort we have indicated *will* be required frequently afterwards. When the protagonist Pasqualino "seduces" the monstrous female commandant in order to escape the fate to which others in the concentration camp are sentenced, we experience a revulsion so great that, for a moment, it threatens to swamp our more considered responses to the film. Pasqualino's behavior had been less than edifying in earlier sequences, but by this point, we feel, he has gone too far. The woman is as close to being a monster as we can imagine any human being to come. That Pasqualino should be willing to seduce her, to plead his love to one so fully terrible, in order to save his life seems at first incredible. Why should she believe him? Why should he assume she'll find him appealing? How can a man who's been through so much seem to have learned so little, resorting to the tiresome deception by which men have so regularly sought to master women? Along with sheer physical revulsion at the prospect of a monstrous and unfeeling coupling, we experience a nausea that frequently accompanies an apprehension of the meaningless and incomprehensible. Though Wertmuller has had the effrontery to show us almost anything we can imagine—in *Seven Beauties* as in other films like *Swept Away* and *The Seduction of Mimi*—we do not believe she will play out the seduction of the camp commandant. What point can possibly be made by pursuing an invention that so strains credulity and the limits of our tolerance?

Wertmuller allows us to resist impulses to reject the ghastly spectacle by detaching us from it and, strangely, by humanizing it. Resistance is an effect of discrimination, and discrimination is made possible by the complicating of an experience which had earlier seemed to offer nothing in the way of an enticing complexity. Revulsion is not so much overcome as, temporarily, held at bay, as the discriminative intelligence registers interesting distinctions between what we are given and what we'd expected. We resist the impulse to dismiss and to turn away because there is something for us in the spectacle, something we may not want to miss. This "something" is signaled in the marks of Pasqualino's possession by his idea, his stratagem. He is so clearly given over to it, so fully convinced that he must act out his "inspiration," that we are almost persuaded he knows what he is doing. It is all thoroughly absurd, more than a little perverse, surely disgusting to think about too closely—but we are disposed progressively to feel that Pasqualino has to do what he has determined to do. We laugh at his overtures to the commandant, enjoy her amazement, anticipate that she may have him castrated and shot—didn't those big, "sexless" German women go in for sexual butchery? we are apt to muse. Wertmuller detaches us from the spectacle by making us laugh at it and, simultaneously, by making us attend in a progressively disinterested way. We want to discover what it is about Pasqualino that drives him to the absurdity of his seduction quest. We want to know why Wertmuller finds him so compelling, and how she manages almost to make him as interesting to us. But we know as well that, to the extent that we share this interest in Pasqualino, it is an interest not so much in his particular fate as in the peculiar, abstract depths of human invention. No one imagines that Pasqualino is Wertmuller's everyman, that anyone would be as likely as he to seduce the commandant. But no one will deny that he represents for us a certain kind of possibility to which present circumstances uniquely contribute. This is the possibility that human beings may well identify their humanity, their very sense of the self and of the values that sustain it, with the energy and cunning to remain alive and scamper, perpetually, beyond the outstretched hands of circumstance. If we are detached as we watch *Seven Beauties*, we experience nonetheless a very large interest in the issues raised, an interest we cannot satisfy by rooting for Pasqualino or against him; by passing secure judgments too quickly; or by giving in to the impulse to deny our laughter.

Bettelheim argues that detachment is fruitful only if we are detached from experiences that justify such a response. It is legitimate to conclude, early in the film, that Pasqualino is a relatively worthless person, and that we are therefore not required to feel concern for him. It is not legitimate to achieve detachment from the imagery of stacked corpses—whatever the way in which they are presented—when to do so is inevitably to harden our responses to the murder of countless Jews. The operant principle here has to do with propriety, and it is not an idea anyone can take lightly. Over and over again, Bettelheim warns his reader that to confuse one mode of presentation with another is to forfeit the capacity to keep things in their rightful place. The comic and the horrible, persistently juxtaposed and intermixed, may make for a certain debased kind of aesthetic delight, but the "combination" will not yield to better purposes. Wertmuller's film, he argues, is a degrading experience because it induces us not to take anything seriously—not even something "that would ordinarily upset us greatly or move us deeply." Talk about detachment all you want, Bettelheim would seem to say. If the result is that the heart is hardened and the intelligence learns to yield too easily to the grotesque and fantastic, no good will come of what we call aesthetic discrimination and disinterestedness.

The problem is that, by failing to resist the impulse to condemn and recoil in sheer disgust, Bettelheim misses the film's invitation to participate in a crucial experience, wherein the dominant perspective is humanized with no corresponding refusal of judgment. This is an unfortunate feature of much self-consciously humanistic thinking. In insisting upon what it knows, it closes itself to all sorts of things it might otherwise have welcomed. To resist a "reflex" judgment is not, after all, to lose capacity to judge, or to reflect, or to forfeit the right to judge at a later time. No doubt there is a sense in which we can take too much time making up our minds; a sense in which to wait, and split hairs, and search, perpetually, for nuance, is to lose any genuine prospect of moral intensity. But a film like *Seven Beauties*, after all, promises *something* in the way of a judgment. It is a work of art, of determinate length and scope and execution. The film, at least, may be judged, if nothing else, and there is bound to be some release of tension in this. We resist the impulse to judge and dismiss abruptly because we are secure in the knowledge that we shall have something on which to pass judgment later on. The film asks us to put up this necessary resistance by complicating our feelings and by humanizing our perceptions of what is going on. Bettelheim considers this sort of complication a disgrace. By making it difficult for us to know what we feel or, exactly, what we should be looking at, Wertmuller makes us doubt our right to judge. From such confusion, one thing looks much like another, a crime might just as well have been an act of charity, and we are left in a muddle from which nothing in the film will extricate us.

Bettelheim's moral knowledge is based upon a number of truths to which every decent person is supposed to be as devoted as he. Because the film seems to go against the grain of these simple truths, Bettelheim feels, it is clearly a violation of the given and a disservice to the survivors of the holocaust, who know what to make of their experience. Example:

> 1—Pasqualino: ". . . charmingly portrayed by Giancarlo Giannini as the prototypical 'little man,' who will be a Fascist under Fascism, a Communist under Communism, and a democrat in a democracy. But this portrait of the little man, which the film makes us believe in, is a lie. The world's little men do not rape or kill—not under Fascism or Communism or in a democracy. These little men do not think of or manage an erection and intercourse with an absolutely abhorrent woman, even if their lives are at stake. The little man is banal, but he is not evil."
>
> 2—The Commandant: "The closer she gets to being a woman, the more grotesque this mass of flesh becomes, but also the more human, and the greater depth she reveals, not least because of the way she is acted by Shirley Stoler. She is not only shown imprisoned in her body but shown to feel it and to suffer from it. Her being disgusted by Pasqualino and his lie of loving her—which she, knowing how repulsive she

is, does not believe for a moment—is but a small reflection of her disgust with herself . . . When she says that Pasqualino, because he managed an erection, will survive and win in the end, while she is doomed, her dreams unattainable, she implies that, unlike Pasqualino, she is unable to have sex without the appropriate feelings . . .

. . . But this portrayal of a concentration-camp commander is no less a lie than the portrayal of Pasqualino as a sometimes charming but always utterly unimportant little man. If any one thing characterized the rulers of the concentration camps, it was their inability to reflect on themselves, to see themselves for what they were. Had they been able to recognize themselves as they really were—which the camp commander in this film is shown as being able to do—they could not have carried on for a moment . . . Somebody with so much insight into herself could not behave toward the prisoners as we see her do."

In the first example, Bettelheim rejects the view of Pasqualino as capable of evil on the scale depicted in *Seven Beauties*. The little man as portrayed by Wertmuller "is a lie." How do we know? Bettelheim seems certain in his declarations on such matters, and assumes we will believe him. If Pasqualino were capable of evil on a grand scale, of indiscriminate killing and rape, he would not be a banal creature. This is the thrust of the argument. It is not, as such, a historical argument; nor is it an enlargement or application of a psychological thesis which has been experimentally validated. The argument is an argument from a body of shared knowledge which is often referred to as our fund of collective wisdom. "Little men do not rape or kill"—the conviction plainly expresses itself, with no hint of qualification or misgiving. Who, then, is responsible for the killing and raping? If not Pasqualino, presumably some other kind of social misfit will be held responsible. This misfit who commits evil deeds, according to Bettelheim, will not be banal. He will have some sense of what he is doing and what it means to do terrible things simply because he has been encouraged or empowered to do them. The evil man will not drift mindlessly into evil deeds, and will not think to defend himself by claiming he could not know how terrible his actions were. He will participate in brutality and terror because he stands to realize something from his participation, and he will know what he wants and how high the price may be. Pasqualino is incapacitated from this kind of participation by virtue of his mindless stumbling about from prospect to prospect with no resolute sense of what he really wants and may actually hope to achieve. He is banal because he is totally subject to the designs of others, and as such he is incapable of the resolve required to perform evil deeds, which require a measure of fortitude, determination, even passion.

If I have properly represented Bettelheim's thought—and I do not see how I can have failed to represent it under the circumstances—I have also demonstrated that it is perfectly insupportable. It is a fact that many human beings in a number of European nations participated in brutal activities over a period of many years. That Hitler's programs were carried out by ordinary persons is not a fact anyone is in a position to dispute. It does not matter whether we call these ordinary persons banal or something else. We know what they did, and what they did was evil, if the word "evil" has any ordinary meaning at all. To kill helpless people, to rape and pillage, is to do evil. Bettelheim argues that it is a slander upon ordinary men and women to show that they may be induced to support or to perform such evil actions. At one point he says he accepts Hannah Arendt's theory of Adolph Eichmann as the very embodiment of banality. But what can it mean to embrace the theory if one does not accept also what follows irrevocably from it? Namely, that banality is a condition to which human beings succumb; that certain cultures nurture in their citizens a complex of attitudes which incline them to deny responsibility for their deeds; and that such persons are to be judged by standards of civilized behavior whether or not they wish to assume responsibility for their actions. In this sense it is clear that banal persons are precisely those who, in our time, will perform evil deeds. Though they may pretend merely to be following orders, or to have acted out of confusion, they will be as capable of evil as though they had earnestly desired to murder Jews in order to steal their shoes or sleep with their daughters. For Bettelheim to deny the possibility of evil to banal little men is to deny that there have been responsible agents performing the many individual acts of brutality which together constitute the experience of the Nazi period.

Why does Bettelheim stake so much on this point? His concern is not really to assert that ordinary persons are fundamentally decent. He knows that any generalization of that kind is bound to seem dubious, at best. His more urgent contention is that Pasqualino, as the prototypical little man, cannot have equated survival with the capacity to do terrible things. This is Bettelheim's central concern, to insist over and over again that survival in the Nazi period depended not upon the ability to kill or in other ways to dehumanize oneself, but to keep up one's sense of decency and honor. Though Terence Des Pres* and other scholars of the holocaust have lately argued that survival often meant learning how to "live beyond the compulsions of culture," Bettelheim argues that persons like Pasqualino cannot be said to represent the meaning of survivorship. Though some, like Pasqualino, may have reverted to sheer animalism, and may somehow have survived, most who came through the concentration camp experience did so because they were lucky, and because they knew better than to succumb entirely to the example of monstrous debasement continually held up to them. The portrait of Pasqualino is a lie because it shows him to have survived by virtue of his capacity to do terrible things—things, moreover, such a person cannot have done in light of the banal characteristics attributed to him.

The argument sends us back, as it must, to Wertmuller's film, or at least to what we can recall of it. At once we are compelled to remember that Pasqualino seemed always a peculiar fellow, slippery and outrageous, something of a buffoon, at times a caricature of what we take to be a familiar Italian figure. It is the figure of the Italian male as the genial, simpleminded butt, hung up in the various ways played upon in a succession of popular films and novels. This is not *man*, but a certain kind of man, a certain kind of caricature of the Italian male animal. How do we know this? The opening sequences of the film had invited the viewer to wonder what might become the dominant perspective for an examination of the Nazi period. The peculiar tensions of the opening minutes—produced by a sound track that seemed to know what it thought, only to impress upon everyone the inherent uncertainty and contradiction of its knowledge—are extended to the entire film. The voice that glibly responds with an "oh yeah" to everything it sees without being able to order its perceptions is the voice that controls the entire film. *Seven Beauties* is a vision of the past and of human possibility under the auspices of a cynicism whose manifest reason for being is the dominating presence of Pasqualino. Again, it is necessary to say, Pasqualino is not *man*—not for Wertmuller, not for the viewer of her film. He is the buffoon, a perennial victim who knows how to save his skin only by adopting the most transparent stratagems customarily available to the type. It never occurs

*In *The Survivor* (1976).

to us to ask whether there is any actual human being who looks and behaves like the type because Pasqualino perfectly embodies what we have always taken the type to be.

Is it unreasonable that such a type should be said to have succeeded in saving his skin? Pasqualino may succeed, but nothing in the film suggests that anyone else would do as well in comparable circumstances. The strokes in Wertmuller's portrait are so broad, the caricature so playful and outrageously implausible, that no general conclusion may legitimately be drawn. We said earlier that the film asks us to focus "not so much on what happened as on what the imagination is wont to make of the holocaust experience." An imagination for which Pasqualino is a dominating presence is likely to be cynical in the extreme about the human truths revealed in the Nazi period. Who is to say, finally, what it takes to survive in a concentration camp? Surely Bettelheim understands that no program or strategy for survival was likely to be effective. Wertmuller's view is that, while "better men" perished, a man like Pasqualino might well have remained alive—not because he'd discovered a clever stratagem, but because he happened to be lucky. The film nowhere "supports" Pasqualino or makes general claims for his shrewdness. On the contrary, he is ruthlessly exposed. We feel that he is detestable even as we want him to succeed in seducing the camp commander and saving his skin. When, finally, he shoots a fellow prisoner, he behaves only as we would expect him to under the circumstances. There is no use in denying that such a man might well do such a thing. Better men did worse things under pressure.

Bettelheim is surely mistaken in arguing that the film elaborates a morality of survivorship. There is nothing exemplary in Pasqualino's success, nothing anyone is encouraged to emulate. Wertmuller simply imposes upon us, with all the imaginative power at her command, an image we are not likely to forget. Though Pasqualino is not *man*, he is a figure of whom it is necessary to take stock when we think about our prospects and calculate the options. The imagination which cannot deal with Pasqualino, which cannot believe that he exists, does not know a very important part of the human condition. It may be that the type is overdrawn in Wertmuller's film; indeed, the elements of patent caricature and burlesque in the portrait encourage the view that Wertmuller deliberately exaggerated the features to provoke us and to indicate what were her major concerns. These have to do with the enlargement of imaginative potential, according to which it is possible to feel involved in

Pasqualino's fate without capitulating to his view of the truth of things. Wertmuller's film succeeds precisely where Bettelheim thinks it fails: In its vivid distortions, in its strange conjunctions and grostesqueries, *Seven Beauties* compels a disinterested apprehension of issues. These are not primarily issues of historical fact but of imaginative resource: What, we consider, can the imagination do with the spectre of terror and banality acted out on a scale no one had previously imagined?

Bettelheim rejects not only the portrait of Pasqualino but of the camp commander as well. The one is "no less a lie" than the other. Though the role is persuasively enacted by Shirley Stoler, though the viewer is led to "believe" in the character, she is a palpable untruth. This camp commander appears to know herself and to understand what makes other human beings behave as they do. In reality, camp commanders were nothing like this, Bettelheim argues. "Had they been able to recognize themselves as they really were . . . they could not have carried on for a moment . . . Somebody with so much insight into herself could not behave toward the prisoners as we see her do." This is one of those arguments it is difficult to win, whatever side you take. If you argue from experience, claiming that there are actual persons full of insight who nonetheless go right on doing terrible things, you will be told that such persons only *seem* to be in possession of the insights they display. Just so, in the film, it is Wertmuller's dexterous manipulation of images that makes the camp commander *seem* plausible. The director's "success" is a form of trickery, and we are duped because we do not know how to resist this kind of deception.

But Bettelheim's side of the argument is no easier to defend. It may be logical to suppose that someone capable of speaking seriously to herself about dehumanization would consequently wish to avoid dehumanizing others and so degrading herself. It is not therefore unlikely that this person will do what she despises and deliberately enact what others already take her to be. The logic of Bettelheim's argument is limited. It has very little to do with the peculiar logic of imagination, according to which truth and contradiction are often indistinguishable. Wertmuller might justly be attacked had she simply yielded to this peculiar logic, but she doesn't. She works at it, strenuously, and finds over and over again that her general suspicion of easy humanistic truths will not be dislodged. She remains cynical and resolutely disabused, largely because she is stuck with the figure of Pasqualino. If he is decidedly a part of *the thing itself*, what can his final antagonist be but a defiantly improbable and all too believable character? The working logic of *Seven Beauties* insists that the improbable is as potentially true to our experience of life as the probable. This has only marginally to do with the familiar notion of the absurd as a determinative factor in our experience. Wertmuller doesn't incline to make broad metaphysical statements. She is intent on following out a number of broad imaginative paths laid out by her involvement with certain kinds of human beings. These figures are, in her films, as likely to work in a factory as to be swept away on a desert island or to find themselves in a concentration camp. To think the portrait of the camp commander is a lie is to reject the kind of imagination for which particular kinds of conflict and paradox are both interesting and important. There is nothing in *Seven Beauties* to prompt so determined a rejection.

But let us return, for a moment, to the question of historical truth. Suppose it was true that camp commanders were not persons of considerable depth, and that it was possible to prove this to anyone's satisfaction. Would Wertmuller's portrait be therefore less "true," less believable than it is? The circumstance as described here is so hypothetical that we are hard put to answer, but we must try. If Wertmuller's character ran counter to everything we know of camp commanders, we should naturally have greater difficulty in believing what we are shown. We should not readily be made to believe in a camp commander who did his best to save the lives of Jews and worked to make other Nazi camp officers cooperate in the effort to prevent destruction. No more can we believe in a camp commander who is nothing but a blundering fool, an idiot who is regularly taken advantage of by inmates and other officers. When we think of qualities of personal depth and insight, however, we are on more treacherous ground. Even if someone had proven beyond the shadow of a doubt that no camp commander possessed such qualities, we might well be induced to entertain further doubts. So vivid a portrait as Wertmuller draws would surely have a chance of shaking our faith in the efficacy of instruments used to test for personal qualities. We would, at least, suspend our disbelief in the possibility of an insightful camp commander. And this suspension of disbelief might well continue for the duration of the film—for so long as we continued to feel that issues raised and conflicts played out had something useful and entertaining to recommend them. Which is to say, the historical truth of the matter is only important to us when the context is such that we have been made to expect that kind of truth. Otherwise we are likely to be tolerant of "violations" and to look for other truths the film may better get at.

Bettelheim assumes that *Seven Beauties* is an example of what we have called, following John Lukacs, cinematized history. It is nothing of the sort. It is a political film; it adumbrates political issues and asks political questions it does not feel required to answer. Like other works of this kind, it refuses to be held responsible for espousing correct positions. Its responsibility is to make us alert to problems it takes to be important, and to trace out the implications of various positions in a reasonably consistent way. It has room for considerable improbability and contradiction, provided only that primary expectations are not wantonly or cruelly violated. History is more than a background used to give depth to character, but it is not an end in itself. At most, history is that circumstance within which political conflicts work themselves out, and in which characters achieve usable designations. Without such "history" as is furnished us in a film like *Seven Beauties*, we can distinguish victims from oppressors only by observing what they do. We need to know as well what characters are supposed to be, what "the record" has made of them. The early newsreel footage of the film indicates amply what we are to make of "the record"; it can say ever so many different things depending on the predisposition we bring to it. Individual acts of brutality or cowardice are more difficult to get around. For Wertmuller, history is an uncertain domain within which we learn to fix particular acts and possibilities whose shape and meaning we both create and, in part, inherit. Politics, in a work for which history is more than background and less than determinate documentary fact, has to do with the problematic bringing to consciousness of social processes which for some persons always remain obscure and impenetrable. *Seven Beauties* is a political film in virtue of its persistent probing of the great social questions in such a way that these questions come to seem unavoidable for each of us. Its use of history is instrumental to this end.

We have concluded that *Seven Beauties* is a political film. Is it possible to say what are its politics? Insofar as we can tell, it elaborates no consistent ideological position. It has its fixed interests, its dominant characters and conflicts, and it seems to make a number of points, to which Bettelheim, for one, attaches great importance. The most important of these points Bettelheim in fact takes to be the theme of the film: that there is no real difference between the world of camps and the world beyond; that, since men behave badly, one way or another, they are never likely to resist the programs to which the Nazis and Fascists of the world will subject them; and that, finally, one contemporary political system is roughly equivalent to another. Whichever way you look, man being what he is, evil triumphs—the good being too weak to realize their decent ambitions. Is this what Wertmuller intended to convey? If she did not, and we do indeed take this to be the theme of her film, we are likely to agree with the film's critics who argue that it is at best confusing and irresponsible. For to suggest that those who "liberated" the camps were no better than those who operated them is to fly in the face of everything we have ever thought to be true and certain. It is, moreover, to challenge the very possibility of genuine politics, which depends, at least, on a capacity to make elementary distinctions.

What did Wertmuller wish to convey? It is true that the postwar Italian world, of which we are given a brief if fevered glimpse, is thoroughly unattractive; true, moreover, that the occupation troops (Americans!) have made it profitable even for otherwise "good girls" to become whores. Bettelheim concludes that in these terms we may as well be back in the concentration camps—this, he argues, is the "message" Wertmuller inevitably conveys. When the "liberated" Pasqualino at film's end describes the future as a fight of all against all, he is articulating the film's final message, which is that there is nothing we can do with the evil all about us.

If Wertmuller had wished to convey this message, though, she would have had to do better than to express it in the words of Pasqualino. Everything we have witnessed in *Seven Beauties* inclines us to feel that Pasqualino is a degraded, albeit a pathetic and sometimes grotesquely funny, human being. His prediction of the war of all against all, which he has heard from someone else, is a pitiful reflection of his degraded conception of himself and of the utter impoverishment of his imagination. *Seven Beauties* stays with Pasqualino to the bitter end because it is he who stands in the way of any hopeful or purely humane exposition of our resources. If there is to be a politics worthy of our hope, Wertmuller suggests, it will have somehow to deal with this man, as Louis Malle knew we would have finally to come to terms with Lucien Lacombe. They are not really as different as they may seem, whatever the differences in their presentation.

For Wertmuller, again, we are to dwell not on what happened in the camps, but on what the political imagination is wont to make of our experience. In the figure of Pasqualino, we see what submission to brute fact amounts to. In his general yielding to the ongoing reality of his time, to what others reductively take to be the facts of life, Pasqualino indicates the failure of imagination to conceive possibility in human terms. The cynicism of Wertmuller's film is a reflection of its focus on this particular character and on the absence of hope to which he inevitably points. The politics of the film are no more than implicit, but not less actual for being so. In its elaborated critique of Pasqualino, in the sense it conveys of his debasement, and in the sense of relief we experience in the daylight world beyond the camp—whatever its modestly infernal dimension—*Seven Beauties* gestures towards a politics that will reclaim the imagination of camp-survival for better purposes. Not survival merely, but a decent survival is what the film encourages us to think about and to want. By challenging us to reject Pasqualino, to discover a perspective from which it is possible to put him in his place, *Seven Beauties* asks us to conceive a politics that is more than a cynical resignation to a limited view of fact. In its energy and cunning, the film addresses the difficulty—but not the utter bleakness—of alternatives. Simply because it does not elaborate these alternatives is no reason to suppose it cannot put us in mind of our need to imagine them, and of the terms in which they will need to present themselves.

Index